My Soul and I

My Soul and I

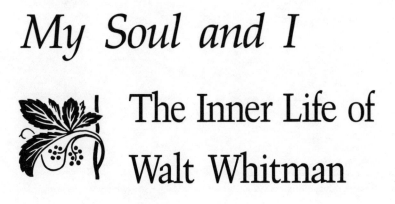

The Inner Life of Walt Whitman

David Cavitch

Beacon Press   Boston

Grateful acknowledgment is made to New York University
Press for permission to reprint from *The Correspondence of
Walt Whitman* edited by Edwin Haviland Miller, copyright
©1961-1977 by New York University, and to Rowman and
Littlefield, Totowa, N.J., for permission to reprint from
Walt Whitman in Camden, edited by Howard Traubel.

Beacon Press
25 Beacon Street
Boston, Massachusetts 02108

Beacon Press books are published under the auspices
of the Unitarian Universalist Association
of Congregations in North America.

92 91 90 89 88 87 86 85   8 7 6 5 4 3 2 1

Library of Congress Cataloging in Publication Data

Cavitch, David.
  My soul and I.

  Includes index.
  1. Whitman, Walt, 1819-1892. 2. Poets, American—
19th century—Biography. I. Title.
PS3231.C37 1985   811'.3 [B]   85-47525
ISBN 0-8070-7000-9

To my children

MAX and ELIZABETH,

this book about poetry and family

Contents

Camerado, this is no book,

Who touches this touches a man,

(Is it night? are we here together alone?)

It is I you hold and who holds you,

I spring from the pages into your arms —

    decease calls me forth.

                "So Long!"

Acknowledgments

A MONG MANY excellent studies of Whitman, I am especially in-debted to psychoanalytic criticism by Edwin H. Miller, *Walt Whitman's Poetry, A Psychological Journey* (Houghton Mifflin, 1968), and Stephen A. Black, *Whitman's Journeys into Chaos: A Psychoanalytic Study of the Poetic Process* (Princeton University Press, 1975). For biographical information I have drawn heavily on Gay Wilson Allen, *The Solitary Singer* (New York University Press, revised, 1967), and Justin Kaplan, *Walt Whitman, A Life* (Simon and Schuster, 1980). My indebtedness to these scholars goes beyond my specific citations, even when I differ with their conclusions.

I am grateful to the National Endowment for the Humanities for a fellowship that enabled me to begin writing this book. Financial assistance from Tufts University aided the preparation of the manuscript.

The discussion of "Song of Myself" in Chapter 3 appeared in an earlier version in *Studies in Romanticism* (Spring 1978).

Among friends, colleagues, and editors who contributed valuable suggestions to my views of Whitman, I wish to thank especially Sylvan Barnet, Marie Cantlon, Donna Hollenberg, Leo Marx, Joanne Wyckoff, and Richard Yoder.

Introduction

"One's-Self I Sing"

WALT WHITMAN was not born to be a poet but he was re-born as one. He published his first book of poems at the age of thirty-six, after an identity crisis inspired him with the importance of his inner life. Nothing in his unpromising background gave evidence of the creative genius that emerged in 1855 in *Leaves of Grass*. And nothing in the long creative life that followed indicates that he fully resolved the problems of identity that stimulated his work. Whitman expanded and rewrote *Leaves of Grass* for the next thirty-six years, repeatedly revising his sense of himself, and changing his life story as poetry uncovered his deeper nature.

To illuminate his creative life, this book tells a story that can be summarized succinctly: Whitman gained his full power to write when he learned how to re-create his family relationships in the voice and structure of his poems, and then in being a poet he struggled against his poetry just as he spent his entire life in loving conflict with his family. He freed his creative spirit by embodying his family in his art; then, inevitably, the poetry began to entrap him in the same way he had suffered at home and from which he had sought to escape. As a poet he found himself partly counterfeited and oppressed by the role of interpreter or translator of experience, a role that he felt deprived him of an authentic emotional life. But while his vocation seemed to become an obstacle to actual fulfillment, he could not abandon the poetry that preserved his family connections and gave him a meaningful existence, even though it betrayed his spirit and left him divided against himself. Obviously, the main events in this story were subjective, and their occurrence is something I have inferred and surmised; but the poems express an inner life that confirms just such a history of his imagination. I do not discuss the poems as if they were naive, direct testimony of his daily life. Poetry is not real life, as skeptics always observe; but the imagination is real life, especially

Whitman's imagination in its central role in his experience. My purpose is to trace the astonishing transformation of his subjective life into an innovative artwork and a national epic, *Leaves of Grass*, and to show the reciprocal relation betwen Whitman and his poetry; in other words, to show the effect of the poems upon Whitman's changing sensibility as he reacted to the reflections of himself in his work.

Though he lived mostly a solitary and introspective life, his withdrawn vantage point did not diminish his view of his contemporary world. Whitman responded actively and sometimes with preternatural sensitivity to the social realities of his era, even though outer events, other persons, ideas and details of the affairs of his time appear in his poems as equivalents of himself or as illustrations of what is already true inside him. As a patriot in a paradoxical new world that exalted both liberty and slavery, and as a poet on the threshold of discovering the psychological meanings of freedom and subjugation, Whitman faced appalling contradictions and refutations whether he looked inside or outside himself. His internal and external perspectives were focused alike on the same mysterious working of the divided human spirit. His observation of paradoxes led him to see reflections of himself everywhere in the world around him, but especially in the ambiguities and unproven coherence of his nation.

> One's-Self I sing, a simple separate person,
> Yet utter the word Democratic, the word En-Masse.

There is a special way in which Whitman's poetry speaks for everyone. He is the only great poet who is surprised to find that someone as ordinary as himself can represent everybody else. The importance of his commonness never stopped delighting him. No European poet has Whitman's democratic sense of personal plainness, and none jumps to the same conclusion that his natural features make him divine. He saw in contemporary democracy a large-scale, public counterpart to his own life. "America isolated yet embodying all, what is it finally except myself?" he proclaims in an early poem. He recognized a magnificent, ready-made myth of himself in the political and social dividedness of the United States; and he found optimism for his future in his country's revolutionary emergence from the constraints of European civilization and the inchoate conditions of its own wilderness. He maintained with inspired conviction that everything important was personal — in short, that the turbulent modern world of democratic revolution, civil conflict, and materialist expansion issued like divine will unfolding from the long-suppressed spirit of each individual like himself.

In the mid-1850s he translated his culture into himself and then found he was unable to write new poetry with the same luminous perception of his identity. While it is widely agreed (though not unanimously) that Whitman's poetry abruptly declined after 1859, the usual explanations claim that Whitman's work became vapid because he found greater satisfaction in erotic involvements with young men in a life without genius. According to this view, Whitman was exhausted by his hospital work during the Civil War, and soon afterward, half paralyzed by a stroke, descended into a premature physical frailty that was notably serene and free of the earlier sexual frustration that his poetry had served to relieve. Or, among scholars who see that Whitman's creativity was blocked, not needlessly sold for porridge, the usual explanation is that Whitman became ashamed of the homosexual feelings expressed in his early poetry and thereafter suppressed the only emotional energy that maintained his creative light. I offer here a different interpretation of Whitman's creativity that demonstrates his commitment and dedication to poetry was more real to him than other life, though the quality of his work declined as soon as he settled into undivided service to his art. He sacrificed both his power of genius and his sensual fulfillment in order to preserve the rigid family structure that supported and defeated him in his poems.

This approach runs contrary to those critical views that maintain that literary texts cannot be shown to contain specific meanings, or that literature reflects primarily other literature or mythic tropes whether seasonal or Oedipal. I reconstruct the thread of Whitman's personal creative intentions, both conscious and unconscious, in the belief that poems need biography and history not only brought *to* them but also extrapolated *from* them, for our full understanding of the artist's power to interpret the world. To present a coherent, readable account of Whitman's creative life I have sometimes made a narrative out of a murkier passage of events in which Whitman's conflicting states of mind reversed and repeated themselves in prolonged ambivalence. It is possible, for instance, that he did not compose some of the more closely related poems in the order in which I have arranged them for discussion. But I have tried to preserve both the long-lasting complexities and the specific sequences of his evolving responses.

With the exception of a handful of good poems written after 1859, Whitman only added voluminous fat to *Leaves of Grass* during the remaining thirty-two years of his writing career, by writing poems that sound like imitations of himself. More ably, he also constantly sorted and polished his earlier achievements, and his revisions are usually artful and mature. Despite his loss of fresh creativity, his years of writing increased his skill as a reader and editor of his own poems. In examining his work I generally follow (except where otherwise noted) the final rather than the earliest versions of the poems, even though I am concerned with the poet's psychological motives and his gains and losses in writing poetry, because the final versions are poetically superior. When he merely censored himself, I restore the deleted material. For the most part, his revisions provide a subtler, ampler expression of his subjective life. Inner experience, particularly his, is not strictly historical; and poetry that has been sensitively revised is likely to tell a truer tale, especially when the subject of the work is the personality of the man who wrote it.

My Soul and I

1

A Stranger in Their Midst

W HEN WALT WHITMAN at the age of thirty-six brought home a copy
of the large, green volume of twelve poems that comprised his first
version of *Leaves of Grass*, no one in the family could appreciate what he
had written. They were not a family that read poetry with any understanding or pleasure. Though the poems speak with scriptural intensity
about the meaning and dignity of common life, his parents, brothers, and
sisters heard neither the point nor the eloquence of these lines.

> I am the poet of the Body and I am the poet of
>   the Soul,
> The pleasures of heaven are with me and the
>   pains of hell are with me,
> The first I graft and increase upon myself,
>   the latter I translate into a new
>   tongue.
>
> I am the poet of the woman the same as the man,
> And I say it is as great to be a woman as to be
>   a man,
> And I say there is nothing greater than the
>   mother of men.*

His brother George recalled that at the time the book did not seem worth
reading, though he thumbed through it. His mother too was baffled and
unimpressed. She disparagingly remarked to the children —most of whom
still lived at home, though even the youngest, a large-bodied and epi-

---

Leaves of Grass, Comprehensive Reader's Edition, ed. Harold Bodgett and Sculley Bradley
(New York University Press, 1965), p. 48. Further quotations from *Leaves of Grass* are from
this edition unless otherwise noted; citations are given by title and line numbers within
the text, or by page number after the abbreviation *LG*.

leptic idiot, was already twenty — that Walt's poetry was as muddled as Longfellow's, and that "if Hiawatha was poetry, perhaps Walt's was."[1] Clearly, nuances of verse were not their business. They were a family of rural people trying to find better work in the city. They had no special education or perceptiveness above the level of their trades, their household tasks, and their pride in being citizens in a country where everyone was encouraged to have something to do and to say — even if both turned out to be as useless as poetry. Whitman's eventual fame as a world-acclaimed poet never made sense to them, though they were more or less pleased to see it. And their indifference to his goals subtly diminished his sense of achievement. Even in his later years, a visit from his favorite brother, Jeff, brought Whitman to reminisce: "No one of my people — the people near to me — ever had any time for Leaves of Grass — thought it more than an ordinary piece of work, if that." Not even his mother? the interviewer asked. "No — I think not — even her; there is, as I say, no one in my immediate family who follows me out on that line. My dear mother had every general faith in me; that is where she stopped. She stood before Leaves of Grass mystified, defeated."[2]

The interviewer is young Horace Traubel, who had the tenacity and the devotion to visit Whitman each day in his last years and to record these meetings in six volumes of conversation. These often barren monologues show us Whitman's stoicism and loneliness in the face of approaching death. He managed to remain remarkably free of nostalgia about any of the old days, except for the warmhearted household of William and Ellen O'Connor, his loving friends in Washington during the Civil War. An old letter from Ellen among the memorabilia he transmitted to Traubel brought Whitman to weep with remembrance of the O'Connors, but the grief in Whitman's voice also conveys a sharper undertone of plaintive disappointment at the failure of his own family to understand him or accept his life's work. That lack of acknowledgment stung him quite literally to his dying days. Traubel reported:

> Whitman was much affected by this letter. He sort of excused himself. Wiped the tears out of his eyes. "It's not so much what's in the letter, Horace, as what it leads me back to, what it stirs up in me, what its tender indirections are. The O'Connor home was my home; They were beyond all others — William, Nelly — my understanders, my lovers: they more than any others. I was nearer to them than to any others — oh! much nearer. A man's family is the people who love him — the people who comprehend him. You know how for the most part I have always been isolated from my people — in certain senses have been a stranger in their midst: just as we know Tolstoy has been. Who of my family has gone along with me? Who?

Do you know? Not one of them. They are beautiful, fine: they
don't need to be apologized for: but they have not known me:
they have always missed my intentions. Take my darling dear
mother: my dear, dear mother: she and I — oh! we have been
great chums: always next to each other: always: yet my dear
mother never took that part of me in: she had great faith in me
— felt sure I would accomplish wonderful things: but Leaves
of Grass? Who could ever consider Leaves of Grass a wonderful
thing: who? She would shake her head. God bless her! She
never did. She thought I was a wonderful thing, but the
Leaves? oh my, hardly the Leaves! But she would put her hand
in mine — press my hand — look at me: all as if to say it was
all right though in some ways beyond her power to explain.

After a few more unhappy comparisons between his family members
and his adoring friends, Whitman felt obliged to deny his obvious
resentment.

Now, you must not set this down for a growl: it's not that.
I never feel unhappy over what is unavoidable: I have no more
right to expect things of my family than my family has to expect
things of me: we are simply what we are: we do not always
run together like two rivers: we are not alike: that's the part
and the whole of it.[3]

Traubel was a discreet and forbearing interviewer; he did not try to draw
out the meaning of Whitman's feelings in the conversations he attentively
transcribed. But he knew how to wait for all the fruit to ripen in Whitman's
recollections. Three months after first broaching the topic, Traubel again
led Whitman to comment on his family's rejection of his genius and
achievements. Traubel asked:

"At what time was it your father died?"
"1855." [Whitman replied.]
"Just your entrance year?"
"Yes."
"Then he did not live to see any of your great work?"
"No — and I don't suppose it would have made much difference if he had."
"But," I pursued, "have none of your folks grown into an
understanding of it?"
"I hardly think so — surely not: they sort of accept me —
do it as a matter of course — but with a feeling as though not
knowing why or what I am: a feeling, a wish, that I might be
more respectable, train more in accustomed lines — let myself
be stitched in with the cluster of celebrities. Even today they

look on me, I am sure, as untamed, stubborn, too much bent
on my own ways — a curio of a sort." He did not "expect of
any of them anything in the way of enthusiasm or even reasonable acceptance."

I asked: "Then there's not one in the bunch who can be regarded as being in touch with what you have written?"

"Not one of them, from my dear mother down — not one
of them: on the contrary, they are dead set against my book
and what it stands for — or what they think it stands for.
George could never overlook the Children of Adam poems:
he has of course never understood them — I doubt if he ever
really read them, though he says he did: he thinks them of
'the whore-house order,' as he has said to me: what mystifies
him is the fact that I wrote the poems: he finds it impossible
to realize them as mine: he don't believe evil of me — yet the
poems seem to him to be evil poems: it's quite a puzzle which
he has told me more than once he absolutely gives up."[4]

Whitman's comments underscore his family's stubborn refusal to listen.
Insistently, his people understood nothing in the poems. It is perhaps
just as well, for what they did not know could have hurt them. Whitman's
poetry is a product of their life together in their long striving against
emotional burdens and family deterioration in an underdeveloped community. Transformed and generalized into poems that celebrate the
natural individual in a democratic society, the experience that bound Walt
to a society of family members remained unrecognized. His principal
subject is the ambiguity of his own life, which he continually reinterprets
and retells, but not as an autobiographer or memoirist portrays a character or describes interesting events. His idea of a man's life is not a
biography; such information struck him as old-fashioned or even
deceptive. He objects to the distortions of conventional biographies in
"When I Read the Book."

> When I read the book, the biography famous,
> And is this then (said I) what the author calls
>   a man's life?
> And so will some one when I am dead and gone
>   write my life?
> (As if any man really knew aught of my life,
> Why even I myself I often think know little or
>   nothing of my real life,
> Only a few hints, a few diffused faint clews
>   and indirections,
> I seek for my own use to trace out here.)
>   (LG, p. 8)

As the verb *trace out* suggests, Whitman's poems are like a series of life studies, or artist's drawings, by which he tried to perceive the essentials of his "real life," beyond the "little or nothing" that he feels he can confidently know. Along with explicit themes and values, the poems present deeper content that he regarded as amorphous or opaque, and they express a sense of himself that otherwise eluded him. That was their "own use" to him: They virtually created his self-image, his recognizable identity. *Self* is the key word in his poetry, and his identity is virtually his only theme; yet within himself he explored the delicious pleasures and frightening confusions of his substantive connections to many, perhaps to all other people. He knew himself primarily as part of a family in which the presence or distance of his parents affected him so powerfully that they seemed to possess his consciousness. By writing poetry he sought paradoxically to enjoy his fusion with them and to assert his individuality. The aim of his creative work was to reconstruct the subjective world of his earlier family experience so that he could retain and improve upon the integrity of his separateness and the intimacy of his deepest unions.

Though his creativity was unrecognized by the people who were the chief source of his inspiration, Whitman's presence in the family was always central and influential, and he held a privileged if ambiguous position. To other Whitmans, it appeared that Walt was superiorly endowed; he was more intellectual, spiritual, and composed than the others. "One of the greatest things about Walt," George reflected, "was his wonderful calmness in trying times when everybody else would get excited. He was always cool, never flurried; would get mad but never lose his head; was never scared....He was forbearing and conciliating. He was always gentle till you got him started — always."[5] Even in childhood he was excused from routine chores, and he escaped most household discipline because he did not seem to need or want instruction in his self-absorbed behavior. He read books, and wandered freely about the streets. He looked after the six children younger than himself with parental attentiveness and assumed authority. All members of the family looked to Walt for sympathy and support in their distress — all except his father and older brother, neither of whom enjoyed the favor that Mrs. Whitman bestowed on her sweet-tempered son.

But among them, in the years before his first publication of *Leaves of Grass* in 1855, Walt's devotion to writing poems was viewed as a misuse of his superior abilities, a waste of privilege and opportunity in a capable man who could have pursued promising careers as a schoolteacher, printer, journalist, or even a house builder like his father and brothers. Instead, he preferred what seemed to be a wholly directionless existence, following mild whims and impulses to jot down lines of poetry or undertaking jaunts around Brooklyn and Manhattan. In his early thirties he no longer kept up his sporadic work as a carpenter; and when he had used up his savings, accumulated from his earlier profitable occupations, he could no longer furnish capital for his family's unlucky speculative ventures in the house-building trade. Unpredictable and bemused, he would rise in midmeal from the table and return to the house long after dinner had been cleared away. He was always just "going out and coming in," said his mother, recollecting behavior that was never condoned but always tolerated.[6]

The family sponsored Walt as an exceptional person, without ever understanding the social causes or family aspirations that underlay his special role. His parents and siblings were largely unconscious of the great dimensions of their experience as part of the new urban poor, ill equipped to face the threats of doom that settled upon nearly every one of them. Against all warnings of their decline, Walt was their luxury and their unreckoned pride. He nourished their dream of a world of dignity and power that in their revolutionary classlessness they would never attain.

Walt's parents were married in 1816, during the first distinctly postrevolutionary era of expansionist activity and democratic values that promised an egalitarian and politically enfranchised society. After the crushing defeat in Europe of Napoleon's last vestiges of French revolutionary zeal, America alone seemed to offer liberty and prosperity to every common, white man. The rationalist idealism of the American gentry who broke with England was about to be translated, partially and for only a short time, into the social realities of free land, free trade, and antimonopolistic capitalism, expressed chiefly in the tenets of the new Democratic party, at least while it prevailed as the party of Andrew Jackson. Young Walter, Sr., and his new wife, Louisa, contended for a few years with the hopelessness of their meager farm on Long Island, which was all that now remained of the hundreds of acres once owned by the Whitman family. After seven lean years, they turned with three small children and a fourth on the way to take up the landless and unprotected life of trades and skills in the new commercial town of Brooklyn. Later in the century, other farmers, perhaps wiser than the Whitmans, would move further westward, not to vigorous towns on the edge of an expanding metropolis, but to homesteads and villages where they could continue the country life they were prepared to lead. But Walt's family chose the strangeness of a developing city and felt its power over their lives like the unmanageable force of nature.

Mr. Whitman worked as a carpenter, initially finding work as a laborer for wages. Soon he plunged into commercial enterprise as a speculative builder of houses, in a fashion that subjected the whole family to the uncertainties of his business. He would buy a lot, build a small house, and move in his family until a buyer appeared and another venture led him to move again. While the family grew, their living arrangements remained unsettled. Within one particularly active two-year period while Walt was six to eight years old, they occupied five different houses. Late in his life, he acknowledged to a young friend that "the time of my boyhood was a very restless and unhappy one; I did not know what to do."[7] Lacking ties to objects and places that might otherwise have provided a stable, outer world, Walt had good reason to devalue material reality and turn inward.

Some of the moves the family made were forced by foreclosure on the mortgage, for Mr. Whitman occasionally lost a house, and even his successful transactions were never adequately profitable. He struggled to take advantage of capitalistic opportunities that in the economic instability of the 1830s and 1840s ultimately defeated the Long Island farmer's attempts to become an urban entrepreneur. He was not a man to take hardship easily. Dour, taciturn, and opinionated, he was apt to drink heavily and to show a violent temper. He steadily deteriorated as a worker and father, probably because of alcoholism and other diseases that it aggravated. He was a doctrinaire who complained bitterly that he never received what he believed were his natural rights. Born to parents who had been youthful American revolutionists, he abided by the political rhetoric of liberty, but the fervor of independence descended on him as the dead weight of rebellious umbrage. Something in his temperament that blinded him to the injustice of slavery for the black man also bound him to a strangely everlasting sense of personal oppression. He lived his life like a released prisoner half trying to make a go of freedom. The coincidence of his birth on Bastille Day 1789 fed his personal myth of portentous facts about himself. That myth also included his introduction as a youth to Tom Paine, whose work he later read, and his friendship later in life with the Quaker radical Elias Hicks, whose preaching he liked to attend. He read Volney's *Les Ruines*, an epitome of rationalistic moral attitudes in eighteenth-century France, and he subscribed to the *Free Enquirer*, a radical weekly. Proud of his connections to great liberal leaders, he projected his sense of democratic celebrity onto his sons: obviously onto Walt, who, before he became the poet of democracy, was a political journalist and a left-wing maverick in the Democratic party, and less effectively onto his younger sons, Andrew Jackson Whitman, George Washington Whitman, and Thomas Jefferson Whitman. Edward, the youngest, escaped his nominal destiny by being born deformed and feebleminded. The father's unachieved ideals cast a net especially over Walt, who absorbed his father's egotistic patriotism and turned it into the truly radical *Leaves of Grass*. But the father also passed along his jealous reproachfulness. Disappointed in himself, he complained that Walt was

never ambitious enough, never practical enough, never good enough —
to achieve the fantasy of grandeur that he had imposed on his son.

In his disappointment and failure, Mr. Whitman was remote and stern,
and the eight children drew close to their mother. Louisa Whitman, voluble and animated, continuously talked about her doings and feelings.
She drew young Walt, her second child, into her obsessive self-regard,
dramatizing her activities to her appreciative son much as some house-
bound people talk their days' events aloud to a responsive pet. "My dear
mother possessed the story-telling faculty," Whitman recollected; "whenever she had been anywhere she could describe it, tell me all about it."[8]
It was to Walt alone that Louisa elaborated on her experience, giving it
the value and color of "storytelling." Charmed and protected by her
attention, Walt agreeably attuned himself to her adult perspective, unob-
trusively fitting into conversations and sympathetically noting the stresses
and perturbations of her overburdened domestic life. In contrast to his
father, who was visibly demoralized and threatening, his mother appeared
buoyant and intact, self-possessed despite her hardships. She became
for him a haven of acceptance and physical intimacy. Because she was
expressive and alert, he thought that she was uncannily perceptive and
full of wisdom. To the end of his life he usually saw her from a child's
perspective as a magnetically attractive, superior woman to whom he was
indebted for his achievements. In his conversations during his last years
in Camden, he maintained that his "dear, dear mother's life was
responsible for the main things. . .in Leaves of Grass itself." He attributed
to his mother's personality all the major traits that defined him in the
poems. In his view, his mother produced the poetry, writing through
him in a creative process that he disclaimed as his own gift and insisted
was a debt.

> How much I owe her! It could not be put in a scale —
> weighed: it could not be measured — be even put in the best
> words: it can only be apprehended through the intuitions.
> Leaves of Grass is the flower of her temperament active in me.
> My mother was illiterate in the formal sense but strangely
> knowing: she excelled in narrative — had great mimetic power:
> she could tell stories, impersonate: she was very eloquent in
> the utterance of noble moral axioms — was very original in her
> manner, her style.[9]

The way she appeared to him is largely the way he presents himself
in his poetry. In Leaves of Grass his own personality is "strangely
knowing," and he overemphasizes his "great mimetic power" by
claiming the ability to "impersonate" everybody. His oratorical tone is
"very eloquent in the utterance of noble moral axioms," and his lasting,

most influential achievement is that he became "very original" in "manner" and "style." Whitman's identification with his mother was so strong that he was never able to distinguish between his sense of himself and his perceptions of her.

Whitman could not separate himself from his mother partly because she did not want to separate herself from him. In his devotion he became the mainstay of her morale, and she actively kept him attached to her, as if her child were her own idealized, doting, and appreciative parent. He was the "good" in her life that enabled her to contain, or even deny, all the "bad" that welled up around her. Louisa Whitman was relieved and even grateful that Walt was not like her first child, Jesse, who from infancy had brought out only her anger. Jesse was an ungovernable boy, as bad in her eyes as Walt was good. Jesse rejected all love and authority. He remained quarrelsome and apart from his brothers and sisters. When he left home to go to sea at about the age of fourteen, the family seemed satisfied to be rid of him. When he returned to the Whitman home at age forty, broken by a fall from a mast and infected with syphilis, he was an invalid subject to dangerous outbursts of anger; he was ultimately committed to an insane asylum where he died and was buried as a pauper, his body unclaimed by his surviving mother or brothers and sisters. Walt's lifelong tacit hostility toward his older brother echoed his mother's long-suffering resentment of her first son, who returned to the family deranged and diseased, as worthless as he had always seemed to them.

Walt, only fourteen months younger than Jesse, constantly witnessed the consequences of his brother's quarrelsome nature in the probably frightening retaliations of anger from his parents. The fixed attitude of condemnation that excluded Jesse from the family circle must have reinforced Walt's good behavior to ensure his safe place in the family. He showed signs of having a bad temper, like his father and Jesse, but he learned to hide it under a generally mild, easygoing, and detached outward manner. The implicit warning in Jesse's experience was compounded for Walt by the fate of another troubling infant. When Walt was six years old — and Jesse then at seven would have been especially recalcitrant — the Whitmans' fifth child was born, probably deformed or subject to convulsions as Jesse perhaps had been. Because the infant was obviously infirm and unlikely to thrive, it was never given a name during its five months of life. Since the baby was treated as one who is expected to die, the six-year-old Walt must have assumed that troublesome children are not loved and that for punishment they are made to die. He connected the horror of the baby's anonymity and doom with his parents' rejection of Jesse. Even as an adult, he carried this association: Unable to recall the baby's birth date, he mistakenly gave it Jesse's. Walt's slip of memory indicates both pity and hatred for Jesse: If young Walt wished Jesse too had died when the baby died, that aggressive impulse would leave the six-year-old feeling as worthless and guilty as the two children whom the parents with apparent heartlessness had cast away for being troublesome. Young Walt had cautionary examples before, behind, and within him that would make him ambivalently wish to cleave to the family and yet at the same time make himself less vulnerable to any possible rejections.

This uncertainty over being accepted or rejected, loved or denied, appears to have set the tone of the Whitman family life not only for Walt but also for his brothers and sisters, who, like Walt, were unable to leave the family or to thrive within it. For seven of the eight surviving children, the family they grew up in continued to hold them emotionally and to a large extent materially, even after marriage, employment, travel, and war. Only Walt's sister Mary, the older daughter and the third child, married at a customary age and managed to establish her family independently of her mother. But in a crisis of unhappiness with her husband, even Mary once fled Greenport for Brooklyn, moving in, ''bag and baggage'' it was said, with her mother and brothers. The second sister, and fourth child, Hannah, lived a life of unhappiness that, unlike Mary's, was never resolved. She made a disastrous marriage at the age of twenty-nine and spent the rest of her bitter, lonely, and childless life in New Hampshire, longing to return to her mother. Hannah and her husband, a former friend of Walt, who never forgave himself for introducing the suitor, incessantly talked about Hannah's returning to Brooklyn, but she never did. Instead they continued to badger each other into madness and death. Andrew, the fifth surviving child, married a prostitute and spent most of his disconsolate days under his mother's care, afflicted by alcoholism and tuberculosis of the throat. Accustomed to being at his mother's nearby house every day, he wanted in his last hours only to be removed there again, away from his child and his wife, when he died in 1863 at the age of thirty-six.

Walt's favorite brother, Jeff, brought his wife to live in his mother's house for nine years before moving to St. Louis, where Jeff took a good post as superintendent of the municipal water system. Until their departure from Brooklyn, Louisa complained repeatedly to Walt about the self-indulgences of her daughter-in-law and Jeff's parsimony, though the daughter-in-law, Mattie, was exceptionally kind and sympathetic to Louisa in ways her own daughters were not. The crowded household soured with further complaints over Jeff's two lively daughters, and Jeff reacted stormily to the presence of his brothers Jesse and Eddie. Jesse was surly and abusive, and Eddie was physically and mentally incompetent, and could not even eat his meals or dress himself without assistance. Jeff wanted both of them sent to an insane asylum, and he argued, with some justification, that his family was unsafe amid the violence that his brothers stirred up in the house. When Andrew died, Jesse, deranged by syphilis and plagued by deliriums of anger against his mother, broke into a rage against Jeff's daughter, and then against the child's mother, threatening to kill Mattie for provoking him by protecting the child. Though it was understood that Jesse was upset over his brother's death, the younger brother Jeff was furious when he learned of the abuse toward his wife. During this fracas in December 1863, Walt was living in Washington, D.C., where he had managed to remove himself from the Brooklyn family household only one year earlier. Jeff wrote to Walt about Jesse:

> he is a treacherous cuss anyway. Probably had I been home he would not have done anything of the kind, but if he had, so help me God I would have shot him dead on the spot. And I must confess I felt considerably like it as it was. I love Mat as I love my life — dearer by far — and to have this infernal pup — a perfect hell-drag to his Mother — treat her so — threaten to brain her — call her all the vile things that he could think of — is a little more than I will stand....I wish to God he was ready to put alongside of Andrew.[10]

Jeff could easily dispense not only with two of his brothers, Jesse and Andrew, but with three out of the five; for after the fracas between Jesse and Jeff he recommended that both Jesse and Eddie be committed to mental institutions. But Louisa was not yet ready to agree to that.

George was the most pragmatic and responsible of the children and the one who modestly achieved the family's goal of middle-class success as an urban businessman. Except for a period of distinguished service in the Civil War, he lived at home as a bachelor until the age of forty-two. When he married he moved to Camden, and brought his ailing mother and Eddie to live with him. When she died, Walt at the age of fifty-four moved directly to Camden and occupied her room in George's house; he slept in her bed, sat in her chair with her pillow nestled under his head, and kept his favorite of her dresses hanging in the closet. He remained with George for eleven years, until George and his wife retired to the country; Walt then took up his final residence in a tiny house on Mickle Street which he bought in 1884.

The emotional constraint that kept the group dependent on one another is reflected in the failure of most of the brothers and sisters to continue the family line. Of the nine children Louisa bore, only Mary Van Nostrand had children who grew to adulthood and became parents themselves. The failure of continuity in the family line and the serious psychological and physical impairments affecting several members of this family suggest that genetic problems may have compounded the doom overhanging Whitman's generation. Whatever combination of circumstances and causes may explain the family deterioration, Whitman seems to have been born into a specially demanding struggle against nature itself, for which he idealized his family line. Despite all the evidence of his disadvantages, he always insisted that he was the heir of superb moral and physical health, wholesome blood, strong stock, and perfect parents.

Walt seemed to learn at an early age that he could survive by detaching himself from the life around him. He stood secretly apart from the family while making himself the ideal member of the household. His immune yet central involvement in external life became his habitual pattern of relating to others while preserving a vivid separateness. In "Song of Myself" he describes the customary withdrawn engagement of what he calls "the Me myself."

> Apart from the pulling and hauling stands what
>   I am,
> Stands amused, complacent, compassionating, idle,
>   unitary,
> Looks down, is erect, or bends an arm on an im-
>   palpable certain rest,
> Looking with side-curved head curious what will
>   come next,
> Both in and out of the game and watching and
>   wondering at it.
>
> (11. 75–79)

As a child, he was able to stay "both in and out of the game" by following a direction tangential to the family's affairs, even though he could increase his independence only by stretching thin his conditional security at home. He lived at least partly separate from the family half of the time from the age of twelve until he was twenty-eight. As a lad his first employment was in an office of noted lawyers, a post that elevated him above the laborer's occupations his brothers were to learn. At the office Walt enjoyed the dignity of having a copying desk to himself and, most valuable of all kindnesses, he received a subscription to the circulating library. "With loving and greedy eagerness," he recalled, he read romantic fiction like Scott's novels, Gothic tales, *Robinson Crusoe*, and the *Arabian Nights*. From works like these, he said while reminiscing over his boyhood impressions, "the minds of boys and girls warm and expand — become rich and generous — under the aspect of such florid pages."[11]

Within a year Walt was apprenticed to a newspaper editor. He lived with other boys next door to the print shop, which was less than a dozen blocks from the Whitman house, where he visited nearly every day. The foreman printer, whom Walt recalled reverently, taught the boy the trade that would become the most important intellectual nurture of his literary genius, substituting for a college education, as it has for other writers from the working class in America. The young compositor came to delight in words concretely, as the poet would; his manual skill with letter types and lines enabled him to "make words sing, dance, kiss,"as he later said the poet does in exultation over the capacity of language "to do any thing that man or woman or the natural powers can do."[12] His practical ability to compose his own words into type must have suggested to the romantically fanciful boy the lore and omnipotence of a magician.

By sixteen he was a man-sized, strong, quick-minded, and well-informed youth who had advanced to the status of journeyman printer. He could remain self-supporting at his work in Brooklyn, and even find a job in New York, when in 1834 the Whitman family abandoned the father's American dream of success and returned to farming on Long Island. For the next ten years Mr. Whitman raised vegetables, took odd jobs, and gathered fortitude for another attempt to win prosperity in the city, to which the family returned in 1845. During that period Walt generally tried to continue as a printer and journalist. When he was out of work in the city, he lived with his family on the farm or found teaching jobs for three-month terms at various Long Island village schools, sometimes boarding in the house of one of his pupils. When he lived at home, his father expected him to help with the farming, which Walt refused to do, and the resulting hostility between the two men drove father and son into quarrels or withdrawn silence. Whitman seldom talked about his father, but nevertheless left a clear impression of his feelings in the minds of Traubel and his associates, who wrote a biographical essay as a preface for Whitman's posthumous *Complete Writings* (1902):

> Like all the Whitmans this father, though fundamentally sluggish, was, when aroused, capable of memorable vehemence. And we know that Walt himself had stormy scenes with the old man. For, while Walt was never critical, he told us that his father sometimes strove to exert an undue parentalism which Walt had, out of self-respect, to resent. Walt would add that on such occasions his mother was invariably the peacemaker.

Perhaps at this time they openly quarreled over the politics and morality of Abolition, for his father's defense of slavery galled Whitman to his dying days long after his father and slavery were gone. The lingering shame in Whitman's memory suggests that the issue was connected with some youthful feeling of humiliation by his unreasonable, quick-tempered father. When Horace Traubel inquired about his father's political affiliations, Whitman replied, "My father was always a Democrat — a Democrat of the old school." Traubel pursued the crucial point: "Was he anti-slavery?" Whitman could not bring himself to respond to that question directly but talked instead about the generally liberal opinions held by his parents, who sympathized with humanitarian Quaker views. Since Traubel would not believe that Whitman chose to evade the question, he rejected the obvious meaning of what he heard: "Whitman did not answer this with a yes or no, whether because he did not wish to (certainly not that) or had not caught it on the fly, I don't know." There is every indication that Whitman caught the question with its full force and was struggling to make his response. Traubel continued his interview: "He went on to say, however, anent my remark that nearly all Quakers were opposed to slavery." It is true, Whitman immediately pointed out to Traubel, that his father "was not, properly speaking, a Quaker: he was a friend, I might almost say a follower, of Elias Hicks." The halting reservations about his father's views disappear when he praises the un-qualified liberalism of his mother: "My mother came partly of Quaker stock: all her leanings were that way — her sympathies: her fundamental emotional tendencies." At last reapproaching the question that was stuck in his mind, he indirectly admits what the old school Democrat must have vehemently maintained: "In those early days, as I remember, the Democrats feared the Abolition ideas — pestilential ideas, they called them, thought them."[13] The hesitation evident in this recollection suggests a personal conflict involving other issues between father and son. Since Whitman was himself always critical of radical Abolitionist politics, he probably could have tolerated his father's conservatism had it not been expressed with intemperance and disrespect toward the son's principles.

Out of place at home and bullied by his father, Walt seldom lived with his family during the years between 1834 and 1845. Whether on Long Island near them or alone in New York, he pursued chiefly newspaper work but either did not like or could not hold onto the posts he obtained. The wife of one Long Island editor, in whose house he boarded for several months, found him slovenly, morose, and lazy. Walt described his feelings in similar terms in a story he wrote around this time about a young man who had to leave the city because of economic misfortune and take charge of a country school. Like Walt presumably, the hero, Archie Dean, "looked on the dark side of his life entirely too often; he pined over his deficiencies, as he called them, by which he meant mental as well as pecuniary wants." During the same period, Whitman wrote poems that echo the conven-tionally morbid, graveyard sentimentality that was characteristic of the popular verse of his day. The maudlin sensibility of contemporary literary taste suited his mood. In plodding rhymes and trite diction that give no hint of the originality he was to command later, he worried over the usual themes of death and obliteration. Nevertheless, personal anxiety located deep within the conventional sentiments occasionally found expression. For example, in "Our Future Lot," written when he was nineteen, Walt shows a special concern for the fate of his "struggling brain." He dreads the dissolution of his conscious mind, which is dissociated from the rest of him.

> The cold wet earth will close around
>   Dull senseless limbs, and ashy face,
> But where, O Nature! where will be
>   My mind's abiding place?
> Will it ev'n live? For though its light
>   Must shine till from the body torn;
> Then, when the oil of life is spent,
>   Still shall the taper burn?[14]

The causes of Walt's depression were more "mental" than "pecuniary." He had opportunities that would have easily led to success for a more pragmatic and autonomous young man. For instance, as a schoolteacher for two terms at Smithtown, he joined a debating society where he associated with the town's business leaders. Perhaps with their support, Walt launched his own weekly newspaper at nearby Huntington, and for a year he operated the flourishing *Long Islander* — until he bolted. "Everything seem'd turning out well," he recollected later, "only my own restlessness prevented me gradually establishing a permanent property there."[15] The prospect of a narrow future amid village life may have caused him to panic, for he hoped to reenter the romantic world of metropolitan journalism and politics.

Though he held up New York work as his goal, even his more promising beginnings in this line turned out badly during this period of his life. In New York in 1841, he worked as a printer for a leading literary magazine while placing his own stories in the notable *Democratic Review,* where Hawthorne, Poe, Bryant, Lowell, and Whittier also published their work. At the same time, he was achieving acclaim for his political addresses and greater responsibility as a publicist within the Democratic party. In the spring of 1842 he obtained a position as an editor on the Manhattan daily *Aurora.* Exhilarated by his new position in a glamorous world of power and fortune, Walt adopted a style of brag and fashion in his manners and dress. He lost his job on the *Aurora* within a few weeks, for reasons that included a political disagreement with the owners, but which also reflect his curious air of detachment from his own activities.

His former employers lampooned him in print as a "pretty pup once in our employment; but whose indolence, incompetence, loaferism and blackguard habits forced us to kick him out of the office."[16] Whitman sharply replied in the newspaper columns of his next employer. The vituperative exchange is not unusual for the journalism of the day, but the remarks indicate that however competently Walt did his work — and evidently he was an excellent editor — he gave the impression of being uninvolved, indifferent, and preoccupied.

Another indication of a deep and unexpressed emotional distraction is that Walt never showed an interest in girls or women, though he was physically mature relatively early in life. Neither his brothers nor any friend could recall Whitman's having a sexual attraction to women. His students in school were aware that he did not like the company of girls or older women. At his newspaper jobs he never displayed a young man's typical excitement over sexual adventures, or iniquities, in the city. "He seemed to hate women," observed a friend who knew Walt when he was managing his own newspaper in Huntington. And like the melancholy Hamlet, Walt was not delighted by either sex. The homosexual passions that erupted in him later were scarcely evident during the early period of his life. His behavior was entirely conventional, strictly moral, and soberly sexless. Yet while teaching in country schools and living with the families of his students, his aversion to girls, casual manner, and dreamy habits roused suspicion that he was too affectionate toward the boys. He once said he had been strongly "reproved" by the father of a fairly grown-up pupil, in whose family he boarded, for "making such a pet of the boy."[17]

After he lost his job on the *Aurora* in 1842, Walt's career declined again, but he did not return to schoolteaching. Short-lived assignments as an editor or hack writer of a temperance novel and other sentimental fiction made up his dwindling activity until he rejoined his family on their return to Brooklyn in September 1845. This reconvergence of the family enterprise and his personal aspirations enlivened Walt and seemed to provide him with the support he needed to take hold of his own life and work. By the following March, in 1846, he had become editor of the *Brooklyn Eagle*, and for two years he devoted himself fully and happily to his career. Once again he was boarding away from home but visiting his family every day. His brother Jeff was old enough to help him at the newspaper office on occasion. He had friends, and best of all, he felt a new bond of familial identification with the community of readers for whom he wrote every day, once commenting on their relationship.

> There is a curious kind of sympathy (haven't you ever thought
> of it before?) that arises in the mind of a newspaper conductor

with the public he serves. He gets to *love* them. Daily communion creates a sort of brotherhood and sisterhood between the two parties. As for us, we like this. We like it better than the more "dignified" part of editorial labors — the grave political disquisition, the contests of faction, and so on.[18]

But however homey he felt working in Brooklyn on the *Eagle,* Whitman lost this job too. The ostensible cause of his dismissal in January 1848 was his longstanding support of the Wilmot Proviso, a bill to limit the extension of slavery; his publisher and employer opposed such restrictions. Discharged again because of his liberal views and chagrined over his failure, Whitman was sufficiently desperate and angry to take a job editing a newspaper in New Orleans, farther from the center of his life than he could expect to endure except as an exile. Nevertheless, he made the decision impulsively: At a theater on a Wednesday evening soon after he was fired, he met a man who was willing to pay him two hundred dollars in advance to take a position in New Orleans; Whitman accepted the offer and left town for New Orleans by that Friday, February 11 — taking his brother Jeff in tow. Both sons quickly turned homesick and stayed that way. Jeff's many letters beg his family to write, and Walt's infrequent additions echo the plea. "I began to feel very uneasy, not hearing from you so long," he writes his mother; he then adds, "O how I long for the day when we can have our quiet little farm, and be together again."[19] It appears that none of the family in Brooklyn bothered to write to the absent boys. After nearly three months away from home Jeff writes lugubriously that they have at last received one letter.

Dear Parents,

Since I wrote to you (the night after we got your only letter) we have heard nothing from you, It is very strange you do not write oftener to us, for we have written to you ever so many times, now we have been from home nearly three months, and we have received only one letter from you, I beg of you to write to us often.[20]

Whitman may have been stimulated by the cosmopolitan, Southern culture of New Orleans in the feverish military atmosphere right after the Mexican War, but whatever attractions he found in the city did not reach deep or hold him long. This single venture far away from home ended in an abrupt disappointment that has never been fully explained, though the utter unlikelihood of Whitman thriving in such a remote place may be enough to account for his return to Brooklyn in just three months. He was too uneasy over the distance between himself and his home life.

It is clear from stories that Whitman wrote during this early period that he was an extremely anxious young man who needed to remain close to his parents for the love and approval that he believed, accurately, were never unconditionally given to him to take elsewhere in a life he might live separately. However he strove to define himself through his growth, ambitions, and experience of a relatively sophisticated culture, he remained basically captivated — both enticed and enslaved — by his feelings about his parents and his place among seven brothers and sisters, who were similarly subject to the central power of life and death that Walt beheld in his parents' love. In the melodramatic stories he had been writing since the age of sixteen, Walt repeatedly portrayed his family and its stresses. The tales that were published in the *Democratic Review* emphasized the cruelty of harsh fathers and other male tyrants who brutally mistreat boys, driving them to death or insanity. In "Death in the Schoolroom," a sadistic teacher unjustly thrashes a sickly boy suspected of a petty theft, but the child has already died before the wrongful punishment begins. In "Wild Frank's Return," a son who left home over favoritism shown by his father to his older brother is trampled to death as he rides home on his brother's horse, the cause of the original dispute among them. In "Bervance" a son must escape the inexplicable hatred that impels his father to commit the boy to an insane asylum. In many other stories as well, the martyred child is apt to be a second son, favored by the mother but scorned by the father, who favors the older son. Mothers are not prominent in most of the stories, but rather grieve over the calamities that occur. Most commentators agree that the point of this trite but self-revealing fiction is Whitman's feeling that children generally need better fathers than they have and that mothers are at fault for allowing such misfortune to befall their favorites.[21]

While Whitman was alternately attempting and evading his entry into an adult career in the 1840s, his father was clearly failing financially and personally, becoming ever more surly, unresponsive, and remote. Walt's efforts to succeed were hampered by an awareness of his father's defeats. But he could not directly recognize the passivity and weakness of his father, who had little ability to provide for his family or to act upon his ideals. He saw, instead, the father who did not value him. The glaring disparity between his father's neglect and his mother's powerful attachment led him to interpret his father's behavior as a deliberate repudiation or even a denial of his basic masculinity. The consequences of that neglect compounded Walt's feelings of worthlessness and vulnerability. In his young imagination, if not in actuality, his father was a threatening tyrant, and Walt felt doomed by the terrible feelings he projected onto his father. It was, after all, a family in which he had witnessed and complied with his parents' apparent retaliations against difficult children. When

Walt later came to recognize, around the age of thirty, that his father's remoteness was less hostile than he had believed, this insight into his father's frustration cleared the way for a fuller identification with him, a crucial step in Whitman's emergence as a mature poet. But in his early anxiety, if he sensed that he was able and eager to outstrip his father, he also anticipated retribution or a catastrophe if he did so, for he would be abandoning the man whose love and support he had always hoped would materialize.

Beginning in adolescence, he tried to overcome this conflict by adopting a double parental role in the family. To gain a sense of manhood in safe, dutiful activity, he became his notion of the ideal father. He fancied that his younger brothers and sisters were his children, and he conducted himself with a mixture of fair-mindedness and sympathy toward all. An air of unquestionable authority protected him behind chasms of isolation from any challenge to his pretenses — in this manner, copying his father's testy remoteness. He helped to teach the children, care for them, protect them from one another, and provide for them, carrying out his tasks better than their remiss actual father cared to do.

Whitman's unilateral acts of fatherhood started early and lasted long. Throughout his life he maintained the emotional conviction, or unconscious fantasy, that he was the true father of his six younger brothers and sisters. When he was old and garrulous, this fantasy emerged as the false claim that he had fathered six illegitimate children whose identities must remain secret.[22] Throughout his adult life in one way or another he treated most people as his children, because the imaginary role of father fed his idea of himself as the spirit who would regenerate the world. He presented himself as a father to his readers, to future generations of Americans whether they read him or not, to his successors in poetry, and eventually to disciples in his old age. As a "kosmos" in *Leaves of Grass* he was also the father of his inner self, and a son "of Manhattan," as he claimed to be, but not of any ordinary progenitor. The ideal of fatherhood symbolized his prodigious efforts in life and poetry to avoid being childish: to become self-creative, important, and immortalized.

In his youth Whitman merely resembled a mature man, and in this guise he tried to attract his father's approval. More importantly, the precocious role also made him forever his mother's practical partner and soul mate. Louisa, who could never bear to be deprived of her grudging total responsibility for any of the children, welcomed her sweetest child into the romance of their mutual endeavor that bound him to her in a continuation of his childhood longings to preserve the closest sympathy he was ever to know. The intimate understanding that flowed from Walt to his mother supplied her with ample demonstration of his devotion and dependence that she required; and it brought Walt the return of her

possessive maternal love, ensuring his connection with at least one responsive human being.

In short, Walt attempted to live without defining himself; instead he
maintained a divided purpose to become the ideal father and to be unified
with his mother. Of course, this prolonged effort could not resolve the
stresses in his life: He lived with two distinctly separate natures, which
he could not harmonize into a cohesive personality. "I cannot understand
the mystery," he wrote in a notebook he began keeping in 1848 after his
return from New Orleans, "but I am always conscious of myself as two
— as my soul and I: and I reckon it is the same with all men and
women."[23] This entry reveals that Walt's anxiety was obsessive and
private: He was "always conscious" of a "mystery" that he evidently
tried but failed to "understand." And in a characteristic way, he looked
to a notion of generalized male and female character — to "all men and
women" — for some clue to the meaning of his divided self. At once helpless and self-indulgent in his plight, he disarmingly understates the misery
of his sense of difference from other people in the casual conjecture and
artless diction of "I reckon it is the same." Dominated by the two looming
figures of his unattainable goals, Walt was divided by his ambivalence
toward a mother who was too close, threatening to become his very person, and toward a father who was too remote, projecting masculinity as
only an object of erotic love rather than an available principle of loving.

Emotionally trapped, the young heir to his father's dream of a prosper-
ous, heroic democracy settled deeper into enslavement to his family experience. After the collapse of his New Orleans venture in 1848, Walt's
professional life appeared to shrink and his daily life became even more
entwined with the household than before he tried to remove himself. His
one significant further involvement with political journalism was frustrated by a fire that destroyed the printing office of his newly launched
Free Soil weekly; after that Walt simply withdrew from managerial journalism and political campaigning, returning to his trade to edit the *Brooklyn Daily Times* only after he was well launched as a poet. He lived at
home with his family and for a while actively joined in their efforts to
make money through house building and speculative real estate transactions. He also began to take on more responsibility for his retarded and
malformed youngest brother, whose care continued to be a major concern for the rest of Walt's life. Eddie shared Walt's room and slept in his
bed. Walt dressed and groomed him, perhaps in his cast-off editor's
clothes, which he had abandoned for jeans and a work shirt. Eddie was
large and muscular, like Walt, and their facial features were similar, so
that Eddie began to look strikingly like him. In later life, their beards,
clothes, shape, and gait were so similar that Walt's friends found the
resemblance uncanny. When Eddie was fifteen or sixteen, Walt's

prematurely gray hair gave him the appearance of being Eddie's father, and Walt's protective attitude toward him reinforced the role of parent he shared with Louisa in the care of this unchanging child. Eddie needed constant attention because he could not control his own behavior. He gorged himself on anything, and he would not of his own will ever stop eating. He was capable of dangerous rages when his wishes were frustrated. Though he was gentle enough when placid, he could not be trusted alone in public except on short, familiar errands. Walt gave all his patience to this ungoverned instinctual creature, whose overt impulses to ingest or obliterate the world may have resonated profoundly in the unconscious of the emerging poet. Whitman's bond with this, the family's third troublesome, unfortunate child reached deep and continued long. When Walt fell ill at the age of fifty-three, his sentimental notion of an idyllic existence was to recover his strength enough to have a small farm where he and his mother could look after Eddie together — even though he had avoided that course when he was healthy.

Walt soon gave up his active participation in house building in the early 1850s, retiring much like his now ailing and helpless father to let the younger men bring in the badly needed money and to make their way together against the world. In moving with them from house to house, Walt sometimes kept part of the first floor for a combined printing office and bookstore. Outwardly, he seemed to embrace his anonymity and limitations. Partly, it suited him to be wholly enclosed within the domestic circle. He felt relieved of the burden to strive alone in the world outside. Independence had clearly come to mean a state of solitude, repeated personal rejections and defeats, and the constant vision of vaguer dangers invented in his fantasies of punishment. He had given up his other hopes, but he had secured more deeply the satisfaction of being his mother's partner and his father's image. Partly succeeding in these regressive aims and strengthened by the family's deference to him, Whitman magisterially took from them all the freedom he needed to go ahead with his writing.

His general taste and aesthetic judgment were improving as he worked more artfully on his poetry. His interest in Italian opera and photography became passions as he discovered in these artistic forms larger ideas and higher standards of the range and complexity of meanings that could be expressed in art. He came to acknowledge more of his feelings through his growing understanding of these fresh arts, and they contributed to his emerging ideas about a new kind of poetry he would write. He fully recognized the beauty of opera, which previously had not interested him, and he lost his earlier preference for the folksy "heart-singing" of popular family choruses like the New England Cheneys and the Hutchinsons. In 1845, writing in a magazine that Edgar Allan Poe edited, Whitman had praised "heart-music" as superior to "art-music" because the former was "something original and beautiful in the way of American musical execution." Its simplicities appeared fresher and more humane than the aristocratic style and conventions of European song. He also promoted Negro minstrelsy with enthusiastic notice in his newspaper features during the 1840s, when with nationalistic pride he claimed that the new minstrel shows offered a native form of theater that could lead to a distinctive American drama. He valued popular entertainments mainly for their nationalistic implications to him. They expressed American originality, and they suggested the possibility of new, freer forms of music reflecting the spirit of the nation. A few years later in 1852, he found such native entertainments distastefully vapid. He reversed his earlier opinion when he began to feel the personal need for a more complicated artistry to articulate the true spirit of the nation, which he was striving to objectify. Complaining about American musical theater at the height of his new passion for imported Italian opera, he wrote in a newspaper column: "Ah, how can such an intellectual people as the Americans really are, countenance before them the nigger monstrosities and the sugar and water of the various 'families' who appear among us from time to time?"[24]

During two splendid opera seasons in New York, in 1851–52 and 1852–53, Whitman thrilled to great performances that enlarged his sense of freedom for the poetic voice. In the rich cascade of works by Bellini, Donizetti, and Verdi, Whitman heard the human voice do things with power and intricacy that he had never imagined possible for a single voice. He became enamored of individual performers, and he felt ravished by the specially melodic, *bel canto* arias, sung in the style he had previously criticized as European decadence. Whitman claimed that during one season he attended every concert and opera performance by the superb coloratura soprano Marietta Alboni. She and the tenor Bettini and the baritone Badiali, whose voices he also praised during the same period, remained for him the greatest singers he had ever heard. He recalled that Alboni's singing filled him with ecstasy: "She used to sweep me away as with whirlwinds."[25] His emotional encounters with such sophisticated vocal artistry opened up the possibilities of poetic expression along similarly musical, brilliantly varied, strong-voiced lines. He confided to his friend Trowbridge in 1860, "But for opera I could never have written *Leaves of Grass.*" In his later recollections with Traubel, Whitman once exclaimed about his opera-going days: "Oh! those great days! great, great days! Alboni, Badiali, in particular; no one can tell, know, even suspect, how much they had to do with the making of Leaves of Grass. . . . My younger life was so saturated with the emotions, raptures, up-lifts, of such musical experiences that it would be surprising indeed if all my future work had not been colored by them. A real musician running through Leaves of Grass — a philosopher musician — could put his finger on this and that anywhere in the text no doubt as indicating the activity of the influences I have spoken of."[26]

During the same period of his intellectual and aesthetic growth, Whitman became fascinated by photography; and more than most people in the nineteenth century with whom he shared this important change in sensibility, Whitman responded to a new idea of personal identity that the photograph suggested. As early as 1846 in his columns in the *Brooklyn Eagle*, Whitman praised the new art form as superior to any other representation "of that subtle thing, *human expression*." The portraits intrigued him, because, as he said with some astonishment, they were "*realities*." He avidly searched for his own reality expressed in photographs: Possibly no other writer of this era was photographed as many times as Whitman, who throughout his life savored the variety of his attitudes that could be registered by the camera.

Daguerreotyping flourished commercially in American cities during the 1840s, with ingenious American daguerreotypists quickly refining techniques and studio equipment, which were later adopted as the "American method" even in France. Whitman became critically interested in the achievements of individual photographers about 1852, when he contributed three free-lance articles to Brooklyn newspapers. He did not fail to take pride in the advancement of the art by Americans, and he asserted authoritatively that "in America alone, and mostly in New York, is daguerreotype taking really an *art*."[27] He avidly visited studios, where the lounges, often luxuriously furnished to attract the carriage trade, usually displayed examples of the photographer's work, arranged on the walls in a dense cluster in the style of nineteenth-century museum hanging. Whitman looked long and closely at a myriad of faces fixed on silvered plates, open to his minutest scrutiny of the exact expression in their features. He saw the faces of public personalities like Victor Hugo, Henry Ward Beecher, Horace Greeley, and even the beloved Alboni, now revealed with more intimacy than in his actual contacts with others, which for him were usually oblique anyway. The sustained concreteness and literalness of expression in those portraits must have overwhelmed Whitman with real evidence of subjective individuality. Personality was seen to be a more substantial, real entity when the photograph demonstrated both its changeableness and its timelessness. Each unique personality was objectified in an image that was not an artist's conception of his subject but the very subject itself made into an artwork through the play of light on silvered plates. The personality projected itself into an external, aesthetic object. The photograph must have helped persuade Whitman that his own personality could be objectified through the natural medium of sound — like light falling on a printing plate the sound of his voice would fix his image in poems.

By making the personal image more explicit and literal, the photograph was also erotically stimulating, and it moved Whitman to acknowledge more of his own sexuality as intrinsic to his identity. Photography made every detail of physical appearance open to any searching gaze, and the physical person appeared unconsciously available to any viewer's possessive thoughts. To Whitman, who was struggling to extricate himself from the sexual compunctions that burdened him, the vividness of the photographic subjects brought their sexual presence closer in a way that was definite without being threatening. He could contemplate the physicality of people, even yearn for the comforts of physical contact with various personalities, without feeling openly shamed. His own erotic awareness rose toward freer expression, bringing him closer to that moment when he could display in poetry a literal image of his own body and dote upon his particular features.

Whitman had the emotional constitution to respond to the poignancy and ambiguity of personality in the photographic image, as well as to the photograph's subjective and sexual literalness. He saw the emotional distance between himself and other people objectified in their fixed images. Because of the necessary long exposure of the plates, faces and bodies in the early photographs projected impassive expressions that withheld even as they promised to give the truth of interior life. They looked distracted or deadened, their gaze mechanically cut off from the next moment of response. The most obvious statement of these images was that they were oblivious of *him*. Viewing pictures was a lot like pondering one's own uncertain visibility through the eyes of another person — like an insecure child looking for himself in his distracted mother's eyes. Whitman was hypersensitive to the suggestions of denial in each unregarding face. Even in his journalism review of daguerreotyping, Whitman evoked the disturbing ambiguity of other people's remoteness and immediacy present in one image, their paradoxical concreteness and disintegration simultaneously revealed, and his yearning for intimacy couched in his anticipations of death.

> A thousand faces? They look at you from all parts of the large and sumptuously furnished saloon. Over your shoulders, back, behind you, staring square in front, how the eyes, almost glittering with the light of life, bend down upon one, and silently follow all his motions. . . . How many of these, whose faces look upon us, are now away in distant regions? How many are dead? What terrible changes have happened to them.[28]

Photography allowed him to project his feelings into the conventions and formal characteristics of the art, helping him in this way to undertake a similar, deeper projection into the medium of poetry. He felt defined by the suggestive literalness of this new art. It so fully symbolized the paradoxes of his sense of self that he chose to identify himself by using only a photograph, not his name, when he published his first book of poetry. The anonymous first edition of *Leaves of Grass* included as a frontispiece the now famous daguerreotype of Whitman posing in his workman's clothes, with a Spanish hat slanted on his head as he nods slightly to gaze directly at the viewer, his stance casually provocative, left hand thrust in his jeans pocket and his right arm akimbo, shirt front open — and not a single word under the picture. To Whitman the photograph was like a poem announcing himself, a poetic inscription like those he used in his later editions, and all the poems to follow were verbal photographs of the self.

By the time he came to write those poems, he was convinced of his direct insight into the realities of individual character — like the *"realities"* he thought he saw in the photographic portraits — and his main philosophical ideas about the nature of personality came from his study of the new, popular science of phrenology. Whitman was deeply interested in phrenology throughout the years of his eclectic development into a poet, and when his first book was ready to be sold, he gave it on consignment to Fowler and Wells, the leading phrenological publisher and bookshop on Fulton Street, which had been an intellectual home for him for several years preceding the publication of the first edition of *Leaves*.

Like his passion for Italian opera and his fascination with photography, Whitman's interest in phrenology was a fresh response to another of the notable cultural achievements of his contemporary world. In the poet's gestation years, phrenology had not yet been degraded as quackery. During its period of integrity, phrenology offered a systematic psychology based on medical and behavioral research. It undertook to demonstrate that the soul of man is concretely and corporeally a mental structure, composed of organs of the will in the brain. It postulated that the dynamic interaction of the brain's distinct faculties constitutes each unique personality. According to this doctrine, conflicts and paradoxes of subjective experience are part of the normal functions of the mind; in this way phrenology accounted for the complexity of internal life without invoking metaphysical preconceptions or moral statements about the aims of the mental processes themselves. Its basic assumption was a simple yet radical belief in natural harmony between the body and the soul, a belief that phrenologists validated by identifying the brain sites of personality traits. Phrenology anatomized character, and offered an approach to the fulfillment of man and society through self-awareness, since the "phrenologized" person would now have solid evidence of his constitutional strengths, weaknesses, and full potential. He could learn to accept, discipline, and develop himself. The title page of Orson Fowler's many books on applied phrenology carried the author's motto Self-Made or Never Made. The practical side of phrenology led to a liberal morality guiding most of the reform leaders and movements in America during this period of many zealous reforms, for it offered a plan that promised better education, better marriage, better laws, manners, diet, recreation, and social order.

Whitman was interested in phrenology even in the mid-1840s when as editor of the *Brooklyn Eagle* he surveyed and recommended to his "family" of readers all that passed for practical and self-improving knowledge. Phrenology fell within his wide-ranging concern at that time for the general welfare, especially for health and hygiene, including reform attitudes about temperance, prostitution, food, drugs, sanitation, exercise for women, and ladies' tight lacing. Phrenology vigorously encouraged a sensible regard for the body: Orson Fowler glorified health and physical beauty as indications of spiritual goodness. Since much of what phrenologists discussed and advised promoted bodily health and forthrightness about sex, Whitman's discipleship at Fowler's encouraged his own sexual definition. He found intellectual and moral support for his inclination to reveal himself utterly in poetry. But a clear perception of himself as a diverse, dynamic personality came into focus only in 1849 when he had a phrenological reading by Lorenzo Fowler. The findings of the cranial survey articulated Whitman's newly emerging self-image, and he devoted the rest of his life to substantiating it in his life and poetry. He kept the chart of the survey among his most precious papers — not even his manuscripts were preserved as carefully — and he repeatedly published the phrenologist's summary of his faculties as a kind of credential of the validity of his poems.

> leading traits of character appear to be Friendship, Sympathy, Sublimity and Self-Esteem, and markedly among his combinations the dangerous faults of Indolence, a tendency to the pleasure of Voluptuousness and Alimentativeness, and a certain swing of animal will, too unmindful, probably, of the conviction of others.[29]

These are the principal traits by which Whitman characterized himself in the poems that were yet to be written about a fully developed, representative American man. Fowler's analysis of his character was an inestimable prize, because it gave Whitman a favorable idea of his abundant humanity. He undertook serious, prolonged study of phrenology in order to learn more about the coherence of personality. For the next five or six years, Whitman regularly read the *American Phrenological Journal*, a publication of Fowler and Wells, and he frequently visited the

Phrenological Cabinet, or museum, maintained by the firm. There he examined busts, casts, and skulls, which were like the expressive faces he scrutinized in photographs. New science and new art were joining in his mind to indicate a new definition of man.

The turbulence of his inner life was now both pleasurable and unnerving. He was making discoveries that connected him spiritually with the larger experience of mankind, yet at the same time he had fallen into a social isolation so deep that his loneliness felt like cosmic darkness, impenetrable, eternal, and deadly. Unlike Thoreau, Hawthorne, Dickinson, or other deliberate "isolatoes" in American history, Whitman could not rest easy in the vividness of his solitude. He carried his social deprivation as a wound and a shame; he hungered for direct contacts with ordinary people that would relieve him of the confusion and strain of his private ordeal. He welcomed the signs of basic familiarity between himself and other people. The illustration of perfect character, he reminded himself in his earliest notebook, was to be found, not in aristocratic or uncommon models, but in the democratic American man, who is proof that human nature is "illimitably proud, independent, self-possessed, generous and gentle."[30] Through his devotion to the political ideal, Whitman came to see himself as a man of congenial character with public associations. He steadily nurtured himself back toward good spirits with an outpouring of love toward humanity. He wrote didactically, as if formulating phrases to deliver in a sermon or moral lecture, but the point of the didactic tone is to soothe and heal his wounded self. "Every American young man should carry himself with the finished and haughty bearing of the greatest ruler and proprietor — for he is a great ruler and proprietor — the greatest." He dwells on what would be the moral qualities of a fully developed "true noble expanded American Character," and he thinks of himself as the companion of the sublime common man. He anticipates that like a kindly father, he will show his charges that the earth is generous and accepting toward all: "None shall be an exception to the universal and affectionate Yes of the earth." Like the earth itself, he moves to embrace "each man and woman of you," and to point out the wondrous equality and balance between mind and matter throughout the universe. He comforted himself, like a cherishing parent speaking to a child.

The wonder of him throughout his ordeal as a young man is that he sturdily faced the important darkness in himself. He secretly lived at the edge of irremediable confusion until he gained enough strength and the imaginative means to accept his peculiarities and to proclaim their universal relevance. The "first inspiration of real wisdom," he continued in his notebook, is to know we are not as unsightly or as wicked as we thought. It is self-acceptance that discloses the sublimity of other ordinary people as well. His new doctrine of acceptance will show others a road where "every breath through your mouth shall be of a perfumed and elastic air, which is love."

Whitman's period of solacing himself eventually came to include moments of sharpened awareness of what was happening within him. Briefly, and possibly on repeated occasions over a period of several months, he experienced ecstasies that felt like outpourings of love from himself to himself directly. He was conscious of unleashing a passion that he himself fully received. He felt transported into contact with absolute reality; he felt he contained what was universal in nature. However strange, pleasurable, or frightening it was, this emotional turmoil had the effect of a revelation that was the turning point of his life. The experience was what his first biographer, Richard Maurice Bucke, regarded worshipfully as Whitman's mystical elevation to "cosmic consciousness."[31] Actually, it was more psychological and creative than mystical or religious. Whitman internalized the entire drama of his family relations, and at last he granted himself the love that he had believed could come only from the parents he imagined himself to be in their stead. The illumination of his fundamental consciousness uplifted Whitman from the mediocrity of his journalism and his early writings and pulled down the walls of his shallow, adolescent egocentricity. He became, instead, profoundly egocentric.

Elated and yet unnerved, Whitman responded to the crisis of his self-definition by inventing the poetry that could objectify his experience. His mature poetry began when he acquired a suitable verse form for dramatizing not just his paradoxes but also his daring, enlivening acceptance of these paradoxes. His notebook shows him proceeding from reflective, sometimes lyrical passages in prose toward the emergence of his first lines in the new verses that enable him to conceptualize and embrace the reality of his divided self. His excited, rambling thoughts are expressed in fragments, not sustained meditations, but they stay close to the themes that continue in his verses, and the prose passages indicate as well the emerging trait of alternation and repetition in the workings of his mind. Always conscious of himself as two, "my soul and I," he seems to be knitting together the opposites of his "mystery": joining spirit and matter, immortality and decay, body and soul, man and woman, father and mother, parent and child, goodness and badness, glamour and ugliness, land and water, earth and air, capitalists and workmen — accumulating the extremes that reveal his feeling for polarities, which he holds together by his response of love for all opposites and contradictions. He begins to see himself as a representative man, enlarged by the very diversities that he embodies. He does not synthesize or integrate the differences he notes; instead, ever more earnestly and ecstatically, he focuses on his capacity as a mediator to accept all differences. At last, the protean verses begin, haltingly and briefly at first, choked back by his excited scurrying between the two sides of him that he can feel:

> I am the poet of slaves, and the masters of slaves
> I am the poet of the body
> And I am[32]

Then, more fluidly, the parallel constructions become more varied and supple, and the lines that sound like the Bible in which he discovered these cadences expand across the page and build up into long rhythmic sentences.

> I am the poet of the body
> And I am the poet of the soul
> I go with the slaves of the earth equally with
>   the masters
> And I will stand between the masters and the
>   slaves,
> Entering into both, so that both shall under-
>   stand me alike.

Whitman had no name for the mysterious process that delivered him from internal oppression to this emotional awakening. He could not intellectually explain his crisis or regard it as a more or less common event in the course of personal development. Nothing like the modern psychological meanings of "self" and "identity" were available to him in the common language of his day. He lived in a parochial American culture in an age that had not yet scientifically grasped the integrity of subjective life, but was already seeking to replace the outworn religious terminology of grace, sin, guilt, and redemption of something long surmised to be the soul of man. From the Romantic literature of England and France, he had absorbed contemporary ideas of the imagination as an autonomous and moral faculty actively involved in the perceptions and responses of real, daily life. But he urgently needed a more empirical, closer account of his strangely separate but beholden existence. If he had been raised in a traditional family culture of Protestant religious attitudes, like his contemporaries Emerson, Thoreau, or Carlyle, he might have more readily defined his experience as a "conversion" of the spirit, and like them he might have interpreted it with customary emphasis upon the moral revelation it conveyed — instead of the emphasis he was to give to the dynamics of consciousness itself. But unlike any of them, he was raised in a nonreligious, radically freethinking household of lower-class workers in Brooklyn during an era of explosively radiating materialism before the Civil War. Despite his early oblique contact with Quakerism, he faced his developmental ordeal with a mind largely unfortified and unprejudiced by mankind's history of encounters with the ineffable and miraculous workings of the divine spirit. Too secular to think of his illumination as a conversion by grace and — unlike Wordsworth — too materialistic to attribute to the imagination any power to create what was so palpably real, Whitman could not explain the crisis of his development with religious or romantic concepts. He was pristinely interested in what was happening to him as a phenomenon of his contemporary world, and his attention flowed unimpeded toward analysis of the process by which he was granted insight and identity. No major writer in English ever met his vision more nakedly than Whitman as he absorbedly pried into the machinery of his redemption. He wanted to unravel the internal mystery of his acute separateness from and his indissoluble union with others. Unprovided with any useful cultural attitude toward his passionate inner experience, he had available to him no theory or dogma with which to generalize his private insight to his divided but cohering nature. Lacking an adequate literary, religious, or scientific language in which to understand himself, he found a way in poetry to define his intuitions about the dynamics and boundaries of individuality.

2

The Anatomy of a Poetic Identity

FROM 1848 to 1855 and the publication of the first edition of *Leaves of Grass*, Whitman intuitively formulated a poetics, a set of ideas about the nature of poetry, which for him as for most other nineteenth-century romantics is a theory of poetic personality. The ideas he drew from phrenology, music, photography, and literature led him to a new understanding of the imagination as the essence of individuality. As a secretly developing poet in workman's clothing, he pondered ontological questions about what is actual, what is ideal, and what is unreal. He was not yet strongly affected, as he later would be, by the moral importunities of Emerson and other Americans who turned such questions into a practical challenge: What are we to *do*? More like English poets of the preceding generation — Coleridge, Wordsworth, Keats — he wanted to know what we subjectively *are*.

Because he wanted to poeticize and thereby confirm his identity, he took particular exception to the famous statement by Keats that "a poet is the most unpoetical of anything in existence, because he has no identity; he is continually in for and filling some other body." Coming upon that statement in 1848 or 1849, Whitman wrote his objections in the margin of the article he was reading: "The great poet absorbs the identity of others, and the exp[erience] of others, and they are definite in him or from him; but he p[erceives] them all through the powerful press of himself."[1] While Keats could find his meanings embodied in literary myths, romances, stars, birds, seasons, and all the poetry of earth, Whitman could not trust analogous extensions of himself beyond his subjective circle. He needed to absorb everything, to draw everything into the immediate context of his own personality.

In the poems he soon wrote for the first *Leaves*, Whitman dwells on the curious phenomena of his imagination, noting especially the pecularities of his memory, dreams, visions, and bewildering states of heightened consciousness in which he sometimes finds the entire universe within himself. For instance, in "There Was a Child Went Forth" (1855), Whitman explains how he came to be the poet he is, by asserting that every childhood experience went into making the person who now remembers as he writes. He finds all his childhood feelings still accessible within him, and all are equally important as long as they remain intact in his memory. With awe and curiosity he touches again his earliest sensations of discovery, happiness, fear, and loneliness, writing in a tone delicately cautious not to shatter the child's ineffable perceptions that remain still vivid. The mystery of personality that developed this child into a poet like Whitman — and not like Keats — occurs between the second and third lines in a momentous reversal of the child's imaginative sympathy; Whitman swings away from becoming the objects he sees to absorbing the objects into himself. The verbal action changes from "he became" to objects "became part of him," and this perception sustains the rest of the thirty-nine lines of the poem. He speaks as the preserver of events, events saved and recovered inside himself.

> There was a child went forth every day,
> And the first object he look'd upon, that object
>   he became,
> And that object became part of him for the day or
>   a certain part of the day,
> Or for many years or stretching cycles of years.
>
> The early lilacs became part of this child,
> And grass and white and red morning-glories, and
>   white and red clover, and the song of the
>   phoebe-bird,
> And the Third-month lambs and the sow's pink-faint
>   litter, and the mare's foal and the cow's calf,
> And the noisy brood of the barnyard or by the mire
>   of the pondside,
> And the fish suspending themselves so curiously
>   below there, and the beautiful curious liquid,
> And the water-plants with their graceful flat heads,
>   all became part of him.
>
>   (ll. 1–10)

The beginning of the poem dwells on the small, intimate facts of nature that would catch a child's wondering eyes and bring the world closer. But the intimacy and concreteness of these natural objects recede when the poet turns to include askant and passive observations of other people.

They are seen on the road, passing by him to go to and from school or the tavern or on their way between city and countryside. He perceives them from a periphery rather than from a center of active life, as if he were standing inside a fenced yard or venturing in solitude among strangers.

> And the apple-trees cover'd with blossoms and
> the fruit afterward, and wood-berries,
> and the commonest weeds by the road,
> And the old drunkard staggering home from the
> outhouse of the tavern whence he had
> lately risen,
> And the schoolmistress that pass'd on her way
> to the school,
> And the friendly boys that pass'd, and the
> quarrelsome boys,
> And the tidy and fresh-cheek'd girls, and the
> barefoot negro boy and girl,
> And all the changes of city and country wherever
> he went.
>
> (ll. 13–18)

The increasingly distant perspective suggests an older, more self-conscious child who is already feeling uneasy over being alone or disregarded. In the slightly anxious mood that arises from this sequence of recollections, Whitman recalls both his parents. The mother's sweet but receding aura of intimacy trails like a "wholesome odor" from her as "she walks by." The father is unapproachably preoccupied with his business and his anger; his willful dealings and his irritability are linked in the insightful boy's summation of his father.

> The mother at home quietly placing the dishes
> on the suppertable,
> The mother with mild words, clean her cap and
> gown, a wholesome odor falling off her
> person and clothes as she walks by,
> The father, strong, self-sufficient, manly,
> mean, anger'd, unjust,
> The blow, the quick loud word, the tight bargain,
> the crafty lure,
> The family usages, the language, the company,
> the furniture, the yearning and swelling
> heart,

> Affection that will not be gainsay'd, the sense
>   of what is real, the thought if after
>   all it should prove unreal,
> The doubts of day-time and the doubts of night-
>   time, the curious whether and how,
> Whether that which appears so is so, or is it
>   all flashes and specks?
>
> (11. 22–29)

The image of his parents involved with their work recalls his loneliness in a crowded household where his turbulent emotions were unacknowledged. His clamor for recognition of the "affection that will not be gainsay'd" — that is, his "yearning and swelling heart" — is nevertheless denied by people who ignore his need for sympathetic responses. The result of this cruel neglect is a perception of himself in which his feelings do not matter, or perhaps are not "real." And worst of all, this depersonalized view of him "became part of him" indeed. As the sequence of thoughts in the poem indicates, his own ideas and feelings lose validity and integrity; his parents' denial of his feelings undermines his sense of what is immediate, real, and substantively himself. He is struck by a generalized, metaphysical sense of unreality, for he is not acknowledged as a separate, distinct child.

In the process of celebrating the cohesiveness of growth and development, Whitman uncovers the scarcely recognized anguish of childhood alienation that made him both want and fear to cling to every vanishing hope of parental love. In the midst of recovering the everlasting freshness and richness of memory, as he does in the first half of the poem, he sees himself becoming a passive observer, alone, saddened by vague losses and mindful of oblivion. This melancholy attitude is fully expressed in the final ten lines when Whitman as a youth wanders through a world that symbolically reflects his exclusion, isolation, and even abandonment. Every object is out of his reach or ken; barriers impede his approach; beautiful objects or prospects of warmhearted community recede. Left alone in the streets, he sees the "façades of houses" or he looks in at "goods in the window"; or he stands alone in the countryside, staring at a distant village two miles away across a river; or he is at the sea's edge, watching clouds and ships and the rim of the world fall away from him. His perception of the experiences that formed him has changed from his initial intimacy with small objects. He reinterprets his personal history as he constructs it, and now acknowledges the lonely child's intense awareness that everything desirable is too far away for comfort. That early sense of luckless exclusion from intimacy "became part of him" forever, giving definitive form to his poetic personality.

Men and women crowding fast in the streets, if
    they are not flashes and specks what
    are they?
The streets themselves and the façades of houses,
    and goods in the window,
Vehicles, teams, the heavy-plank'd wharves, the
    huge crossing at the ferries,
The village on the highland seen from afar at
    sunset, the river between,
Shadows, aureola and mist, the light falling
    on roofs and gables of white or brown
    two miles off,
The schooner near by sleepily dropping down
    the tide, the little boat slack-tow'd
    astern,
The hurrying tumbling waves, quick-broken
    crests, slapping,
The strata of color'd clouds, the long bar of
    maroon-tint away solitary by itself,
    the spread of purity it lies motionless
    in,
The horizon's edge, the flying sea-crow, the
    fragrance of salt marsh and shore mud,
These became part of that child who went forth
    every day, and who now goes, and will
    always go forth every day.

(11. 30–39)

The final line returns to the activity of the adult poet, who confirms his continuity with the child he was and the child he partly remains. Though formed long ago, his sensibility "now goes, and will always go forth." Through close repetition of the major verbs, Whitman emphasizes the resolute physical action that reflects his receptive state of creativity: "went forth," "now goes," "will always go forth every day." The feelings of confidence and integrity in the reiteration suggest that the inner child is stalwartly forging ahead, full of determination that indeed he *must* go. The understated grief in Whitman's discovery of his continuing past is that his experience was always slipping from his grasp; to the child as he went forth in solitary ways, it seemed he was compelled away from the intimacy he longed to preserve. In the last few lines, remembering himself at various points of departure from home, Whitman fully notes the absence of companionship, adventure, and love that his life does not provide; but he glamorizes his wan loneliness because he feels that the stoical and heroic destiny of that child is to be alone and to embody the lives of others. It was his fate to become the subjective reality of other people, and to incorporate in himself whatever symbolized them.

Throughout his poetry Whitman refers to his childhood with similar reverence and wariness, for he understood both the dignity and degradation of being a child. He saw a child as a sensitive individual being whose experience and responses are important because they shape the developing personality of the adult. From Whitman's secular, evolutionist perspective, childhood is what one comes from, which makes it important to remain open to childlike impulses, but childhood also poses the danger of dependence. He never simplistically thought — as many contemporary writers did — that man's highest or finest attributes of wisdom and virtue could be symbolized by the naiveté or pleasures of childhood. He expressed his ideal of a better human nature in the figure of a mature man, not a child. The figure of the child in Whitman's poetry conveys neither the challenging "innocence" of Blake's radical infants nor the natural piety of Wordsworth's "best philosopher." Whitman's child is not Rousseau's animal with perfectly balanced instincts, nor is he the noble victim of society popularized in Victorian fiction on both sides of the Atlantic. Whitman is less sentimental than most writers who participated in the aggrandizement of childhood in the nineteenth century. He is also less demanding than his own parents had been, for he accepts children more or less as they are.

By contrast, he could not accept his parents for what they were, and he seldom expressed feelings about his past without explicitly idealizing and implicitly criticizing his family. He idealized his childhood as a time of specially privileged intimacy with everything around him, a state of unusually idyllic closeness not just to his mother but also to his earliest sights of the world, which are still part of him, as he says. His poetry re-creates this intimacy as well as the loss of such intimacy that accompanies growth. Yet for Whitman these losses were abrupt, inconsistent, bewildering, and not simply the kind of progressive widening of personal horizons recounted in "There Was a Child Went Forth." His relationships with both parents were more often unpredictable and illogical swings between intimacy and detachment. As a child he took necessary advantage of the confusion of a large family by making himself both mother and father to everyone around, thereby acquiring not only his parents' subjective companionship but also part of their higher status. The self-aggrandizement remained part of his creative motivation. But as a poet, it was hard to put into words these ambiguous ties and transpositions of identity that made him what he was.

To express his internal complexities, he sometimes needed to ignore or deliberately repudiate the objectifying assumptions embodied in the

English language. Nearly everything uttered in standard English reaffirms a differentiation between action and being, or between subject and object. Whitman does not always accept such differences among objects and himself, or between active and passive states of being. Often, he deconstructs the impersonal order of circumstance and logic — and with it, the entire context of metaphor — so that he can supplant the external world with his unique sensibility. In many of his poems he adopts this strategy for lengthy passages, turning reality inward, where the only absolute facts are his feelings. The most succinct illustration of this triumph of imagination over circumstances is "Spontaneous Me." Though the poem was first published in the second edition of *Leaves*, in 1856, it exemplifies the spirit and technique of his major early poems, and it clearly shows the dual, contrasting sexual identification with both parents separately that constitutes his sense of self.

Whitman opens with the line "Spontaneous me, Nature"; the ellipsis immediately requires an explanation of what he means. Nothing in the line or in the rest of the poem has an ordinary grammatical function that would indicate how the statement should be understood. The first line appears to present Whitman objectively, as if he were showing himself to the reader, saying *look at spontaneous me*, and "Nature" appears to be an appositive, implying something like *behold in me the spontaneity that is the essence of nature*. But this apparently acceptable construction of the grammatical sense of the line fails to establish a perspective or a rhetorical framework that carries forward into the next line or organizes any other part of the poem. It is inadequate even for the first line when this is read in the context of the full poem. There is neither subject nor predicate in the entire forty-five lines. The poem is written as one sentence, but contains no independent clause to serve as a foundation for making logical sense. The attempted paraphrase fails because Whitman is not being merely elliptical, giving us the task of filling in the unstated parts of a statement. He rejects logical syntax. His language avoids almost all copular and analytical words that would admit or develop the substance and relations of things in themselves apart from Whitman's perception of their correspondence with his exalted self, the "spontaneous me."

> Spontaneous me, Nature,
> The loving day, the mounting sun, the friend I
>   am happy with,
> The arm of my friend hanging idly over my
>   shoulder,
> The hillside whiten'd with blossoms of the
>   mountain ash,

The same late in autumn, the hues of red,
  yellow, drab, purple, and light
  and dark green,
The rich coverlet of the grass, animals and
  birds, the private untrimm'd bank,
  the primitive apples, the pebblestones,

Beautiful dripping fragments, the negligent
  list of one after another as I happen
  to call them to me or to think of them,
The real poems, (what we call poems merely
  being pictures,)
The poems of the privacy of the night, and of
  men like me,
This poem drooping shy and unseen that I always
  carry, and that all men carry,
(Know once for all, avow'd on purpose, wherever
  are men like me, are our lusty lurking
  masculine poems,)

$$(11. \ 1–11)$$

The juxtaposition of images in the second line unites a Whitman who is happy in the company of his friend with the similarly loving day that welcomes the company of the ''mounting sun.'' The reaching or embracing action of the sun reappears in the friend's easy embrace in the next line, and his arm adorning Whitman's shoulder is like the blossoms draping the hillside, in line 4. The images in these lines are not metaphors, because they do not refer to other things to establish their sense, in the way, for instance, that Shakespeare's metaphor of ''bare ruin'd choirs'' refers to deteriorated choir stalls and barren trees and to his advanced age. Whitman's images have no ''vehicle'' and ''tenor'' to signify different levels of meaning distinguished by literal and figurative elements. Nor are they implied similes, any more than the first line implies a simile, for Whitman does not acknowledge that one image is merely ''like'' another and its meaning therefore derived from this relationship. The images are mutually suggestive when they occur side by side; their juxtaposition indicates the meaning each embodies separately. He and nature equally reveal that spontaneous life consists of numberless happy embraces.

He writes from a double sense of himself as personally erased, incapable of even a nominative or a predicate reference to himself apart from nature, wholly fused with nature and living its acts; while at the same time he is the center of exquisite self-consciousness as he absorbs and equates with himself all the sharp-edged imagery of the external world. The ''hillside whiten'd with blossoms'' of springtime in line 4 turns to rich autumn colors in line 5, and the change from innocent to intense dark hues provides a sensual atmosphere for the more secluded details of the landscape in line 6. Each of the "beautiful dripping fragments" of life, however randomly noted as he claims in line 7, suggests sexuality and, more precisely, the delicate sensitivity of sexual organs that are everywhere evident in the forms of nature and man alike. The vitality of nature is perceived as sexual excitation from lines 12 to 22, so that climbing vines, flowing sap, hands that caress, breasts, lips, bellies that touch, the hairy bee that grips the flower, the longings of the boy who confides his dream to Whitman — all forms of natural life express the same straining toward orgasm.

> Love-thoughts, love-juice, love-odor, love-
>   yielding, love-climbers, and the
>   climbing sap,
> Arms and hands of love, lips of love, phallic
>   thumb of love, breasts of love, bellies
>   press'd and glued together with love,
> Earth of chaste love, life that is only life
>   after love,
> The body of my love, the body of the woman I
>   love, the body of the man, the body
>   of the earth,
> Soft forenoon airs that blow from the south-
>   west,
> The hairy wild-bee that murmurs and hankers up
>   and down, that gripes the full-grown
>   lady-flower, curves upon her with amorous
>   firm legs, takes his will of her,
>   and holds himself tremulous and tight
>   till he is satisfied;
> The wet of woods through the early hours,
> Two sleepers at night lying close together as
>   they sleep, one with an arm slanting
>   down across and below the waist of the
>   other,
> The smell of apples, aromas from crush'd sage-
>   plant, mint, birchbark,
> The boy's longings, the glow and pressure as
>   he confides to me what he was dreaming,
> The dead leaf whirling its spiral whirl and
>   falling still and content to the ground,

                                        (11. 12–22)

Overcharged with sexual energy, the world spends itself both in fecund intercourse and in spontaneous release of aromas and moisture and tensions that culminate pictorially in the relaxation of the single falling leaf: "The dead leaf whirling its spiral whirl and falling still and content to the ground." The deflating rhythm of this line, which nearly settles into prose, underscores the juxtaposition of the spent leaf and the boy's nocturnal emission.

Having equated sexual arousal and satiety with nature, Whitman then turns, not to the pleasure of gratification, but to the torment of sexual frustration. For eleven lines he sympathizes with the distresses of baffled and overwhelmed young men and women who suffer the shame of masturbation because they contain, as Whitman says he also feels, "the vex'd corrosion so pensive and so painful, / The torment, the irritable tide that will not be at rest." Even as he accepts the pathos of their attempted self-restraint or secrecy, he makes their sexual misery appear grotesquely unnecessary, out of harmony with nature where even ripe apples and crushed herbs freely exude their sexual aromas into the air. Self-gratifying sexual acts are the same as the innocent, spindrift turbulence of nature. In a sequence of images absolving a tortured young man from blame, Whitman equates masturbation with the rush of ocean waves breaking upon him.

> The no-form'd stings that sights, people, objects,
>   sting me with,
> The hubb'd sting of myself, stinging me as much
>   as it ever can any one,
> The sensitive, orbic, underlapp'd brothers, that
>   only privileged feelers may be intimate
>   where they are,
> The curious roamer the hand roaming all over the
>   body, the bashful withdrawing of flesh
>   where the fingers soothingly pause and
>   edge themselves,
> The limpid liquid within the young man,
> The vex'd corrosion so pensive and so painful,
> The torment, the irritable tide that will not
>   be at rest,
> The like of the same I feel, the like of the
>   same in others,
> The young man that flushes and flushes, and the
>   young woman that flushes and flushes,

> The young man that wakes deep at night, the hot
>   hand seeking to repress what would
>   master him,
> The mystic amorous night, the strange half-welcome
>   pangs, visions, sweats,
> The pulse pounding through palms and trembling
>   encircling fingers, the young man all
>   color'd, red, ashamed, angry;
> The souse upon me of my lover the sea, as I
>   lie willing and naked,
>
> (11. 23–35)

When the tide of sexual feeling overwhelms him, Whitman becomes both the lover and the loved. He gives himself to an orgasm in which passion from himself is directed to himself. He is conscious of the erotic glamour of his own body — "as I lie willing and naked" — and he feels exalted by the magnitude of his own sexual ardor — "my lover the sea." He is both the powerful, natural tide breaking on him and the desirable person who is delighted to be embraced.

In such moments of intense self-consciousness, Whitman's sense of himself reveals both genders. Whitman's first-person sense of himself as "I" was strongly feminine — that is, his immediate subjective traits signified womanly qualities to Whitman, and surely to his American Victorian society. His personal ego is passive, enticing, caring, receptive, and vulnerable — "as I lie willing and naked." A masculine sense of himself is evident as the autonomous and irrational force that exists obscurely with nature. The sensibility of "me" in this poem is willful, impersonal, unconfined, remote, and undefined. It is the center of ungovernable, "spontaneous" volitions; it gives masculine animation to his genitals and it unites him with undifferentiated life throughout the universe. It can overwhelm or supplant Whitman's ego, making him feel entirely externalized, protean, unattached, and infinite, or lost to himself.

In bringing these two elements of his personality closer together, Whitman literally embraced himself. His youthful masturbation continued into adulthood because it came to convey the only assurance of love that he expected to receive. Until well into his middle age, no other form of affection moved him as deeply as this sort of auto-erotic transport. Always the child who goes forth, he steadfastly awaited love from the withholding or possessive parents who "gainsay'd" his affections — and whose images he had incorporated into himself. In his divided personality, Whitman could harmonize his male and female qualities only by submitting to each sexual identification separately but simultaneously. Never fully integrated, he could only become from time to time a fully realized, accepted contradiction.

This was the sense of "self" he wanted always to preserve, and it was the sense of "self" that became his poetic personality. The moments when Whitman felt fully in possession of his whole self were moments of dynamic balance and active poise between his subjective personality and his objective, natural being. It was a state of illogical but harmoniously double consciousness: a capacity for feeling "both in and out of the game and watching and wondering at it," as he says in "Song of Myself." Such moments lifted him above his usual alienation from his "soul" of masculine sexuality, which generally seemed external and unpredictably distant-or-close, indifferent-or-overpowering toward him.

Whitman states in the concluding eight lines that his self-enclosed sexuality is not unnatural, unmanly, or even infertile. As a moral vindication, the imaginative record of his experience has germinated in poetry, where it will shape the sensibility and character of present and future readers. As carelessly but as purposefully as nature, the poet tosses his poem like a seed, to fall where it may.

> The continence of vegetables, birds, animals,
> The consequent meanness of me should I skulk
>   or find myself indecent, while birds
>   and animals never once skulk or find
>   themselves indecent,
> The great chastity of paternity, to match the
>   great chastity of maternity,
> The oath of procreation I have sworn, my Adamic
>   and fresh daughters,
> The greed that eats me day and night with hungry
>   gnaw, till I saturate what shall produce
>   boys to fill my place when I am through,
> The wholesome relief, repose, content,
> And this bunch pluck'd at random from myself,
> It has done its work — I toss it carelessly
>   to fall where it may.
>
> (11. 38–45)

The conclusion is more than an apologetic argument or a rationalization. His reasoning in the final lines constitutes a reorientation toward more standard modes of thought and expression. His intuitive vision is superseded by another, conventional sense of order that acknowledges time, succession, analogy, logical limits, and ordinary relationships. In the now restored, ordinary world, the ego is active, not passive, and the personal "I" dominates the conclusion, enriched and vivified by union with the expansive "me" that dominates the beginning of the poem. Characteristic of the conclusions of his poems, Whitman turns to the American public or the forthcoming lover or to all men and women now living and yet to live, democratically extending to all a bond of identification.

Whitman needed this bond as a confirmation of his identity. He required external substantiation for the conception of himself that, however accurate, was an exceptional idea which was impossible for him to maintain alone. Through writing and revising poems he discovered that the strongest confirmation of his identity came from the book itself, and not necessarily from the people he addressed as lovers or readers. As the volume of his poetry increased over the years, Whitman found the full and deepening diversity of his personality objectified in the coherence of the book he never stopped writing and revising. Always close to him in the inner space of his ongoing creativity, the book, in turn, gained reciprocal influence over him. It led him to continue the definition of his personality by creating his biography as he added new poems, which relate the main events of an internal history. Once it was begun, he would never be able to let go of this book, never finish it and put it aside for other work. For thirty-seven years of his adult life, through a total of six editions and three additional reprintings of *Leaves of Grass*, he constantly altered the volume by adding new poems, revising old ones, rearranging the order of presentation, grouping poems into sections, thinking up new titles for poems and headings for sections.[2] To detach himself from *Leaves of Grass* — and to think of it as a closed, finished entity — might be to succumb to the alienation and oblivion he feared in an existence without any personal relations.

Accordingly, the recognition he hoped for was not that people would praise his poems but that people would accept the poetic identity of Walt Whitman as lovingly as he had created the figure of himself. "Camerado, this is no book," he says to the reader who is about to conclude the volume: "Who touches this touches a man." That is why in the 1855 preface to his first edition of *Leaves*, he looked to "great audiences" to absorb him "as affectionately," he hoped, as he had absorbed his country. He wanted the entire nation to support the ideal of the balance of opposites, or contraries, that he had clarified in his own personality, and he expected society to respect the ambiguities of a diversified national identity with the same delicacy of mind and feeling that he had attained only in writing poetry. Of course, nothing in the actual life of his country, particularly at that time, could fulfill Whitman's desire to find a stable reflection of himself in public events and values. On the brink of war, its ideals betrayed everywhere by political corruption and social violence, the nation in the 1850s presented the spectacle of citizens driven by deadly antagonism against one another. As an imperfect but nevertheless insidious image of his most irrational fears, national life could only exacerbate the stresses within his personality. After a few short, creative years of speaking to Americans about the essence of democratic experience, by the outbreak of the Civil War he was virtually worn out as a poet: undermined morally not by public neglect of his poetry but largely by his culture's massive repudiation of the meaning of his inner life.

3

The Triumph of Imagination, 1855

IN THE poems of the first edition of *Leaves*, published in 1855, Whitman's main purpose was to follow the strangely autonomous life of his imaginative self. He was inspired with new emotional power and freedom that had emerged from his momentous experience of self-acceptance in the early 1850s. He regarded his transformed self as an entirely contemporary man, born of the American mid-nineteenth century and wholly expressing the nation and the era. In his greatest poem from *Leaves*, which he eventually titled "Song of Myself," he writes a life-history in which he constructs his first complete poetic identity. In this detailed and exuberant story of his origin and destiny, he sees his imaginative self as the offspring of parents within him.

To recreate the emotional context of his life before his self-definition, he imposes on the reader the feelings of helplessness and alienation that he experienced as a young man. We are put in the position of dependence that he suffered, particularly in his relationship with his mother, including his detachment from the unreality of life beyond the family circle. But in the poem Whitman allows the reader to feel dominated, while the poet adopts the freedom and limitless powers that he attributed to his parents. Unlike any other major poet, Whitman makes his readers feel totally dependent on his speaking voice. Our attention is restricted to him and everything that comes to our attention is interpreted by him. "He was the first totalitarian poet," Pablo Neruda remarked about Whitman's dominating presence in his poetry; "his intention was not just to sing, but to impose on others his own total and wide-ranging vision of the relationships of men and nations."[1] The ironically admiring epithet by this ardently republican Chilean poet contains a trace of the ordinary reader's feeling of being crowded or badgered by Whitman. We have the sensation that our only valid responses are being directed — indeed, conducted with bravura — by Whitman from the page. Other poetry may control our responses, but still allow us to believe that we are freely noting and valuing what the poem presents. Whitman, by contrast, demands that we acknowledge and yield to his external administration of our feelings and thoughts as he explicitly anticipates and defines what we must accept as our own responses formed in him. His overmastering readiness to stand in our place is offered as sympathy, but it can miscarry its intended effect, as in these lines from "Song of Myself," and make us feel shouldered aside, undervalued as individuals, our privacy invaded, our uniqueness belied.

> I do not ask who you are, that is not important
> to me,
> You can do nothing and be nothing but what I will
> infold you.
>
> (11. 1001–1002)

He places himself at the center of our activity, disallowing our separateness or detachment, insistently drawing out an acknowledgment of him as the authority, the mediator, the person who loves, invents, commands, promises, dismisses, cheers, entices, eludes, rejects, or even denies us in the life we share, potentially creating or annihilating our world, all in the name of defining our own feelings and interests. His stance suggests the power and the violence of Louisa Whitman's maternal possessiveness, for in being like her he repeats to us the way she presented herself to him. She was the single, vibrant interpreter of any shared experience. His poetry, as Whitman noted to Traubel, "is the flower of her temperament active in me."[2] This temperament reappears in Whitman's dictatorial arrogations of our feelings and thoughts, and the intimate dependence he imposes on his readers.

He subordinates the reader immediately in the opening three lines, in which Whitman's offer to share experience puts up a bridge that can be crossed emotionally in only one direction, from him to us.

> I celebrate myself, and sing myself,
> And what I assume you shall assume,
> For every atom belonging to me as good belongs to you.
>
> (11. 1–3)

The fantasy of our assuming different roles together with Whitman makes our range of feelings available to him while it prevents our empathizing with the poet except by sharing his enjoyment of fantasied roles and relationships. We become familiar with his character only through his detailed and ceaseless externalizations of himself as we follow his program of activities. Everything he is, is brought out; we do not receive impressions of his unspoken depths that would allow us to construct an intuitive understanding of him. Instead, he claims the power to possess everyone else, by absorbing and representing everyone.

In the first four stanzas of the poem, he repudiates any allegiance to polite standards of behavior and manners, traditions in art and expression, logical argumentation, and rationalistic ideas of causality and temporality. He dismisses external forms that would distort the miracle of creation from which he emerged. He accepts, in short, the possibilities of unconscious and irrational life, and he proclaims as a heroic challenge to the conventional and intellectual scruples of his age that he will articulate "Nature without check with original energy" (l. 13).

In stanza 5, his familiar account of his initial self-definition recalls an episode when his soul became his lover who embraced him as they lay in the grass. He felt exalted by the adoration of this masculine side of himself; the vivid sensation of the fusing of his soul and his person was accompanied by elation, and then by religious awe over the influx of power and beauty to the self. The brief, highly sexualized coupling leaves Whitman with a quietly blissful conviction of an inner harmony that seems to emanate from him, organizing the entire universe into a supportive, personal relation to himself.

> I believe in you my soul, the other I am must
>   not abase itself to you,
> And you must not be abased to the other.
> Loafe with me on the grass, loose the stop from
>   your throat,
> Not words, not music or rhyme I want, not custom
>   or lecture, not even the best,
> Only the lull I like, the hum of your valvèd
>   voice.
> I mind how once we lay such a transparent summer
>   morning,
> How you settled your head athwart my hips and
>   gently turn'd over upon me,
> And parted the shirt from my bosom-bone, and
>   plunged your tongue to my bare-stript
>   heart,
> And reach'd till you felt my beard, and reach'd
>   till you held my feet.
> Swiftly arose and spread around me the peace
>   and knowledge that pass all the arguments
>   of the earth,

And I know that the hand of God is the promise
    of my own,
And I know that the spirit of God is the brother of
    my own,
And that all the men ever born are also my
    brothers, and the women my sisters and
    lovers,
And that a kelson of the creation is love,
And limitless are leaves stiff or drooping in
    the fields,
And brown ants in the little wells beneath them,
And mossy scabs of the worm fence, heap'd stones,
    elder, mullein and poke-weed.

                                          (11. 82–98)

It is important to note what is seldom observed, that the fusion of the soul and the person does not occur in these lines at all. The moment of union is not part of the dramatic action. It is a remembered experience, which, for five lines that drop into the past tense, Whitman recalls as having happened some time ago: "I mind how once we lay." The remembering occurs as part of an apostrophe to the soul, as if Whitman is cajoling his lover into a sentimental reverie over a sweet episode in their past. With coaxing tactfulness, he promises good faith; "I believe in you my soul" he says; and he offers new rules of fair play, that will proscribe the wounding attitudes of denial and shame that expressed conflict between his soul and person: "the other I am must not abase itself to you, / And you must not be abased by the other." Touchingly grateful for the love once received from the soul, Whitman guards against the betrayal of his happiness by seduction or abandonment by his impulsive lover. The form of the stanza is a love-plaint full of hope and caution that the soul will remain with him, placidly, as in an idyll. Wary of another passionate consummation of love, he invites the soul to join with him in a milder rendezvous on the grass that will allow his person to feel equal with his soul, but not once again to be ecstatically possessed by it.

In contrast to his present assertiveness in examining the experience, the poet is passive during the remembered event. The soul embraces him and opens his clothes; with a plunging tongue, the soul penetrates his heart; it clasps his face and feet in widespread arms. The account glorifies Whitman's body as the object glamorized by desire — his hips and open shirt and bosom-bone, his heart, beard, and feet — while the vaguely represented soul is not glorified or otherwise individuated except as the activity itself of sexual cherishing.

In the remembered moment of union, the absolute and erotic love that

Whitman hungered for flooded him from a remote part of his own personality. This step toward sexual definition is more peculiar, however, than a normally integrative step in ordinary personal development. His sexual definition occurs with sudden, frightening, and apocalyptic completeness. Further, it occurs intrapsychically, without any corresponding sexual involvement with another person of either sex. Neither man nor woman gave Whitman the love that led him through his prolonged adolescence toward adulthood: He alone gave love to himself. Though he may very likely have had sexual intercourse on several occasions that encouraged his more generous and accepting attitudes toward himself, the effective acknowledgment of his sexuality occurred much as he describes it in the poem, as an ardor arising in one part of himself and directed to another part where it is ecstatically received. His sexual definition did not integrate his masculine and feminine qualities into one gender identification; instead, Whitman accepts his identification in both genders: partially, separately, and simultaneously.

This moment of internal union led Whitman to a beatific recognition of his personal value and the intrinsic loveliness of all existence. His new vision is expressed with the biblical language of supernatural wonder.

> Swiftly arose and spread around me the peace and
>   knowledge that pass all the argument
>   of the earth,
> And I know that the hand of God is the promise
>   of my own,
> And I know that the spirit of God is the brother
>   of my own. . . .

Like the transports of saints or mystics, Whitman's illumination includes his definitive moral assent to the vocation of a dedicated visionary and poet. The combination of sexual and spiritual ecstasy that he recalls resembles the holy passion of a Christian conversion or the transfiguration of a mystic, including a preliminary descent to mortification and to feeling "abased." But Whitman does not see God as the agent of his deliverance or the meaning of his illumination. Rather, he assumes that his mystery has an *internal* cause; and God does not do anything or play a necessary part in Whitman's explanation. God and the merest grass are equally accepted in his devotional, and he holds a wholly secular attitude toward the world.

Notwithstanding the utter naturalness of the experience, Whitman recognized that he gained a new quality of being as a result of his illumination. He tells us that this erotic experience permanently changed his identity. By accepting erotic feelings he had previously denied, he recovered an earlier, sensual experience that had been lost to him. His redefinition of himself at once gave him access to all his past. He does not need to *remember* the past: It continues in his living personality. In his ecstasy, time itself softened into vaguer dimensions easy to transcend. And the subtlety of expression that makes the shifting verb tenses almost unnoticeable — they are purposely articulated as scarcely felt and reduced from normal significance — emphasizes the heightened sense of personal continuity that accompanied his sexual definition. Between the illumination in line 91 and its exposition in the final seven lines, stanza 5 returns to the present tense. During the shift of tenses, the verbs also change the center of action. The active element switches from the absolute truths that rose up in him as if by revelation — "Swiftly arose and spread around me the peace and knowledge that pass all the arguments of the earth" — to Whitman after the event, when he is reestablished as the agent of his thoughts. He knows what he has felt, and the final lines of stanza 5 are governed by his incantatory assertion of his convictions. The progress of principal verbs, from "I mind" (I remember) to "I know" (I believe), reveals that Whitman's purpose in this passage is to recover certitude that this experience has continuing meaning. His new sense of his wholeness is formed, after all, upon the shaky foundation of an inexplicable "mystery." In "Song of Myself" he wants chiefly to objectify and stabilize his original ego-shattering convergence of person and soul into a new self.

Whitman sees himself on the one hand as the personal agent of every action, yet sometimes, even simultaneously, he sees himself not at all: His personal sense is replaced by the fragments and flux into which he himself is dissolved. Things become himself. The fluctuation of these modes of awareness occurs as internal conversation in voices that alternate between long sections of the poem, or between stanzas, or between lines, and sometimes between phrases in a single verse. In his catalogs, for instance, which illustrate some of his procedures in emphatic, simple ways, his personal sense is nearly overwhelmed — it is lost for dozens of lines at a time — by his involvement with external things. He feels the immediacy of remote and discontinuous forms.

> The pure contralto sings in the organ loft,
> The carpenter dresses his plank, the tongue of
>   his foreplane whistles its wild ascending
>   lisp,
> The married and unmarried children ride home to
>   their Thanksgiving dinner,

The pilot seizes the king-pin, he heaves down
with a strong arm. . . .

(11. 264–267)

This catalog continues with similar unelaborated concreteness for sixty-two lines! He finally manages to reclaim possession of his thoughts after they nearly disorient him with their density and disconnected rapidity. These catalogs reflect the shower of perceptions he received as a child from his mother, when every thought or feeling seemed to originate in her or flow to her. His childhood sensations were never simply internal events; they were confused with external sensations that came to him or fled from him as part of his double consciousness of sharing his mother's experience. As a poet he seizes her role, and finds this double awareness reassuring in poetry. It absorbs and dissolves away any separate, detached viewpoint. The air of immediacy in Whitman's poetry arises partly from this knack he has of apprehending alternative ways of looking at things.

The shifting perspective of his double consciousness is reinforced by the parallelism of biblical verse. The repetitive pattern accommodates two points of view defining each perception, one impersonal and projective, the other personal and analytical. The contrasting viewpoints are most harmoniously aligned in those passages where Whitman uses the personal pronoun to balance the random external facts that with strange urgency press upon his restlessly moving, inspired attention:

> The little one sleeps in its cradle,
> I lift the gauze and look a long time, and
>   silently brush away flies with my hand.
>
> The youngster and the red-faced girl turn aside
>   up the busy hill,
> I peeringly view them from the top.
>
> The suicide sprawls on the bloody floor of the
>   bedroom,
> I witness the corpse with its dabbled hair,
>   I note where the pistol has fallen.
>
> (11. 148–153)

The first line in each of these sentences describes a world without Whitman, who materializes only in the second line as a covert presence within the scene. It is as though he arrives in each sentence only after an impersonal viewpoint has conveyed the perception. A similar suggestion of the shifting point of view occurs when the personal voice begins a sentence but fades away. The objects of his initial attention become so vivid and detailed that they ultimately overwhelm and exclude Whitman from the remainder of the sentence.

> I saw the marriage of the trapper in the open
>   air in the far west, the bride was a
>   red girl,
> Her father and his friends sat near cross-legged
>   and dumbly smoking, they had moccasins
>   to their feet and large thick blankets
>   hanging from their shoulders,
> On a bank lounged the trapper, he was drest
>   mostly in skins, his luxuriant beard
>   and curls protected his neck, he held
>   his bride by the hand,
> She had long eyelashes, her head was bare, her
>   coarse straight locks descended upon
>   her voluptuous limbs and reach'd to
>   her feet.
>
>   (11. 185-188)

This and the preceding passage are meant to show Whitman's wide-ranging sympathy for all life; but his sympathies are brief and circumstantial. He is struck by this or that situation and appearance, yet the thoughts and feelings of the people concerned are omitted. Throughout the poem other people do not think, speak, or complete acts, as the absence of characterization, narrative, fixed settings, or other novelistic elements makes clear. The world outside himself appears fragmented and static. But by drawing these pieces into himself, Whitman becomes the context in which these pieces gain order and meaning. By embodying reality he restores harmony and finds a place for the rest of mankind — busily looking after the chaotic household in his mother's fashion — and in this poem the rest of mankind is surely downtrodden and incapacitated without him.

After stanzas of absorbing other people, Whitman emerges in stanza 18 as a militant champion of oppressed humanity, playing "marches for conquer'd and slain persons" as well as for victors, and heralding a revolution of feelings. His procession is like a triumphal approach to a city that will receive him as a reconciler of age-old conflicts.

> With music strong I come, with my cornets and
>   my drums,

I play not marches for accepted victors only,
  I play marches for conquer'd and slain
  persons.

Have you heard that it was good to gain the day?
I also say it is good to fall, battles are lost
  in the same spirit in which they are won.

I beat and pound for the dead,
I blow through my embouchures my loudest and
  gayest for them.

Vivas to those who have fail'd!
And to those whose war-vessels sank in the sea!
And to those themselves who sank in the sea!
And to all generals that lost engagements, and
  all overcome heroes!
And to numberless unknown heroes equal to the
  greatest heroes known!

(11. 361–371)

He offers dignity to the defeated because he believes that equality of spirit is ordained by nature and should be brought openly into modern civilization, in the form of democracy. His internal struggle gave him the moral sensitivity to uphold democracy as the naturally evolving perfection of social order and to celebrate the egalitarianism of the United States over the hierarchies of Europe. Yet his commitment to democracy in this poem (as in his family life) is distorted by his authoritarian role. The political stance in "Song of Myself" implicitly idealizes the benign autocrat, not the common man. Whitman's idea of the fair and good in social terms remains close to the supreme will of a kind, firm parent. As a beloved and loving authority, he proclaims and nurtures the integrity and dignity of deadened or demeaned individuals, the slaves and refuse of society. His struggle is for their good. He extends democracy to all and invites all to a eucharistic sharing of physical love for everyone's "natural hunger." His idea of the Union would exclude no one. As in a family, *being* is the only necessary enfranchisement.

This is the meal equally set, this the meat for
  natural hunger,
It is for the wicked just the same as the righteous,
  I make appointments with all,

I will not have a single person slighted or left
    away,
The kept-woman, sponger, thief, are hereby invited,
The heavy-lipp'd slave is invited, the venerealee
    is invited;
There shall be no difference between them and the
    rest.

This is the press of a bashful hand, this the float
    and odor of hair,
This is the touch of my lips to yours, this the
    murmur of yearning,
This the far-off depth and height reflecting my
    own face,
This the thoughtful merge of myself, and the
    outlet again.

                   (11. 372–381)

He places himself humbly among the world's rejected and ruined de-
pendents, denying that they are unworthy of his love. He exalts the
wounded, the vulnerable and deprived, by embracing them with his
splendor and power. His identification with common people is like a god's
assumption of mortal form, an act of beneficence that reveals the divinity
it disguises. Walking among mortals in his democratic flesh, Whitman
at last takes possession of his ordinary name, Walt, which up to stanza
24 had been withheld. Whitman proclaims his name (in a book of poems
that was first published anonymously) only after he has deified his association with the degraded and helpless circle of his birth. The four-line
announcement in stanza 24 contains no verb or grammatical subject that
would reduce him to personal and finite scale; he cries out the name of
his primal, universal being: ''Walt Whitman, a kosmos, of Manhattan the
son.''

    Walt Whitman, a kosmos, of Manhattan the son,
    Turbulent, fleshy, sensual, eating, drinking
        and breeding;
    No sentimentalist, no stander above men
        and women or apart from them,
    No more modest than immodest.

    Unscrew the locks from the doors!
    Unscrew the doors themselves from their jambs!

    Whoever degrades another degrades me,

And whatever is done or said returns at last
    to me.

Through me the afflatus surging and surging,
    through me the current and index.

I speak the pass-word primeval, I give the sign
    of democracy,
By God! I will accept nothing which all cannot
    have their counterpart of on the same
    terms.

                      (11. 497–507)

These lines vibrate with the energy of release, release from constraints and escape from suppression by privilege, standards, or bad fortune. The overriding energy gives the poet freedom even to drop the rhythm of his own prosody in the final line that stretches out into prose. His poetry sends into the world, as if for the first time, the liveliness and power of all human attributes and experiences that have heretofore lacked expression, he says. Offering himself to others so that no one will need to feel misshapen or exceptional or deprived or alone, he prepares to consecrate his identity so that all men may share. He elevates himself for viewing, in the language of sacramental ritual. He is a "miracle"; he is "divine"; his touch is "holy"; and he finds "the scent of these arm-pits aroma finer than prayer." He undrapes and worships his physical form to show that nothing is alien or disgusting to him or in him: "If I worship one thing more than another it shall be the spread of my own body, or any part of it," he says as he begins to "dote on" himself and to exult that he is "all so luscious."

The public scene fades and Whitman, adoring his nakedness, is once again alone in a natural setting, recalling here his initial illumination in the grassy scene in stanza 5. The recapitulatory organization of the poem becomes clear here when Whitman reenacts his earlier ecstasy. The experience that was treated earlier in the poem as a guardedly remembered, cautiously mentioned moment becomes the dramatic foreground event from stanza 24 through 31. Reconstructed and expanded at this point, an experience of sexual arousal and consequent humiliation occurs as the central crisis of the poem. The recapitulation suggests that the episode it recalls contains the clue to his creative drive to define himself anew.

In stanza 24 Whitman's body is suffused with ecstasy like an infant's in a mother's embrace. The boundaries between himself and the sustaining world soften and dissolve as he admires his masculine shape, his genitals, his hair and beard, the sun and wind and vapors that touch his skin. His pleasure in exquisite sensations repeats the erotic detailing that gave stanza 5 the atmosphere of a seduction, in which Whitman is the relatively passive object of desire. The general environment is sexualized as though enveloping and caressing him — broadly reaching, as it were, to hold him again from beard to feet — and in his revel of delight his entranced wonder over himself changes to deeper, more urgent tones of sexual desire.

> If I worship one thing more than another it
>   shall be the spread of my own body,
>   or any part of it,
> Translucent mould of me it shall be you!
> Shaded ledges and rests it shall be you!
> Firm masculine colter it shall be you!
> Whatever goes to the tilth of me it shall be
>   you!
> You my rich blood! your milky stream pale
>   strippings of my life!
> Breast that presses against other breasts it
>   shall be you!
> My brain it shall be your occult convolutions!
> Root of wash'd sweet-flag! timorous pond-snipe!
>   nest of guarded duplicate eggs! it shall
>   be you!
> Mix'd tussled hay of head, beard, brawn, it
>   shall be you!
> Trickling sap of maple, fibre of manly wheat,
>   it shall be you!
> Sun so generous it shall be you!
> Vapors lighting and shading my face it shall
>   be you!
> You sweaty brooks and dews it shall be you!
> Winds whose soft-tickling genitals rub against
>   me it shall be you!
> Broad muscular fields, branches of live oak,
>   loving lounger in my winding paths, it
>   shall be you!
> Hands I have taken, face I have kiss'd, mortal
>   I have ever touch'd, it shall be you.
>   (ll. 527–543)

The last line is surprising because Whitman is suddenly tender and adoring toward a specific human figure. From among the fields and winds and branches that incline with love toward him, he singles out the hands and face and poignant mortality of a particular lover. The change from generalized bodily pleasure to focused sexual desire is important enough for Whitman to record it three times in the poem. The line here recalls his autoerotic fantasy idyll upon the grass, for the movement in this passage develops another tentative, suggestively sexual episode in the present that is interrupted by another remembering pang of longing — like the flashback in stanza 5. The action switches from ecstatic self-absorption in the present to an evocation of the lingering past — as it did earlier — which is memorialized in the three successive perfect tenses: "I have taken," "I have kissed," and "I have ever touch'd." The parallel construction emphasizes the suggestion of a completed, satisfying gesture rather than another hypothetical act of erotic play, and the adverb *ever* reinforces the concreteness and specificity of an immortal moment of direct embrace by Whitman. His suddenly overt active expression of love for another contrasts sharply with the preceding list of his conditional, venturesome responses to sexual excitation. He remembers reaching out at last to the "mortal," but simultaneously the line withdraws the loved one from the scene. Describing the loved one by the word *mortal* suggests that the loved one is now inaccessible, even though the line claims to be recovering the immortality of a moment's perfect fulfillment. This anomaly can be understood if the mortality of the loved one is not simply through death but through the barriers of age and identity that separated the two even at the moment of Whitman's happy embrace. His greatest pleasure culminates in a child's sexual response to a *mother*, who is "ever" the *mortal*: older and inaccessible. The tragic link between *mortal* and *mother* is examined by Whitman in many of his later poems; here he is solely imagining the event of his earliest expression of sexuality, from which he dates the origin of his creativity. His insight seems to have reasoned that if creative rebirth is astoundingly sexual, as it recently was for him, then sexual assertion must be creative. In any case, his imagination was so highly sexualized by the division between male and female that he found or invented the originating point of his poetic sensibility in the childhood awakening of his sexual response, with all the ambiguity and introversion that descend on him from that moment.

During his seemingly secure bliss with mother in stanza 24 he is thrilled with the pleasure he can take in anything — how his ankles bend, or the magical exchanges of friendship, or the sight of a morning glory at his window. In his brief return to paradisal experience, moments become too intensely good to be true: "That I walk up my stoop, I pause to consider if it really be." At this pitch of elation, he does not doubt that he or the stoop exists; rather he can scarcely believe the exquisite pleasure of unconsidered things. The beauty of daybreak captures his attention long enough to become an image of his awakened joy in himself. The frail bit of pre-dawn light rolls back the immensely larger darkness, the "diaphanous shadows" that hung upon himself as well, and in the new air of morning he tastes his fresh breaths. The swiftly changing sky of clouds suggests romping, playful children at "innocent gambols...scooting obliquely high and low"; that is, he enjoys the spectacle of lamblike pleasures that express his preference for innocent idylls of love. Wherever he looks the world mirrors his happy fancifulness. But this placid romance of poetical consciousness does not last. It appears to be taken away from him. Currents of turbulent emotion move the external world into images of phallic arousal that are first ominous and then overtly threatening. This change in atmosphere explains retroactively Whitman's apprehension in stanza 5 over a resurgence of his soul's adult passion. The daybreak changes to an image of the "sun-rise" as a phallic erection and orgasm, and the morning scene then suggests the end of a nightlong embrace between the earth and sky. But this spectacle, in contrast to the innocence of clouds, is not witnessed as the glory of his own natural sexuality (such as he welcomes in the image of his "spontaneous" erection). Instead, Whitman at first disavows the force of phallic sex as an overmastering, external imposition upon him. The surrealistically transformed sunrise encroaches on Whitman with bullying arrogance and goading supremacy.

> To behold the day-break!
> The little light fades the immense and diaphanous
> shadows,
> The air tastes good to my palate.
>
> Hefts of the moving world at innocent gambols
> silently rising, freshly exuding,
> Scooting obliquely high and low.
>
> Something I cannot see puts upward libidinous
> prongs,
> Seas of bright juice suffuse heaven.
>
> The earth by the sky staid with, the daily
> close of their junction,
> The heav'd challenge from the east that moment
> over my head,
> The mocking taunt, See then whether you shall
> be master!
>
> (11. 550–559)

These lines suggest an episode, remembered or invented, in which the child Whitman is abruptly ousted from his morning of bliss by a frightening and powerful father claiming sexual union with the mother, who was cuddling and rousing the child. Apparently humiliated and mocked by a jealous father, the child is driven away with blame and mockery. His happiness violated, his ardent love disregarded (his affections "gainsay'd" as always), Whitman struggles with his feelings of roused desire and smoldering rivalry. His immediate response as a child is to overprize his own erection. His initial sexual defeat leads him to compensate by an imaginative triumph in which all the sexuality in the world is expressed by his fantasies.

> Dazzling and tremendous how quick the sun-rise
>   would kill me,
> If I could not now and always send sun-rise
>   out of me.
> We also ascend dazzling and tremendous as the sun,
> We found our own O my soul in the calm and cool
>   of the day-break.
>
> (ll. 560–563)

The passage suggests that Whitman attempted to redress his wrongs and rationalize his relations with his parents by working out compromises in the family romance. Within the fourteen lines, nature's animated feminine beauty in the early morning, when Whitman receives its boundless affection, is reduced to the more modest and restrained demeanor of "the calm and cool of the day-break," in which he cannot be aroused again by "hefts of the moving world." Nature's stimulating love is made impassive, mild and soothing. The atmosphere of random, playful pleasures changes to the fixed grandeur of sunrise that is remote and hostile but still glamorous with phallic power. Whitman surmises great danger, but averts it with the ingenuity of a weaker rival: "how quick the sun-rise would kill me, / If I could not now and always send sun-rise out of me." To reaffirm his potency against the challenge that he infers, Whitman adopts an ambiguously bisexual role. He perceives himself as the erotic object, prizing the wonder of his erection and receiving the loving, sexual attentions of his masculine soul, which can "ascend dazzling and tremendous as the sun." Flooded with sexual consciousness, he admires his own genitals — as if compensating for an anticipated defeat in the larger world of adult experience. By rehearsing the early childhood feelings underlying his sexual ambiguity, Whitman here returns to the threshold of Oedipal conflict when he felt most unstable in his sense of self, subject to profound changeableness for better or worse in his effort to attain his identity.

In his later work Whitman will repudiate this account of his beginnings, omitting the equation between creativity and sexual intro-version. In "Song of Myself" his spiritual birth is a struggle against compunctions over masturbation, in which the triumph of his sexual will over shame and emotional deprivation unlocks the barriers to self-definition. The apocalyptic, sexual union of his person and soul recalled in stanza 5 is later repeated in greater detail to dramatize the emergence of poetical identity through redemptive self-love. The earlier line "I mind how once we lay such a transparent summer morning" becomes "We found our own O my soul in the calm and cool of the day-break." Sexually roused, he is engulfed once again by emotions and energies that seem to arise in the surrounding world and invade his actions. He is directed by passions over which he loses his usual control; even speech fails him, and he claims that he is powerless to articulate what he is made to contain. Plunged into a chaos that is both sweet and terrifying, he struggles to keep from dissolving entirely away.

> I am cut by bitter and angry hail, I lose my
> breath,
> Steep'd amid honey'd morphine, my windpipe
> throttled in fakes of death,
> At length let up again to feel the puzzle of
> puzzles,
> And that we call Being.
>
> (11. 607–610)

His crisis opens up a vista of inchoateness. Swept back into rudimentary consciousness, he recovers his kinship with all forms of being. "To be in any form, what is that?" he asks, and the dismissive answer indicates that he feels both helpless and favored in his exposure to radical transformation. Any object can represent him because he has become an elemental being: "(Round and round we go, all of us, and ever come back thither,) / If nothing lay more develop'd the quahaug in its callous shell were enough." Stimulated and harassed by alien, ungovernable energies, he abandons himself to the upsurge of sexual forces that possess him.

> Is this then a touch? quivering me to a new identity,
> Flames and ether making a rush for my veins,
> Treacherous tip of me reaching and crowding to help
> them,
> My flesh and blood playing out lightning to strike
> what is hardly different from myself,
>
> (11. 619–622)

His sexual excitement rekindles his sense of betrayal by phallic power, which is now even more confusing because it is his own roused sexual feelings that threaten to overpower him. He feels humiliated if his entire self-awareness can be outmatched by this one compelling sensation. He protests that his innocence is betrayed; he cries out against traitors, treachery, and desertion by his protective wits that ought to be rescuing him from this plight as his clothes are once again unbuttoned and his own hands succumb to the villainy of masturbation. Like a child, he feels overpowered and exposed, unfairly tricked and badly taken advantage of by stronger agents who have turned out to be prurient, licentious, immodest, exploitative, inconsiderate, and taunting. His embarrassment is full of castigation and anger against the misleading powers that have trapped him in this debasing torment for the purpose of their own callous delight. Abused and demeaned, he devotes exaggerated attention to his excruciating shame, enlarging upon his feelings of victimization and resentment as a way of blaming others for his misery. Yet it is also pleasurable to fantasize his thrilling seduction.

> On all sides prurient provokers stiffening my limbs,
> Straining the udder of my heart for its withheld
>   drip,
> Behaving licentious toward me, taking no denial,
> Depriving me of my best as for a purpose,
> Unbuttoning my clothes, holding me by the bare
>   waist,
> Deluding my confusion with the calm of the
>   sunlight and pasturefields,
> Immodestly sliding the fellow-senses away,
> They bribed to swap off with touch and go and
>   graze at the edges of me,
> No consideration, no regard for my draining
>   strength or my anger,
> Fetching the rest of the herd around to enjoy
>   them a while,
> Then all uniting to stand on a headland and
>   worry me.
>
> The sentries desert every other part of me,
> They have left me helpless to a red marauder,
> They all come to the headland to witness and
>   assist against me.
>
> I am given up by traitors,
> I talk wildly, I have lost my wits, I and
>   nobody else am the greatest traitor,

I went myself first to the headland, my own
    hands carried me there.

You villain touch! what are you doing? my breath
    is tight in its throat,
Unclench your floodgates, you are too much for
    me.

                                    (11. 623–641)

After passionately disclaiming his sexual impulse and pleasure, he at last accepts what he anticipates as guilt: "I and nobody else am the greatest traitor." He surrenders to an orgasm, expecting the flood of feeling to defeat him. Instead, the passion exalts him with tender love for himself. In this passage, as in "Spontaneous Me," Whitman's relief is far more than sexual: It includes the inexpressible elation of discovering that his misery over rejection has never been necessary. Restored by love that seems to arrive from the farthest, impersonal reaches of himself, he is wrapped in the splendor of its completely free expression. Peculiar as it is, Whitman's masturbation at this midpoint crisis of the poem dramatizes the apocalyptic experience of love from which he dated the emergence of his true identity. He is pierced by a love that wounds and possesses him, like the divine arrows that pierced Saint Teresa. The force of the tongue that "plunged...to my bare-stript heart" in stanza 5 assails him again in stanza 29.

Blind loving wrestling touch, sheath'd hooded
    sharp-tooth'd touch!
Did it make you ache so, leaving me?

Parting track'd by arriving, perpetual payment
    of perpetual loan,
Rich showering rain, and recompense richer
    afterward.

Sprouts take and accumulate, stand by the curb
    prolific and vital,
Landscapes projected masculine, full-sized and
    golden.

                                    (11. 642–647)

Less discreet and conventional than the transports of saints and mystics, Whitman's masturbation is not simply a metaphor for the spiritual event;

his illumination undoubtedly occurred as he recounts it, recurring perhaps more than once during his young manhood. But at least once his masturbation led to a fateful acknowledgment and complete acceptance of love for his person issuing from his deepest self. Unadorned by dogma and relatively undisguised, Whitman's ecstasy gives full expression to both sides of his sexual feelings, and he reports the internal dynamics of the process of acceptance as a sacred event. His unabashed and almost scientifically curious observations avoid the usual supernatural and obscurantist elements surrounding "mystical" illuminations. Delighted to find the germination of his poetic self in a sexual act, he is wonderstruck over the spiritual dimensions of his masturbation. "All truths wait in all things," he observes ingenuously, unable to explain except by showing the mysteries of his nature.

The event is fully dramatized in the poem because Whitman needs to ensure that no one in the larger world will distort the meaning of his experience, or "gainsay" it, or make it seem not true.

> (Only what proves itself to every man and
>   woman is so,
> Only what nobody denies is so.)
> (11. 655–656)

He uses the confidentiality of a parenthesis to emphasize that there need be nothing secret about sexuality; the truths of sex must be shared knowledge or they are falsified by shame. Yet, in brushing away the secrecy, Whitman seems to be requiring confirmation, or agreement, from "every man and woman" to assure him that his sexuality is valid and his to keep. His self-possession is not firm; he appears inordinately vulnerable to the threat of denial by other people: "Only what nobody denies is so."

Assured by the repeated transfiguration, Whitman knows that love is a principle of his inner being. He is blessed with another beatific vision of the beauty and harmony of all creation. In the famous confession of faith in stanza 31, beginning "I believe a leaf of grass is no less than the journey-work of the stars, / And the pismire is equally perfect, and a grain of sand, and the egg of the wren," Whitman elaborates at greater length the sense of absolute love pervading the universe that he expressed in shorter form in stanza 5. More than a restatement, though, this joyous acceptance of existence delivers Whitman from his earlier uncertainty in which he could record only patterns of repetition and reconstruction of experience. His sense of overlapping and interweaving time turns into a more progressive, historical sense of continuity. A comparison of his present and earlier jubilations, in stanzas 31 and 5, reveals that Whitman no longer suffers from recurrent pangs of longing or fear for the past:

He has recovered what he felt was lost, and what could have been lost again. In stanza 31 he expresses his sense of personal intactness through time. He sees himself in the long train of geological time, a creature formed by it, with evolutionary affinities.

> I find I incorporate gneiss, coal, long-threaded
>   moss, fruits, grains, esculent roots,
> And am stucco'd with quadrupeds and birds all
>   over,
> And have distanced what is behind me for good
>   reasons,
> But call any thing back again when I desire it.
> (11. 670–673)

The assurance of being able to "call any thing back again when I desire it" comes to him from writing the poem itself in its dramatically repetitive form, and the contemporary idea of evolution corroborates his personal insight. His present illumination shows him not only that he was loved, as he remembered in stanza 5, but also he now has the assurance that the love remains with him forever. The past and the distant no longer mock him or cause anguish. The spectacle of their apparent remoteness — like the apparent remoteness of his "mortal" loved one — is all "in vain...," as he reiterates for nine lines, because he can "follow quickly" wherever they are.

> In vain the speeding or shyness,
> In vain the plutonic rocks send their old heat
>   against my approach,
> In vain the mastodon retreats beneath its own
>   powder'd bones,
> In vain objects stand leagues off and assume
>   manifold shapes,
> In vain the ocean settling in hollows and the
>   great monsters lying low,
> In vain the buzzard houses herself with the sky,
> In vain the snake slides through the creepers
>   and logs,
> In vain the elk takes to the inner passes of
>   the woods,
> In vain the razor-bill'd auk sails far north
>   to Labrador,
> I follow quickly, I ascend to the nest in the
>   fissure of the cliff.   (11. 674–683)

Whitman delightedly finds that his imagination triumphs over circumstances. In his imaginative revel he can recreate everything subjectively, making his thoughts so palpably real that he finds a blessing in his solitude. He no longer needs to vie for external objects that are ages removed or elusively unattainable. The surprising, comic relief (which accounts for his amusing good humor in this passage) is that he gets what he always wanted anyway. Flushed with victory, for apparently nothing can withstand him, he has overcome even the stinging defeat that swamped him with childish Oedipal chagrin. Imaginatively and symbolically, he wins everything back, including his sexual possession of the dangerous but enticing mother: "I follow quickly, I ascend to the nest in the fissure of the cliff." A good poem can contain a supreme erection, one that outmatches his father's and that outwits his mother.

Restored to intimacy with his parents, he no longer feels the inadequacy of ordinary, rational explanations of his experience. In the second half of the poem he more readily accepts the stable dimensions of science and history to explain his world. For example, in stanza 6 the innocent child who asked "What is the grass?" provoked Whitman into speculative, hesitant answers, but in stanza 32 he speaks with resonant self-assurance as he again faces "tokens" and "remembrancers" of his vision when he dwells on the relevance of animals. "I think I could turn and live with animals, they are so placid and self-contain'd, / I stand and look at them long and long." A historical, evolutionary bond links him to "a gigantic beauty of a stallion" and a shared past equalizes all creation. No longer equivocal and wistful about imperfectly "translating" his intuitions as in stanza 6, he confidently enjoys his human capacity for imaginative understanding.

> I think I could turn and live with animals,
>   they are so placid and self-contain'd,
> I stand and look at them long and long.
> They do not sweat and whine about their condition,
> They do not lie awake in the dark and weep for
>   their sins.
> They do not make me sick discussing their duty to God,
> Not one is dissatisfied, not one is demented
>   with the mania of owning things,
> Not one kneels to another, nor to his kind that
>   lived thousands of years ago,
> Not one is respectable or unhappy over the
>   whole earth.
> So they show their relations to me and I accept
>   them,

They bring me tokens of myself, they evince
    them plainly in their possession.

I wonder where they get those tokens,
Did I pass that way huge times ago and negligently
    drop them?

Myself moving forward then and now and forever,
Gathering and showing more always and with
    velocity,
Infinite and omnigenous, and the like of these
    among them,
Not too exclusive toward the reachers of my
    remembrancers,
Picking out here one that I love, and now go
    with him on brotherly terms.

A gigantic beauty of a stallion, fresh and
    responsive to my caresses,
Head high in the forehead, wide between the ears,
Limbs glossy and supple, tail dusting the ground,
Eyes full of sparkling wickedness, ears finely
    cut, flexibly moving.

His nostrils dilate as my heels embrace him,
His well-built limbs tremble with pleasure as
    we race around and return.
I but use you a minute, then I resign you,
    stallion,
Why do I need your paces when I myself out-gallop
    them?
Even as I stand or sit passing faster than you.

                            (11. 684–709)

In stanza 33 Whitman triumphantly sums up the intellectual point and method of his poem's repetitive form. He is assured not only that something cosmically wonderful happened to him but also that he correctly grasped and reverenced its importance even while he remained perplexed:

Space and Time! now I see it is true, what I
    guess'd at,
What I guess'd when I loaf'd on the grass,
What I guess'd while I lay alone in my bed,
And again as I walk'd the beach under the paling
    stars of the morning.   (11. 710–713)

By referring back to earlier parts of the poem in which Whitman uncon-
fidently hypothesized and "guess'd at" the relatedness of all things, these
lines implicitly emphasize the completion or demonstration of a proof.

He has made his case: In a fully explicit masturbation fantasy he has
revealed (or invented) the actions of his parents in a primal scene of sexual
rivalry and Oedipal mortification that he now accepts as the origin of his
creative spirit. He has reinterpreted the fantasy of seduction in stanza
5. To the extent that there was a sin or a crime committed earlier or later,
Whitman has relieved himself of shame and reclaimed the sexual innocence of babes and animals. Most importantly, the vivid sexual polarities
of his divided nature are identified with his mother and father, with whom
he now feels more intimate. Empowered as a man and acknowledged
— even cherished — as a woman, he has proved that his perfect self
reflects others: internally, separately, simultaneously, universally.

In the second half of the poem, Whitman finds logical, metaphorical
reflections of himself throughout an ordinary, familiar world. Like the
resolution of "Spontaneous Me," the final twenty stanzas of "Song of
Myself" deliver Whitman to a life of historical dimension and social significance. He projects himself into a series of historical narratives — a
shipwreck off New Jersey, the bombardment of a fort, a military mas-
sacre in Texas, an old-time sea fight — claiming that "I am the man, I
suffer'd, I was there." The more realistic details of time, place, and
character help restore to the poem the objective dimensions of the external
world.

He dips back into historical and geological eras to note that his essence
was formed and destined even then. The wonder of the far past is that
even prehistory was never loveless, impersonal, or mechanical; that love
for his person, so recently discovered by Whitman, has in fact been the
organizing power in the universe since earliest creation. Some of
Whitman's most dazzling lines proclaim that love was *always* meant for
him.

> Rise after rise bow the phantoms behind me,
> Afar down I see the huge first Nothing, I
> know I was even there,
> I waited unseen and always, and slept through
> the lethargic mist,
> And took my time, and took no hurt from the
> fetid carbon.
>
> Long I was hugg'd close — long and long.
>
> Immense have been the preparations for me,
> Faithful and friendly the arms that have help'd
> me.

Cycles ferried my cradle, rowing and rowing
    like cheerful boatmen,
For room to me stars kept aside in their own
    rings,
They sent influences to look after what was to
    hold me.

Before I was born out of my mother generations
    guided me,
My embryo has never been torpid, nothing could
    overlay it.

For it the nebula cohered to an orb,
The long slow strata piled to rest it on,
Vast vegetables gave it sustenance,
Monstrous sauroids transported it in their
    mouths and deposited it with care.

All forces have been steadily employ'd to
    complete and delight me,
Now on this spot I stand with my robust soul.
(11. 1152–1169)

Protected against obliteration and nurtured through the ages by an adoring nature that never pushed him aside — "Long I was hugg'd close — long and long" — Whitman at last enjoys perfect familial security in a setting free of Oedipal conflict. The limits of the universe bend closer to shelter the small but cherished figure of Whitman standing firm in the company of his "robust soul."

The combination of literary and scientific allusions in the passage reflects the continuation of his separate, simultaneous male and female roles. His identity has not been psychologically integrated, despite his new sense of wholeness. On the one hand, Whitman sees the formation of his identity as a corollary to mid-nineteenth-century ideas of evolution drawn from astronomy, biology, and geology. As such, his self-definition was not miraculous but inevitable; his identity was implicit in the most rudimentary conditions of nature. Mythologizing the evolutionary process, so that natural forces become personal agents responsible for his care, he sees himself passively delivered, continuously being born by a maternal, all-providing, loving nature. At the same time, the literary allusions suggest his personal heroism in the metaphorical journey of the soul from the misty pre-world of phantoms and noxious poisons to the present moment of his triumphant emergence from the "huge first Nothing." This convergence of scientific and literary imagery represents him as the mothered baby and the divine, mythological hero.

Whitman appears to grow older and more detached as his experience takes the form of a life story. He observes himself passing through stages of an exemplary life as he assumes in succession the roles of military hero, martyr, wise teacher, and deceased comrade. But there is something more in his idea of personality deeper than growth and age can quite express, which he hopes to transmit as a legacy to the future. He frequently talks about faith, gives testaments, and makes bequests. Yet approaching the end of the poem, he admits he is dissatisfied with his explanations. Reluctant to conclude the only activity in which he possesses his true self — and on the verge of separation from numberless readers who are supporting his identity — Whitman blenches with the thought that he has not successfully communicated his nature. He again faces the worrisome possibility of disintegration. Naturally enough, he finds it difficult to say goodbye and to distance himself from the company he has constructed in poetry. He turns to his "brothers and sisters" with a lingering appeal for intuitive sympathy that will perpetuate among his readers the family relationships he has integrated in his poem.

> There is that in me — I do not know what it
> is — but I know it is in me.
>
> Wrench'd and sweaty — calm and cool then my
> body becomes,
> I sleep — I sleep long.
>
> I do not know it — it is without name — it
> is a word unsaid,
> It is not in any dictionary, utterance, symbol.
>
> Something it swings on more than the earth I
> swing on,
> To it the creation is the friend whose embracing
> awakes me.
>
> Perhaps I might tell more. Outlines! I plead for
> my brothers and sisters.
>
> Do you see O my brothers and sisters?
> It is not chaos or death — it is form, union,
> plan — it is eternal life — it is
> Happiness.
>
> (11. 1309–1318)

His true happiness lies in thinking that he will never again be unattached. To keep himself treasured, his ultimate bequest to his readers is, of course, himself; after his death he shall be the legacy. His final role in the poem is that of a disembodied, friendly spirit who awaits us in the grass under our feet. We are left expecting future confirmation of the reality of Walt Whitman: We are left desiring the insight, deliverance, and love that are vaguely promised by continued intimacy with him beyond the conclusion of the poem. With the relationship perpetuated by this stratagem, Whitman overcomes his reluctance to end the poem.

> The spotted hawk swoops by and accuses me, he
>   complains of my gab and my loitering.
>
> I too am not a bit tamed, I too am untranslatable,
> I sound my barbaric yawp over the roofs of the
>   world.
>
> The last scud of day holds back for me,
> It flings my likeness after the rest and true
>   as any on the shadow'd wilds,
> It coaxes me to the vapor and the dusk.
>
> I depart as air, I shake my white locks at the
>   runaway sun,
> I effuse my flesh in eddies, and drift it in
>   lacy jags.
>
> I bequeath myself to the dirt to grow from the
>   grass I love,
> If you want me again look for me under your
>   boot-soles.
>
> You will hardly know who I am or what I mean,
> But I shall be good health to you nevertheless,
> And filter and fibre your blood.
>
> Failing to fetch me at first keep encouraged,
> Missing me one place search another,
> I stop somewhere waiting for you.
>   (11. 1331–1346)

The final subordination of the reader in stanza 52 — one of the most astonishing yet satisfying conclusions in all poetry — fulfills the ulterior purpose of the poem given in the opening lines: "what I assume you shall assume." In a sudden but inevitable reversal of his preemption of other peoples' identities through most of the poem, he surprises us in the end by making us absorb him. Now we feel the same unrest in being ourselves, the same longing for an ideal relationship, and the same anguish over received love. In dying, he resembles his masculine soul exclusively, and he draws us into taking on the idealizing role of a dependent. He gives himself the vague invisibility of a wholly spiritualized, willful presence whom we are to cherish as an inner companion. He attributes to himself the mysteriousness and unembodied remoteness in our lives that made his soul a difficult, unpredictable lover, comrade, master, and muse for him; and he urges us to seek him out perseveringly in the grass, just as he needed to invite and encourage the soul's resurgent affection. Like the soul whose alien presence confused him, he will inscrutably influence us — "You will hardly know who I am or what I mean," he warns — and he will sometimes delight us by again granting the love that we search for.

While the imagery of the stanza shows him agreeably disintegrating into his elements that pass again into vegetation that will nurture anyone's blood, Whitman does not give up his ghost as selflessly as he implies by his scene of departure. The stanza can make us feel small in spirit, or guilty, if we shrug off his appeal for an everlasting attachment. He proliferates himself, even shreds himself, into aspects and attributes that are clues to his presence; his suggestions need to be assembled into the wholeness of his personality by our loving regard for what he has come to mean. Exactly like his father toward him, Whitman projects onto us his unattained goals and we are left with responsibility for his ideals. He gives himself to us as a moral force, a teacher of democracy and a model of humane love, even while paradoxically he undercuts the individual's intactness which is fundamental to democracy and love. But with his promises of affection and unending adventure, his high spirits — and most of all, in the end, his poignantly transferred, absolute need for companionship — he makes us feel glad to be stuck with him forever.

The highly syncretized personality that Whitman creates in "Song of Myself" satisfied his conflicting wishes to be his father and a child, his mother and himself. But such delicately precarious harmonies of the imagination never entirely forestalled his obsessional thoughts of sudden doom. This dreadful suspicion of his unreality was the dark antithesis to his transcendent selfhood, and the swing from one belief to the other was the ritual order of his creative life. He could not glorify himself without also anticipating annihilation. He constantly glances ahead beyond the limits of personal existence to the abyss of death in which he finds no one at all in the emptiness: imagine there is nothing, he taunts himself, imagine there is no self, imagine no thoughts. Even during the first splendid upwelling of his creative genius, his ascent to imaginative freedom and joy had to be weighted by his deep habituation to anxiety and depression.

In "To Think of Time," which was included among the original twelve poems of the first edition of *Leaves*, Whitman dismantles his conception of himself as a representative man. He fears that his poems will not maintain his connections to other people and his own part in the universe will be undone by oblivion. The immense stretch of time mocks the pointlessness and trumpery of the living self. The cause of his distrust remains obscured beyond the reach of his probing in this not very successful poem, but one powerful stanza, which stands out as better poetry, gives a clue to his immeasurable grief over death. Whitman recounts the funeral of "an old Broadway stage-driver" as a reminder that death is applicable to all lives, "A reminiscence of the vulgar fate."

> Cold dash of waves at the ferry-wharf, posh and
>   ice in the river, half-frozen mud in
>   the streets,
> A gray discouraged sky overhead, the short last
>   daylight of December,
> A hearse and stages, the funeral of an old Broadway
>   stage-driver, the cortege mostly drivers.
>
> Steady the trot to the cemetery, duly rattles the
>   death-bell,
> The gate is pass'd, the new-dug grave is halted
>   at, the living alight, the hearse
>   uncloses,
> The coffin is pass'd out, lower'd and settled,
>   the whip is laid on the coffin, the
>   earth is swiftly shovel'd in,
> The mound above is flatted with the spades
>   — silence,
> A minute — no one moves or speaks — it is done,
> He is decently put away — is there anything
>   more?
>
> (11. 36–44)

For the next eight lines, Whitman sketches out the dead man's personal details, his tone of understatement acknowledging that death is the implausible but common fate of each person. Eulogizing the workman with a list of words and gestures of his driver's trade, Whitman's sympathies are more deeply engaged and he recharacterizes the dead man as a type of poet. Neither the corpse nor the poet participates in external events that solidly define the self. Mere words define Whitman, and words can undo him.

To restore his pleasure in being a poet despite the "slow moving and black lines" of numerous burials that "go ceaselessly over the earth," Whitman tries to outface his fears by insisting on the reliability of his own self-definition. Returning to the "you" upon whom he projects his doubts in this poem, Whitman tries to regain the conviction of his identity.

> You are not thrown to the winds, you gather
>   certainly and safely around yourself,
> Yourself! yourself! yourself, for ever and ever!
>
> It is not to diffuse you that you were born of
>   your mother and father, it is to identify
>   you,
> It is not that you should be undecided, but that
>   you should be decided,
> Something long preparing and formless is arrived
>   and form'd in you,
> You are henceforth secure, whatever comes or
>   goes.
>
>   (11. 70–75)

Despite the reference to his parents and his rededication to a belief in his destiny, he does not rest assured that he is "henceforth secure." His ability to embody other people and diverse elements also means the vulnerability of his own individuality to that of another. He anticipates death as a special punishment for something worthless in himself. For Whitman, "to think the thought of death" means to feel obliteration now.

> If maggots and rats ended us, then Alarum!
>   for we are betray'd,
> Then indeed suspicion of death.
>
> Do you suspect death? if I were to suspect
>   death I should die now,
> Do you think I could walk pleasantly and
>   well-suited toward annihilation?
>
>   (11. 104-107)

Unlike "Song of Myself," the poem ends without resolution or discovery. With all the confidence he can muster for a salvo of faith in the final stanza, he still equivocates between belief and disbelief by repeating the declamation: "I swear I think now that every thing without exception has an eternal soul!" and "I swear I think there is nothing but

immortality!'' The convoluted phrasing belies his uncertainty: to swear
a thought of nothing without exception but immortality confounds sense
with blustering.

In a more direct companion piece to "Song of Myself," Whitman tries
to disarm not merely his bad thoughts, as in "To Think of Time," but
even his bad dreams. In "The Sleepers" he seeks in his dreams the most
ordinary connections with other beings. Like his special states of transcendent, apocalyptic insight in "Song of Myself," dreams break down
the limits of time, space, and logic to reveal the power of his sympathy
with others. In dreaming we all can make others assume what we assume.
Everything can be taken into ourselves; people, remote places, the past
or future can be directly felt in the present instant of dreaming. Everything expresses ourselves: the rigid circumstances of an external world
melt away into flexible associations that rearrange experience into a
reflection of the mind itself. But in order to dream, we must fall asleep,
and that poses special problems for Whitman. Childhood reasons for
being afraid to sleep continued into his adulthood: Like a child he feared
he might lose himself in the dark. He faces the humiliation, which he
acknowledges, that he is afraid of the night; and as he recounts his dreams
during a night of turmoil, he dispels his fears by identifying some of the
causes of his distress.

In the randomly flitting turns of mind between sleep and wakefulness,
his first thought is of children sleeping in their cradles, looking as if death
is already upon them. Their lifelessness suggests the violent and sensual
sleepers who lie at the edge of death.

> The wretched features of ennuyés, the white
>   features of corpses, the livid faces
>   of drunkards, the sick-gray faces of
>   onanists,
> The gash'd bodies on battle-fields, the insane
>   in their strong-door'd rooms, the sacred
>   idiots, the new-born emerging from gates,
>   and the dying emerging from gates,
> The night pervades them and infolds them.
>   (11. 8–10)

Thrown together with horrors in the night, Whitman sleeps amidst
evidence of decadence and mutilation crowding upon him in the
reappearing "features" and "faces," the "gash'd bodies" and the bodily
helpless young, old and crazed.

After the first ten lines establish the thoughts of death and violence
that disturb his night, Whitman turns to family members sleeping con-
tentedly, the married couple touching each other, the sisters side by side,

men side by side, a mother with her baby close to her. Their sleep is markedly different from his own, or that of the other sleepers, because they are oblivious to any of the horrors that fill the night. The family sleepers are the image of loving security in their complacent sleep, yet they also suggest an indifference to his fears. The suggestion that they are even denying him is articulated clearly in the following lines, which return to images of misery, guilt, rage, and helplessness. The repeated verb *sleep* now recurs insistently, both internally and at each line's end where it emphasizes not only the quiet that soothes troubled people but also the futility of their desperate lives. Sleep is an ironic, recurrent memorandum that death erases all pains and desires.

> The married couple sleep calmly in their bed,
>   he with his palm on the hip of the wife,
>   and she with her palm on the hip of the
>   husband,
> The sisters sleep lovingly side by side in
>   their bed,
> The men sleep lovingly side by side in theirs,
> And the mother sleeps with her little child
>   carefully wrapt.
>
> The blind sleep, and the deaf and dumb sleep,
> The prisoner sleeps well in the prison, the
>   runaway son sleeps,
> The murderer that is to be hung next day, how
>   does he sleep?
> And the murder'd person, how does he sleep?
>
> The female that loves unrequited sleeps,
> And the male that loves unrequited sleeps,
> The head of the money-maker that plotted all
>   day sleeps,
> And the enraged and treacherous dispositions,
>   all, all sleep.
>
> (11. 11–22)

When at last he sinks into deeper sleep his dreams are at first a relief and a pleasure to him.

> I dream in my dream all the dreams of the other
>   dreamers,
> And I am become the other dreamers.
>
> I am a dance — play up there! the fit is whirling
>   me fast!   (11. 30–32)

He dreams of cavorting with a band of sexually playful comrades who treat him as their darling pet — echoing his lambkin revel in his parents' bed in "Song of Myself." His dream quickly changes and he is transformed from the favored youth into a woman who receives her lover in the night. Next, darkness itself becomes an erotic presence as vague and overpowering as Whitman's "soul," and with a touch sweeter than her lover's, deep sleep embraces the woman he now is, as Whitman dreams the exquisite intimacy of her possession by the masculine darkness. In a passage that he eventually deleted twenty-six years later, he next dreams that he is suddenly thrust from bed and shamefully exposed in his nakedness. He would hide if he could. This sudden embarrassment in sexual activity repeats the mortification he described in "Song of Myself," and his remedy for this burning shame is, as before, a fantasy of sexually introverted triumph that enables him to feel both male and female. He dreams of genitals as food and mouth, and sexual intercourse as eating.

> O hot-cheek'd and blushing! O foolish hectic!
> O for pity's sake, no one must see me now! my
>   clothes were stolen while I was abed,
> Now I am thrust forth, where shall I run?
>
> Pier that I saw dimly last night, when I look'd
>   from the windows!
> Pier out from the main, let me catch myself with
>   you, and stay — I will not chafe you,
> I feel ashamed to go naked about the world.
>
> I am curious to know where my feet stand and what
>   this is flooding me, childhood or manhood — and
>   the hunger that crosses the bridge between.
>
> The cloth laps a first sweet eating and drinking,
> Laps life-swelling yolks — laps ear of rose-corn,
>   milky and just ripen'd;
> The white teeth stay, and the boss-tooth advances
>   in darkness,
> And liquor is spill'd on lips and bosoms by touching
>   glasses, and the best liquor afterward.
>
>   (*LG*, pp. 626–627)

The sequence of his dreams brings Whitman closer to his dangerous goal of uniting with the body of a woman, where he will receive tender love — both hers and her lover's. But a sustained passionate attachment to the sensual woman is not possible for him even in his dreams. He chooses next to unite with the old, the dispassionate, and the melancholy: "Perfume and youth course through me and I am their wake," he says as he feels his vitality leaving him, presumably after an emission, and his skin turns flaccid. In the dreams that follow his sexual climax, he experiences the restrained, saddened love that grandmothers and widows have remaining to them in old age, while darning socks or looking at the frozen earth on a winter night. Still united with womanhood, he is safely withdrawn from the power of his ardor, and from hers. In a striking reversal of his identification with the sensual woman who responded to the vibrant intimacy of darkness, Whitman becomes a shroud that envelops a corpse and he goes down with that unfeeling body to the darkness of the grave. Paralyzed by his desire and his fear, he sees himself as a husk encasing an emotionally deadened life:

> A shroud I see and I am the shroud, I wrap a
>   body and lie in the coffin,
> It is dark here under ground, it is not evil
>   or pain here, it is blank here, for
>   reasons.
>
> (It seems to me that every thing in the light
>   and air ought to be happy,
> Whoever is not in his coffin and the dark grave
>   let him know he has enough.)
>
> (11. 66–69)

His own admonishment, which in parenthesis speaks as if from beyond the grave, goes unheeded in the poem as Whitman dwells on his wishes and terrors in dream after dream.

> I turn but do not extricate myself,
> Confused, a past-reading, another, but with
>   darkness yet.
>
> (11. 81–82)

In the dreams of stanzas 3 through 6, which are intensified by more detailed and sustained elaboration, Whitman is overrun with unvarying, chronic feelings of wretched helplessness as he is exposed to heartbreaking deaths that cannot be prevented. The beautiful gigantic swimmer "in the prime of his middle age" drowns in the eddies among the rocks despite his valiant, pathetic striving to save himself. Whitman in his dream can hardly believe that the waves, slapping and rolling upon the swimmer's tormented body, really do kill him and carry him away. A ship

in winter runs against the rocks during a storm at night and all on board
are lost in the surf, as Whitman on the beach cannot go to the aid of the
doomed but helps in the next morning to "pick up the dead and lay them
in rows in a barn." General Washington in his defeat at Brooklyn Heights
stands weeping over the slaughter of the young men entrusted to him
"by their parents." Later in victorious peace, the General weeps again
to say goodbye to his beloved soldiers. His open displays of love and
grief partly redeem Washington from the implied guilt of his relentless,
unheeding power, which is like the sea's. In all three dreams Whitman's
theme is that situations of dependence and bonds of trust are shattered
by betraying force, leaving him deadened and helpless. But the sequence
of the dreams reveals his imaginative purpose, for in each dream he
appears to become younger and less alone.

His regression to comfort and full solace is completed in the fourth
dream. Whitman recounts his mother's reminiscence — dreaming a story
of hers that he cannot forget — of a beautiful Indian woman who once
stopped by her girlhood home, sat in the house with her while Louisa
admiringly served her through the day, then departed, to the child's
profound dismay. The dream emphasizes the emotional desolation that
his mother experienced as an innocently adoring child who is confused
by a remotely attractive, potentially hostile, ambiguously responsive adult
who goes away.

> Now what my mother told me one day as we sat
>   at dinner together,
> Of when she was a nearly grown girl living home
>   with her parents on the old homestead.
>
> A red squaw came one breakfast-time to the old
>   homestead,
> On her back she carried a bundle of rushes for
>   rush-bottoming chairs,
> Her hair, straight, shiny, coarse, black, profuse,
>   half-envelop'd her face,
> Her step was free and elastic, and her voice
>   sounded exquisitely as she spoke.
>
> My mother look'd in delight and amazement at
>   the stranger,
> She look'd at the freshness of her tall-borne
>   face and full and pliant limbs,
> The more she look'd upon her she loved her,

Never before had she seen such wonderful beauty
    and purity,
She made her sit on a bench by the jamb of the
    fireplace, she cook'd food for her,
She had no work to give her, but she gave her
    remembrance and fondness.

The red squaw staid all the forenoon, and toward
    the middle of the afternoon she went
      away,
O my mother was loth to have her go away,
All the week she thought of her, she watch'd
    for her many a month,
She remember'd her many a winter and many a
    summer,
But the red squaw never came nor was heard of
    there again.

                (11. 100–116)

Whitman assumes the viewpoint of his child-mother, equating his feelings of lost love and parental neglect with her early experience. He identifies with her as a child rather than as the aged, hopeless woman he dreamed of earlier in the poem. In drawing near to her as a child, he is dimly recognizing the childishness of her search for an ideal parent, such as Louisa tried to fashion her son into becoming for her. The dream acknowledges the helplessness and deprivation that mother and son both prolong in the possessive relationship they impose upon each other. Yet he is not critical; instead, he feels united with her in the yearning they share. By finding his intimate identification with his mother in his discovery, or projection, of her wistful desire for parental love, Whitman dreams his way to a tenable life situation.

Whitman made one of the most artful and revealing revisions in *Leaves of Grass* when, late in his life, he removed eight lines that followed the dream about his mother's story. From the first edition of 1855 until 1881, "The Sleepers" included at this point the dream of a male slave calling for vengeance against a white oppressor who has taken away his woman and sold his brothers and sisters. The slave's murderous rage against a cruel master repeats the sense of betrayal and helplessness that Whitman expressed in the three dreams leading up to his mother-dream. The reassertion of anger and frustration is out of place in the poem's emotional structure, even though it reveals that Whitman's psychological conflict was not fully resolved by resolving a poem. The section fits an earlier point but Whitman chose to remove it entirely, recognizing that its bitterness contradicts the argument, or plot, of the poem. The revision illustrates his powerful self-expressiveness being brought into line by his aesthetic judgement over the poem's integrity.

In the final version of 1881 Whitman proceeds directly from his mother-dream to other dreams of reconciliation. Sufficiently restored to his child-mother by sharing the passive love of their mutual longing, Whitman can restore all losses in the poem. His dreams turn brighter — ''A show of the summer softness — a contact of something unseen — an amour of the light and air.'' And he guides the swimmer, the travelers, the homeless, and the lonely homeward to havens of remembered love in their dreams.

> Elements merge in the night, ships make tack
>   in the dreams,
> The sailor sails, the exile returns home,
> The fugitive returns unharm'd, the immigrant
>   is back beyond months and years...
>   (11. 123–125)

In stanza 7, all the sleepers are beautiful as they dream their peace and consolation.

Reconciled with the mother he feared to gain or to lose, Whitman sees his soul at last come forth in the night like a god ''from its embowered garden.'' The soul reestablishes the masculine balance of opposites in the order of the universe. Blessed by the soul's favor, Whitman sinks into a quiet sleep, sensing the coherence of contrary things. He sees that all sleepers will be restored in loving embrace with their opposites: ''The diverse shall be no less diverse, but they shall flow and unite — they unite now.'' In the final stanza, he dreams of diverse people lying beautiful and unclothed as they flow with love over the whole earth, including fathers and sons: ''The father holds his grown or ungrown son in his arms with measureless love, and the son holds the father in his arms with measureless love.'' Whitman, of course, stays mainly with his mother: He remains closely enveloped by the night in which he sleeps, but he claims that he will come and go into the daylight as he needs to. Having faced the darkness, but unwilling to pursue his fears any further, Whitman fits the night world of dreams into a well-ordered domestic routine.

> I too pass from the night,
> I stay a while away O night, but I return to
>   you again and love you.

Why should I be afraid to trust myself to you?
I am not afraid, I have been well brought forward
   by you,
I love the rich running day, but I do not desert
   her in whom I lay so long,
I know not how I came of you and I know not where
   I go with you, but I know I came well and
   shall go well.

I will stop only a time with the night, and rise
   betimes,
I will duly pass the day O my mother, and duly
   return to you.

                                    (11. 177–184)

In the conclusion of this poem, unlike "Song of Myself," he continues to face inward, to his solitude. Though he says he will turn away, he does not. The poem is self-analytical to the point of prophetic insight, for it dramatizes the unbreakable link with his mother that will prevail against all his Oedipal striving for sexual autonomy and confirmation in the external, daytime world. He returns to nightmares that will grow worse.

Dreams, obsessions, delusions of guilt, ego-shattering illuminations, beatific visions, hypomanic fantasies, these are the significant experiences of life in the poems of his first edition of 1855, in which his attention focuses on the tumultuous definition of the self that suited him at last. But while his basic subject material in these poems is similar to Poe's and to Blake's, for instance, Whitman did not dramatize his spiritual crisis with similar assumptions and concessions evident in their work. To make the imagination the common, natural possession of all men and women, he avoided the suggestions that it was aberrant, or demonic, or angelic, or mystical, or even private. In his poetry he treated his intensified, illogical states of consciousness as natural and common occurrences; they indicated to him the bed-rock reality of the spirit. His new vision of spiritual existence was personally *democratic* — in the largest sense of Whitman's usage that means equal accessibility and harmonious attachment through all time and space. In the poems that he continued to write for the rest of his life, he tried to extrapolate from the democracy of personality a principle of social unity for the use of "These States" — as he rather warily called the syncretized nation of opposing factions that was the outer country of his mind.

4

Roads of Adventure and the Attachment to Home, 1856

ALL SUMMER after the first appearance of *Leaves of Grass*, in July, 1855, Whitman was absorbed in thoughts of his beginning role as America's national poet, and he held himself in readiness for an exalted destiny. This period in his life seemed like a miraculous unfolding of his myth of himself. It was a year of supremely good fortune in which he roused the literary world to dramatic reaction, if not acceptance, and he met a number of important writers beyond his bohemian circle of Brooklyn journalists. High-minded princes of the universal Soul — Emerson and his disciples and emissaries arriving from the universe's village center in Concord, Massachusetts — began pilgrimages to his workman's house in the city to take the measure of this new literary wonder. During the year he completed twenty new poems, and brought out a second edition of *Leaves of Grass* by September 1856. He told his biographer Richard Maurice Bucke that the late summer and fall of 1855 had been the happiest period of his life.[1]

For the most part, Whitman's happiness was a continuation of the ecstasy of becoming a poet. "When the book aroused such a tempest of anger and condemnation everywhere," he told Bucke, "I went off to the east end of Long Island, and spent the late summer and all the fall — the happiest of my life — around Shelter Island and Peconic Bay. Then came back to New York with the confirmed resolution, from which I never wavered, to go on with my poetic enterprise in my own way, and finish it as well as I could." He felt confirmed in his vocation, but other events during the month of July made the summer and fall of 1855 a period of challenge and rededication in a different sense. He was affected by more serious affairs than the cries of shock over his book that he exaggerated to Bucke as a "tempest of anger and condemnation everywhere." Greater tempests, including his own feelings of anger and condemnation, swept him with contrary sensations of deliverance from his doom as an evil son and deliverance into the hands of a nemesis revealed, while he was hailed by a new father who seemed too good not to be forever true.

Within a week after the first publication of *Leaves of Grass* in which Whitman was proclaiming himself the liberator of all the downtrodden spirits in the world, the poet's begrudging father died, on July 11, 1855, as if erased by his inspired son's declaration of independence. He had been seriously ill for several years, partly paralyzed, according to one newspaper obituary, and had suffered so many "bad spells," as Mrs. Whitman called them, that on the day of his final attack the family was not aware of a critical change in his condition. Walt, George, and Jeff spent the day away from home, presumably separately working, until they were called home. Walt and Jeff arrived too late, and Mrs. Whitman reported in a letter to her daughter in New Hampshire that "they felt very much to blame themselves for not being home but they had no idea of any change."[2] Mrs. Whitman appears to have remained characteristically placid and encouraging toward her children while projecting on them any "blame" she might have felt. The inevitability of their father's death had been accepted dispassionately long before it happened. The old man's final removal was apparently a relief to all members of the household, who found it easy to stop caring about the unappreciating and dour invalid.

Although it produced some distress (which will be examined), the death of his father was in some ways emotionally liberating for Whitman. He no longer needed to feel like a murderer for wanting to be rid of an oppressor, and his spirit soared free of this heavy dread. Now he could more openly pursue love from other people, no longer falsified by his nagging hatred toward one of the parents whose love he sought. And with his father entirely removed from the scene, Whitman was freer to explore his love for men, without suffering the risk of shame in his father's sternly condemning eyes. Whitman's chronic feelings of rivalry, diminishment, rejection, and unrequited affection did not end with his father's death, but the event helped to vindicate his unconscious goals. It appeared that simply to have written poetry like "Song of Myself" changed the entire composition of his life. He had gained a new idea of his manliness by writing freely about his emotional states, and life seemed to be immediately answering him by elevating him to actual seniority and liberated manhood: reality appeared indeed to be a personal construction of meanings, like a poem.

While part of him worried about the implications of such terrible success, his blither spirit surged with confidence and self-congratulation that is best expressed in "Song of the Open Road." As one of Whitman's many poems organized around a symbolic journey, "Song of the Open Road" recalls his first poem about his primary life journey, "There Was a Child Went Forth." But the stoicism of the onward-trudging child, who took his lonely fate in stride, turns into a bright anticipation of adventure, comrades, and love, a celebration of release from a restricting fate. Life ahead

of him on the road offers freedom for the imagination, and the poet
assumes that by embracing new experiences he will achieve great deeds.
With charming expressions of youthful optimism he breaks away from
his former mode of life. He casts off his past timidity and his complaints
about misfortune; he rejects conventional routine.

> Afoot and light-hearted I take to the open road,
> Healthy, free, the world before me,
> The long brown path before me leading wherever
>   I choose.
>
> Henceforth I ask not good-fortune, I myself am
>   good-fortune,
> Henceforth I whimper no more, postpone no more,
>   need nothing,
> Done with indoor complaints, libraries, querulous
>   criticisms,
> Strong and content I travel the open road.
>
> The earth, that is sufficient,
> I do not want the constellations any nearer,
> I know they are very well where they are,
> I know they suffice for those who belong to them.
>
> (Still here I carry my old delicious burdens,
> I carry them, men and women, I carry them with
>   me wherever I go,
> I swear it is impossible for me to get rid of
>   them,
> I am fill'd with them, and I will fill them in
>   return.)
>   . . . . .
> From this hour I ordain myself loos'd of limits
>   and imaginary lines,
> Going where I list, my own master total and
>   absolute,
> Listening to others, considering well what they
>   say,
> Pausing, searching, receiving, contemplating,
> Gently, but with undeniable will, divesting
>   myself of the holds that would hold me.
>   (11. 1–15, 53–57)

The "old delicious burdens," the affections and heartaches expressed
earlier, are freely carried into the future, in contrast to the "limits" and
"holds" he repudiates. Whitman dwells at length on these "holds,"
which are conventional relationships and the horrors of a settled life. He

deplores the isolation of the individual imprisoned by social and family hypocrisies; such people in their ordinary lives are grotesques; disfigured, in contrast to the naturally expressive personalities he expects to encounter on the open road. Throughout the poem he refers to two ways of life — one, honest and spontaneous; the other, hypocritical and suffocating. The attractions of the road are companionship and adventure; the evils of staying home are alienation even from one's self. In an angry passage in this otherwise joyous poem, he denounces the abject misery of the secret, falsified self.

> Whoever you are, come forth! or man or woman
> come forth!
> You must not stay sleeping and dallying there
> in the house, though you built it, or
> though it has been built for you.
> Out of the dark confinement! out from behind
> the screen!
> It is useless to protest, I know all and expose
> it.
> Behold through you as bad as the rest,
> Through the laughter, dancing, dining, supping,
> of people,
> Inside of dresses and ornaments, inside of
> those wash'd and trimm'd faces,
> Behold a secret silent loathing and despair.
> No husband, no wife, no friend, trusted to hear
> the confession,
> Another self, a duplicate of every one, skulking
> and hiding it goes,
> Formless and wordless through the streets of
> the cities, polite and bland in the
> parlors,
> In the cars of railroads, in steamboats, in the
> public assembly,
> Home to the houses of men and women, at the
> table, in the bedroom, everywhere,
> Smartly attired, countenance smiling, form
> upright, death under the breast-bones,
> hell under the skull-bones,
> Under the broadcloth and gloves, under the
> ribbons and artificial flowers,
> Keeping fair with the customs, speaking not a
> syllable of itself,
> Speaking of any thing else but never of itself.
> (ll. 189–205)

His commanding invitation to step out from behind the screen subjects the ordinary poor soul to withering humiliation by Whitman's expression of sympathy. He loathes the compromised life, calling it into the shame of public exposure. His tone is chastizing and unforgiving; and he mocks the pretense of well-being among people who suffer hopelessly. Vehemently he attacks lives so blocked from fulfillment that the caged soul cries with "secret silent loathing and despair."

Touting life among the warmhearted, open-souled travelers who delight in freedom and love, he expects to adopt their way of living — "Allons! after the great Companions, and to belong to them!" The denunciation of what appears to be behind him changes to a concluding promise of absolute trust in the new companion who may come forth.

> Camerado, I give you my hand!
> I give you my love more precious than money,
> I give you myself before preaching or law;
> Will you give me yourself? will you come travel
>   with me?
> Shall we stick by each other as long as we live?
>
> (11. 220-224)

These lines are tenderly moving because their tone is full of uncertainty over the return of the pledge. The lines repeatedly proffer his love and they questioningly urge acceptance, but they end the poem on an expectant feeling of vulnerability and hope. Whitman's choice of *Camerado* to replace the original appellation, *Mon enfant*, removes the suggestion of any fatherly claim to affection; rather it emphasizes equality and freedom of fellowship, a revision that increases the danger of rejection of Whitman's unguarded love. The casual diction of "Camerado" and "stick by each other" reinforces through the irony of understatement his ardent commitment to another traveler who may choose to leave him. The happiness of adventuring through life is suddenly consolidated in the conclusion by his gently pleading offer of steadfastness and loyalty, suggesting that his ultimate happiness lies beyond the end of the open road of poetic self-contemplation. Even in his present elation he acknowledges that he has yet to achieve the fruit of his creativity in the security of actual love. Like any poet, Whitman was gratified principally by composing poetry, but unlike most others he believed that a wide range of life, including his own and other people's sexual experience, would change according to what he wrote (and in unplanned ways his life did). He expected to be loved because he wrote: loved by his nation of readers, of course, and in more illogical ways he looked for lovers who would actually materialize in the spirit of his poems.

The conclusion of "Song of the Open Road" indicates how strongly Whitman wanted the love of another man, a desire that he was possibly not yet pursuing actively. But the wistfulness of the conclusion also indicates his doubt that his love for anyone would be reciprocated. Perhaps he also felt his offer came too late, now that his father was irrevocably lost. Whitman's sense of loss did not emerge openly as mourning until three years later in his "Sea-Drift" poems, in which he seeks a reconciliation with the spirit of his father, and his entire work thereafter turns predominantly elegiac over all the sons and fathers lost in the Civil War. His feelings at the time of his father's death are suggested only obliquely in his poetry by his renewed anger and anxiety over death.

In the immediate aftermath of his father's death, which was all too calmly accepted by most of the family under Louisa's influence, Whitman struggled with what seemed to be the indifference and possible treachery of nature. The apparently invulnerable calm of the inhuman world roused his fascinated horror. Perhaps as part of his effort to deal with his father's death, Whitman describes in "This Compost" his shock and revulsion over corpses and burials while nature serenely remains unaffected by the grotesqueness of man's mortality. The earth's complacency frightens him, and he scarcely knows whether the chemistry of decomposition that distills the sour dead in the earth produces healthful nurture or subtle poison. He recoils from contact with the earth he loves: "Something startles me where I thought I was safest." The word *something* begins the poem with a flourish of dramatic mystery about the cause of his uncharacteristic behavior. The poem reveals that his father's death is the unnameable "something" that startles him into anxiety over the natural world that he usually regards as protective. Overcome with revulsion from the thought of mortal decay, Whitman cannot take off his clothes to touch the woods, the pastures, the grass or the sea where the rotting corpses seep and drain, or expose himself to the air infected by the gas of decomposing bodies. Deprived of nature's customary, sensual caresses, his fearful recoil into himself away from the places where he enjoyed his securest pleasures is a symptom of his grief, which bursts out in his anger over bereavement. He is abusively gross about the foul carcasses: resentful over man's weakness and nakedness; and he is angry that the earth placidly receives even more putrefaction.

> Something startles me where I thought I was safest,
> I withdraw from the still woods I loved,
> I will not go now to the pastures to walk,
> I will not strip the clothes from my body to meet
>   my lover the sea,

I will not touch my flesh to the earth as to
    other flesh to renew me.

O how can it be that the ground itself does not
    sicken?
How can you be alive you growths of spring?
How can you furnish health you blood of herbs,
    roots, orchards, grain?
Are they not continually putting distemper'd
    corpses within you?
Is not every continent work'd over and over with
    sour dead?

Where have you disposed of their carcasses?
Those drunkards and gluttons of so many
    generations?
Where have you drawn off all the foul liquid
    and meat?
I do not see any of it upon you to-day, or
    perhaps I am deceiv'd,
I will run a furrow with my plough, I will press
    my spade through the sod and turn it
    up underneath,
I am sure I shall expose some of the foul meat.

                                 (ll. 1–16)

He is desolated over a death and burial that have unmanned him but
had no effect on the earth. He rages against the earth's imperturbable
capacity to hide the dead, and perhaps indeed its readiness to snatch men
into oblivion. He speaks as if he will shock, interrogate, challenge, bait,
threaten, and eviscerate the earth into disclosing the enormity of death
and corruption within it.

But finally he curbs his turbulent, dangerous impulse to expose the earth
as a sickening charnel house. A new season of growth in the springtime
restores his wonder for the mystery of regeneration. He marvels that the
full-grown crops of summer are "innocent and disdainful above all those
strata of sour dead." Relieved, he returns to the physical pleasures of
life, resuming his walks and sea baths, just as Whitman did after his
father's death, and he renews his taste for fruit and his hours of repose
upon the grass. Comforted by the earth's natural resurrection — the poem
in 1856 was originally titled "Poem of Wonder at the Resurrection of the
Wheat" — Whitman follows almost to the end a simple pattern of first
loss and then consolation in witnessing the renewal of the world. But
the final six lines of the poem reach beyond the logical structure of con-

solatory verse. Whitman remains transfixed by an earth that turns human corruption into fresh air and grasses. He is frightened by its impervious resilience; nature is distressingly unmindful of any value but her own equilibrium:

> Now I am terrified at the Earth, it is that
>   calm and patient,
> It grows such sweet things out of such corruptions,
> It turns harmless and stainless on its axis, with
>   such endless successions of diseas'd
>   corpses,
> It distills such exquisite winds out of such
>   infused fetor,
> It renews with such unwitting looks its prodigal,
>   annual, sumptuous crops,
> It gives such divine materials to men, and
>   accepts such leavings from them at last.
>
> (11. 42–47)

Ostensibly, the poem calls into doubt and then reaffirms procreative life and the ongoing vitality of Whitman's father, who will prevail over death through resurrection in his son. But Whitman lingers disquietingly on the impassivity of the earth that overcomes and perhaps even drains away the vigor of men. The earth remains steady "on its axis," unaffected by the degradations of absorbing the dead. Its "unwitting looks" anticipate the inconsequence of individuals who are everlastingly diminished, shamed and replaced: "It gives such divine materials to men, and accepts such leavings from them at last." This poignant disparagement of mortal men expresses pity for the disappointment of everyone's high hopes of life — like Yeats's pity in "Among School Children" for nuns and mothers who worship idealized images. But Whitman also conveys a strong sense of danger in the power of the earth to deactivate and reconstitute the substance of men. To think of men as earth's compost, as he does throughout the poem, is to worry over the earth's irrational opposition to their humanity.

Whitman does not recognize the full meaning of his feelings and his symbolic material in this poem. He did not identify Louisa in the attitudes of the earth, and consequently he did not directly incur the personal threat of the earth's power over him. The irony of burying the dead in the fruitful earth is an entirely conventional, elegiac subject that Whitman treats in a conventional way; he suggests but does not develop more revelatory meanings in the usual imagery of springtime and burial and distress and consolation of the mourner.

When Whitman responded to his father's death in less conventional poetry, he more clearly acknowledged his complicated personal feelings and the ambiguous relationships that underlay his suspicion that the heart of nature was destructively possessive toward men and manhood. In "Song of the Broad-Axe" he works with his more original imagery of democratic life. Taking a hint from his social observations of the veneer of femininity over the coarseness of American life, what he uncovers unnerves him deeply. "Song of the Broad-Axe" at first develops and then disguises a spectacle of masculine, workaday power that is sapped by feminine complacency.

Whitman begins with a riddle: The ax is described with metaphors that make it enigmatic and promise meanings yet to be unraveled. The deliberate symbolism is emphasized and set off from the rest of the poem by the stylized versification in the opening six lines of pronounced meters and insistent rhymes:

> Weapon   shapely, naked, wan,
> Head from the mother's bowels drawn,
> Wooded flesh and metal bone, limb only one and
>   lip only one,
> Gray-blue leaf by red-heat grown, helve produced
>   from a little seed sown,
> Resting the grass amid and upon,
> To be lean'd and to lean on.
>
> (11. 1–6)

The exaggerated figurativeness of the language draws attention to the paradox, which Whitman intends to demonstrate, that the overtly phallic object representing man's law and masculine power throughout the ages contains an inner core of feminine power, which expresses nature's law.

The ax, as Whitman develops its meaning, is the great instrument with an organ-range of creative and destructive acts from ancient times to the present. It is the most common, most flexible tool of the individual will, an extension of personal strength and impulse that can be multiplied into armies and hordes; invested with the power of a monarch to execute traitors and rivals and to appropriate property; or used by countless millions to clear forests, build houses, bridges, ships, and cities. Whitman makes the ax symbolic of the immanent but undervalued human spirit in every use and feature of the implement. Even the materials come from lands that do not produce obvious riches like crops, gold, timber, grazing for cattle; the ores that are smelted and forged into the ax are hidden in the earth under the apparent barrenness and harshness of the "Lands of iron — lands of the make of the axe." Its original sources lie unseen within places that are forbidding, austere, and not counted precious.

The uses of the ax celebrated in stanza 3 indicate a world at work without stint or relief. For sixty-nine lines humanity is shown striving to inherit the earth through skills, trades, greed, and ambition, always employing the ax as the instrument of material achievement. The external signs of civilization are defined by the work of the ax that exerts "the power of personality just or unjust" — a crass energy like the blows of the hurried and crafty father in "There Was a Child Went Forth."

At the height of glorifying the productive work of the ax — and extolling the material values of his family of Brooklyn house builders — Whitman turns to the ephemeralness of man's works and of the external world generally. What seems substantial and fixed in the world is only transitory; material achievements indicate chiefly the immaterial powers that form them. "Muscle and pluck forever!" Whitman calls out as he redirects his praises from man's feats of muscle to celebrate the human pluck that rises and rises again through the falling monuments of the ages. Whitman dismisses the works of the ax because they do not last — "Do you think a great city endures?" he asks. Only the spirit that the ax expresses is real and immortal. The universal occurrence of the ax amid the changes of the mutable world indicates that "nothing endures but personal qualities." That gnomic aphoristic line sounds more like a sentence by Emerson than Whitman's usual verse. Whitman asserts that the ax symbolizes not only the individual will but specifically the natural democracy of the great spirit of mankind, because only the vigor of individuals survives and endures through the pomp and decay of empires.

> What do you think endures?
> Do you think a great city endures?
> Or a teeming manufacturing state? or a prepared
>   constitution? or the best built steamships?
> Or hotels of granite and iron? or any chef-d'oeuvres
>   of engineering, forts, armaments?
>
> Away! these are not to be cherish'd for themselves,
> They fill their hour, the dancers dance, the musicians
>   play for them,
> The show passes, all does well enough of course,
> All does very well till one flash of defiance.
>
> A great city is that which has the greatest
>   men and women,
> If it be a few ragged huts it is still the
>   greatest city in the whole world.
>
> (ll. 100–109)

When he has established the moral and social significance of the symbol as distinctively democratic, the continuation of the poem becomes partly repetitive and concentric as Whitman reiterates the themes developed in the first half; but as he elaborates the meaning of the ax, unexpected features surface. His perspective changes to a more visionary one that discerns a general truth about the way all of nature, not just the ax, expresses the supremacy of the spirit. He again notes the unpromising landscape that contains the hidden, common ore; he again recounts through history the service of the ax to the living and the dead; and he sees again the emblem of the American future in the scourge of the world's past, now washed clean of its blood and disgrace. The rapid condensation of these symbolic facts produces the evidence in the poem that nature ceaselessly externalizes the spirit. Whitman finds the meaning of experience in nature's manner of revelation through objective form. The essences of all created things arise as the penumbrae of their now hallowed shapes. "The shapes arise!" he repeats through the final fifty-four lines, as these shapes speak of the reality of internal life.

> The shapes arise!
> Shapes of factories, arsenals, foundries, markets,
> Shapes of the two-threaded tracks of railroads,
> Shapes of the sleepers of bridges, vast frameworks,
>   girders, arches,
> Shapes of the fleets of barges, tows, lake and
>   canal craft, river craft,
> Ship-yards and dry-docks along the Eastern and
>   Western seas, and in many a bay and by-place,
> The live-oak kelsons, the pine planks, the spars,
>   the hackmatack-roots for knees,
> The ships themselves on their ways, the tiers of
>   scaffolds, the workmen busy outside and
>   inside,
> The tools lying around, the great auger and little
>   auger, the adze, bolt, line, square, gouge,
>   and bead-plane.
>
>   (11. 207–215)

He sees a world transformed into the embodiment of spirit; from huge factories to small tools, the implements have become wholly personal while remaining concrete objects. This inspired perception of details resounds with echoes of Whitman's beatific vision in "Song of Myself," in which he recognized love immanent in the plenitude of the universe and he enjoyed spiritual intimacy with starkly objective nature. But in

"Song of the Broad-Axe" the beatific feeling turns melancholy as the celebration of commercial manufacturing concludes with the imagery of man's production, skillfulness, designs, and mastery. Whitman cannot bring the joy of spiritual work back home without resuming tones of deep depression. The shapes of domestic life that subsequently arise are shadowed with pathos, frustration, and suppressed rage. The routines of a contented home life are intermixed with the miseries of dying, family strife, drunkenness, criminality, punishment, and despair. The shapes that arise in stanza 10 are the enclosing or rejecting structures of beds, coffins, houses, courtrooms, taverns, prisons, gallows, and doorways of forced exits and ignoble entrances. These places are all closely associated with parents, spouses, the old and young generations, children, and outcasts. It is as though Whitman can find no place at home for his essential shape to arise amid the bitter chaos of his private life. Facing that diminished and oppressive world, Whitman recognizes figures of his brothers trying to find the natural balance, the order and sanity of their life even though they understand nothing of the emotional turbulence that besets them. In the first version of this poem that passed through several stages of revision as Whitman struggled with the painfully intractable materials of its concluding portion, the shapes of "full-sized men" arise — that is, adults who are still thought of as children. They want to know what is being asked of them, imposed on them, what more can they give to forestall the constant indications of their debts:

> Their shapes arise, above all the rest — the
> shapes of full-sized men,
> Men taciturn yet loving, used to the open air,
> and the manners of the open air,
> Saying their ardor in native forms, saying the
> old response,
> Take what I have then, (saying fain,) take the
> pay you approached for,
> Take the white tears of my blood, if that is
> what you are after.
> (*Variorum*, I, p. 188)

Whitman dropped this entire passage, removing from the poem his sympathy for the inarticulate brothers, himself among them, who submit to the strangely demanding household atmosphere in which love is implicitly required as "the pay you approached for. . .the white tears of my blood." This contemporary phrase for semen links sexual passivity — and perhaps masturbation — with their prolonged bachelorhood. Whitman implicitly complains that his sex is forfeited as a debt, the pay he is not free to spend elsewhere. Nor were his bachelor brothers.

The intense ambivalence of being in that situation is directed toward the mother at home. Her shape immediately arises in the next ten lines, which Whitman retained without any revision. The mother is portrayed as the center of equanimity, poise, and justice; she knows everybody's concealed thoughts, yet she remains undistressed. She is impassively generous, secure, inviolate; and amid the disorder of relationships that seem to direct hostility against her, she is the calm law of nature itself.

> Her shape arises,
> She less guarded than ever, yet more guarded
>   than ever,
> The gross and soil'd she moves among do not
>   make her gross and soil'd,
> She knows the thoughts as she passes, nothing
>   is conceal'd from her,
> She is none the less considerate or friendly
>   therefor,
> She is the best belov'd, it is without exception,
>   she has no reason to fear and she does
>   not fear,
> Oaths, quarrels, hiccupp'd songs, smutty expressions,
>   are idle to her as she passes,
> She is silent, she is possess'd of herself,
>   they do not offend her,
> She receives them as the laws of Nature receive
>   them, she is strong,
> She too is a law of Nature — there is no law
>   stronger than she is.
>
>   (ll. 239–248)

Some of the mother's preternatural powers appear as mere idealizations of womanhood in the final version of the poem. But in light of the original verses, the fact that she knows everyone's secret thoughts, remains insulated against harsh criticism, denies the grossness of other people's suffering and anger, exercises her will without any hesitation or particular response to individuals, all these qualities of majestic self-possession are maddening and desolating traits when they are seen from the eyes of a child, however old, who is thereby trapped by his love and hate, neither of which ever gets through to her. The apparently benign, sweet temper of the woman suggests from the viewpoint of a family in distress, an impervious will to please herself. That view of her character, or "shape," explains Whitman's change of tone to melancholic thoughts of humiliation, degeneracy, and oblivion as soon as the plot of the poem brought him home with his band of working brothers, where the door shut behind them upon the promise of achievement and freedom in the vigorous world of other men. But these negative aspects of her essence are disguised and idealized as the equanimity and grace of female sensibility that expresses the impersonal lawfulness and strength of nature itself in its spiritual essence. The shape of the new American woman is presented as the underlying basis of reality; her revealed shape is the ultimate expression of human depths made evident, of the invisible world made visible, of the inchoate personality given perfect form. Acknowledgment of her supremacy completes the symbolic work and revelatory meaning of the broad-axe.

In another tussle with his ambiguous and disturbing aggressive feelings in the concluding section, Whitman initially included a portrait of his own shape, or self, arising immediately after his mother's. In the first version of the poem, the brawny shape of the new American man, resembling Whitman in every feature he popularly projected as his own, balances the female shape with equal strength and poise — and outmatches her by being more affable and responsive. He celebrates his own image, trying for the second time within this poem to achieve the harmonious self-acceptance that he expressed in "Song of Myself," in which his acknowledgment of his inner core of feminine sensibility led to transports of relief and to doting on himself in liberated pleasure. But the imaginative structure of "Song of the Broad-Axe" is not similar to that of "Song of Myself." The analysis of the symbolic meaning of the ax leads Whitman to recognize an untrustworthy feminine shape that denies him but is nevertheless part of him. He faces a malign egotism that is both outside and inside him, and he experiences not relief but the burdens of his inadequacy, his resentment and guilt.

Ultimately Whitman refused to face the full intensity of the feelings he uncovered by exploring this symbol of manhood; and despite all his revisions, he never connected his anger with his feelings of frailty arising from the death of his father, or with any anxiety over emasculation by the cutting ax. In this threatening capacity, the ax as a symbol of a powerful will could suggest to him both mother and father as a combined parental force. But as far as his insight took him in this poem, his feelings led him away from transcendence, and away from fulfilling himself through identification with the family and nation that he tries to embrace. His initial self-portrait as a triumphantly representative man who embodies and enriches the culture that formed him is evidence of his failure to admit the truth of the poem, that the mother-in-the-ax is not a warm breast of nature, as he wished her to be. When he dropped the eighteen-line passage of ostentatious self-description, and dropped as well the passage in which he is a deeply troubled son and brother, he left a curiously warped but intense poem in which flashes of his creative intuition outleap the belief he intended to poeticize. Although he meant to show the triumph of the spirit in the unfolding of American history, Whitman could not accept or integrate into the poem meanings of the symbol he found in his private life.

The calm possessiveness of the earth in "This Compost" and the withering complacency of the woman in "Song of the Broad-Axe" reveal Whitman's horrified suspicion that he was betrayed in his deepest trust. He saw from a child's perspective the threatening self-centeredness of his mother to whom he again felt vulnerably exposed. She could allow her sick infant to die; she could exile her oldest child, who would not acquiesce to her denial of the squalor and misery of their life; she overrode her second child's feelings with her own, making him her favorite; she imposed on all her children a dependence and obligation as rankling as Eddie's helpless idiocy, which mirrored their plight; and now she could bury the worn-out and useless husband and father — all while acting as if nothing were seriously amiss. She appeared possibly treacherous, even while they continued to "stick by each other" as long as they lived.

Whitman's tumult during the summer of 1855 was compounded by the one acclamation that mattered most in his career. In direct response to the publication of *Leaves of Grass* he was immediately heralded by a publicly grand, loftily spiritual, gently caring and appreciatively literary father when Emerson, upon first reading the book, sent Whitman his unbounded praise. Like the timely advent of his manly soul stepping forth to him from its embowered garden, as in "The Sleepers" he had dreamed it would, the remote and august voice from Concord warmly said everything that Whitman wanted to hear; and with feigned impetuosity Emerson even proposed to come visit him sometime. If acknowledgment of Whitman's genius were needed, the letter that arrived on July 24 confirmed Whitman's vocation as a poet. He fed his self-esteem on that letter of recognition for the rest of his life, exploiting and treasuring Emerson's words, and keeping the letter at the center of the controversy over his reputation among the socially accepted writers, whom he jealously disdained — always implying that he was the secretly more favored son of their idealist father.

Whitman had of course sent copies of his book to all the notable authors in New York and Boston, hoping for favorable reviews and conversational notice even from the primly conventional poets of New England domesticity. Whittier is said to have burned the book, recognizing at least that it was powerfully repugnant to him; Longfellow spurned it; Holmes reviled it; Bryant, though a friend of Whitman, did not believe that his work was worth including in an anthology of verse (he included instead familiar American mediocrities); the younger William Dean Howells could not believe that Whitman wrote poetry at all; and not one among the writers who represented refined literary taste in the nineteenth century ever gave public approval to the best book of poetry written in America. Late in life, the humanitarian Whittier contributed to a collection for the ailing Whitman, but sent his undying admonishments along with his ten dollars. Longfellow along with a mutual friend made a formal visit to Whitman during an illness, and later allowed Whitman to return the call at his Brattle Street mansion in Cambridge. Emerson later waffled in his opinions and he also excluded Whitman from an anthology of poetry he compiled; but initially, in 1855, he had the untrammeled good judgment and the magnanimity to recognize Whitman's achievement. When he read the copy sent to him, "I rubbed my eyes a little," he responded, "to see if this sunbeam were no illusion." He took the trouble to find out how to reach the author named only in the copyright notice, and wrote immediately to say extraordinary things to the unknown workman in Brooklyn, using a phrase soon made famous by Whitman's publicizing of it: "I greet you at the beginning of a great career."

Concord, Massachusetts, 21 July, 1855.

Dear Sir — I am not blind to the worth of the wonderful gift of "Leaves of Grass." I find it the most extraordinary piece of wit and wisdom that America has yet contributed. I am very happy in reading it, as great power makes us happy. It meets the demand I am always making of what seemed the sterile and stingy nature, as if too much handiwork, or too much lymph in the temperament, were making our western wits fat and mean.

I give you joy of your free and brave thought. I have great joy in it. I find incomparable things said incomparably well, as they must be. I find the courage of treatment which so delights us, and which large perception only can inspire.

I greet you at the beginning of a great career, which yet must have had a long foreground somewhere, for such a start. I rubbed my eyes a little, to see if this sunbeam were no illusion; but the solid sense of the book is a sober certainty. It has the best merits, namely, of fortifying and encouraging.

I did not know until I last night saw the book advertised in a newspaper that I could trust the name as real and available for a post-office. I wish to see my benefactor, and have felt much like striking my tasks, and visiting New York to pay you my respects.

R. W. Emerson

(*LG*, pp. 729–730)

Emerson could not know how well his letter and ensuing involvement in Whitman's career fitted neatly into the "long foreground" of poetic development that he surmised. As Whitman's sponsor he took on a role that was to some extent imposed by Whitman's anticipation of what his ideal, tutelary comrade would most likely be and do. Whitman could not have chosen better. At the age of eight Emerson had lost his father, and then in devastating close succession as an adult he had lost his first, romantically loved wife after only eighteen months of marriage; two intimately close brothers, of whom Charles was his irreplaceable favorite; his literary associate, Margaret Fuller, with whom he spun a sexually repressed, overwrought sympathy; and then most traumatically, his adored six-year-old son, who was approaching the age at which Emerson had first suffered the death of his father. The Emerson who still persisted in strong family ties came to his acquaintance with Whitman already haunted by specters of lost comradeship. Both men knew the wringing limitlessness of solitude, and each had determined to make his separate best of it. Expectedly, the long story of their relationship is marked by inflated nuances of ambiguous responses to each other.

Out of gratitude for his praise, Whitman began rereading Emerson's essays with eager intention to understand them intellectually. Throughout the summer of 1855 he took Emerson's books with him on jaunts to the Long Island shore, where he spent his days in creative indolence, bathing, walking the sands, and reading the essays that now thundered with confirmation of his ideas and experience. "There, for the first, he read *Nature*," John Burroughs reports in his biography written with Whitman's assistance. "Soon, on similar excursions, the two other volumes followed."[3] Whitman realized that he had absorbed important perceptions from his earlier reading of Emerson, and these along with his analysis of his own intuitions had led him to an idealist outlook that he found fully expressed in Emerson's writings. He could welcome the doctrine and embrace the master without reducing himself to a disciple. Much of what he read he could accept easily as descriptions of his own feelings and thoughts; for in historical terms Whitman's sense of himself is part of American transcendentalism, which dwelt on intuitive perception of the correspondence between the individual and the natural world. In *Nature*, the chief tract of transcendentalism, published in 1836 when Whitman was seventeen, Emerson writes about moments of heightened awareness that supersede the merely personal sense of oneself, when the individual becomes conscious of a grander man or soul existing within him and extending everywhere. For Emerson, these moments of transport came through contemplation of the natural world, when his being seemed to fuse into the immediate landscape or far into the stars. In a brief, reticent account of one of his experiences of transcendence, Emerson describes his sensations of union with nature.

> Crossing a bare common, in snow puddles, at twilight, under
> a clouded sky, without having in my thoughts any occurrence
> of special good fortune, I have enjoyed a perfect exhilaration.
> I am glad to the brink of fear. . . .Standing on the bare ground
> — my head bathed by the blithe air and uplifted into infinite
> space, — all mean egotism vanishes. I become a transparent
> eyeball; I am nothing; I see all; the currents of the Universal
> Being circulate through me; I am part or parcel of God.

His detractors were delighted with Christopher Cranch's cartoon of
Emerson as an immense "transparent eyeball" standing on spindly legs
in Boston Common; but Emerson's diction, despite its susceptibility to
ridicule, accurately conveys his double sense of merging with nature and
yet attaining heightened consciousness of perceiving: "I am nothing; I
see all." Emerson seemed to be commenting on Whitman's life: "The
Universe is the externization of the soul," Emerson proclaimed in various
ways in his major essays.

Whitman was delighted to find his experience explained and ampli-
fied as if by a wise storyteller, such as his mother seemed to him whenever she too had put their shared life into her words. Like a maternal
voice, the essays provided him with conscious emotions and self-
awareness as they interpreted what he knew more or less for himself.
And from the personal contact Whitman found an intimacy of mutual
understanding in Emerson's confirming praise. In Whitman's old age,
after his mother had died, he remembered Emerson as his receptive,
angelic, and secret ally, with a clean, shining, impassive face — and nearly
his mother's white cap on Emerson's prematurely senile head.

Whitman's serious study of Emerson's writings made a dual impression on Whitman, and the other, more radical influence resulted from
their intellectually aggressive tone. In his writings, Emerson could never
rest in sensual nonchalance upon the grass, listening to the hum of his
placid soul. Moments of transcendence and union with nature are acknowledged as sacred events that signify the health and dimensions of
the spirit, but Emerson wrote to galvanize and advance the spirit, not
especially to grow fondly intimate with its peculiarities. Emerson maintains in *Nature* that the glamour of individual self-realization is not the
dizzying sensual beauty of the physical world and its sensations, such as
Whitman had experienced during his identification in "Song of Myself."
For Emerson, the perfection of the self lies in the apotheosis of intelligent
being in general. He presses for achievement after achievement over the
realm of obdurate, senseless fate; he strives without rest to enlarge his
human will into the splendor and inevitability of a natural force. His

charge to his audience is this: "Build therefore your own world. . . .The kingdom of man over nature, which cometh not with observation, — a dominion such as now is beyond his dream of God, — he shall enter without more wonder than the blind man feels who is gradually restored to perfect sight." Develop a fuller human nature that is meant to be the soul of the world, Emerson says. This goal of purposeful self-assertion against every impersonal and deathly circumstance in the universe took command of that similar disposition in Whitman. The inspired authority and the relentlessness of Emerson's imperatives temporarily captivated Whitman, and the period of Emerson's influence helped to make a more independent man of him. Emerson's explanations of the spiritual reality of external nature made Whitman less sentimental and self-indulgent about loafing his way into communion with the divine order, and they helped wean Whitman away from his naive yearning to unite with nature, with darkness and with death. Emerson led him to sustained thoughtfulness about his potential supremacy over nature by teaching that the spirit of nature is realized only when living people, whose efforts may continue over generations or may succeed in a flash of genius, conceptualize and absorb into their humanity the essence, principle, or law of materials and events, thereby placing man where nature was. In reading major essays like "Experience" and "Fate," Whitman discovered that Emerson connected individuality with the common experience of other people, not through a hero's emotional identification with others, as Whitman did, but chiefly through the heroic effort of Thought, which creates our shared reality. People are united forever because together they create and share the interpreted world. In "Fate" Emerson wrote:

> History is the action and reaction of these two — Nature and Thought; two boys pushing each other on the curbstone of the pavement. Everything is pusher or pushed; and matter and mind are in perpetual tilt and balance, so. Whilst the man is weak, the earth takes him up. He plants his brain and affections. By and by he will take up the earth. . . .Every solid in the universe is ready to become fluid on the approach of the mind, and the power to flux it is the measure of the mind. If the wall remain adamant, it accuses the want of thought. To a subtle force it will stream into new forms, expressive of the character of the mind. What is the city in which we sit here, but an aggregate of incongruous materials which have obeyed the will of some man? The granite was reluctant, but his hands were stronger, and it came. Iron was deep in the ground and well combined with stone, but could not hide from his fires. . . . The whole world is the flux of matter over the wires of thought to the poles or points where it would build.

In Emerson's view, as long as nature's spiritual meanings remain undiscovered, unhumanized nature is crassly deterministic, and even broadly uncongenial to human life. Emerson's sense of the heartlessness of the unhumanized universal spirit reminded Whitman that nature would accept only those who became as autonomous, equable, complacent, insistent, stubborn, and dominant as *she*.

In Emerson's radical attitudes, conveyed in his dogmatic style, Whitman heard the voice of a *good* father, a man of impeccable spiritual integrity who lived up to his outspoken principles. At a crucial moment in Whitman's imaginative eagerness and openness, Emerson gave him the perspective of an intellectual, sophisticated culture that was conveyed chiefly through ideas about man's relation to a symbolic world.

Everything Whitman wrote during the following year he offered for Emerson's approval. When he completed his second edition of *Leaves*, in September 1856, he embossed the spine of the volume with Emerson's praise and name: ''I greet you at the beginning of a great career. — R. W. Emerson.'' Though they had met in person the previous winter when Emerson came to visit Whitman at his Brooklyn house, Whitman continued to treat the letter as a public communication, answerable only by his poems and literary opinions. As a preface to the second edition, he appended an open letter to Emerson (together, of course, with Emerson's note to him), in which he implies that the continuation of his work is in response to Emerson's influence: ''Here are thirty-two Poems, which I send you, dear Friend and Master, not having found how I could satisfy myself with sending any usual acknowledgment of your letter.'' He honors Emerson as the leading writer of the new American age in letters — the repeated term *master* is not merely slavish, but carries as well the sense of *maestro*, the chief craftsman — whose work explains ''the supremacy of Individuality.'' Emerson, he says, first touched the shores of an inner continent of freedom, ''that new moral American continent'' which is the spiritual counterpart of the democratic nation. And Whitman is delivered upon the shore of new liberty — with Emerson's letter in hand like ''the chart of an emperor,'' as he referred to it later. He implies that all his creative effort on behalf of the meaning of These States is to be thought of as an extension of Emerson's leadership.

> Those shores you found. I say you have led The States there — have led Me there. I say that none has ever done, or ever can do, a greater deed for The States, than your deed. Others may line out the lines, build cities, work mines, break up farms; it is yours to have been the original true Captain who put to sea, intuitive, positive, rendering the first report.
>
> (*LG*, p. 739)

Whitman equated Emerson's praise with public and national encouragement to renew his social leadership; after all, it was "the chart of an emperor" he had received. Buoyed by this confirmation of his authority to speak for America, he defined himself more politically in many of the poems he wrote for the second edition. He stepped up his polemical address to a recalcitrant nation that was still neither free nor democratic nor unified — nor even safe from betrayals and assaults within the national family. In his 1856 preface to Emerson, he assures his "dear Master" that the day has come for the reassertion of moral principles in America through the actions of young "literats" — poets, journalists, orators — who can transmit to the people the spiritual meaning of democracy and end the corruption in America's leadership. Dismantling his earlier, unified poetic vision of the United States in relation to Europe, which he expressed in his brilliant 1855 preface, Whitman differentiates between the symbolic ideal of America and its political and social reality. The preface discusses at length the many distinctions Whitman made between the actual moral landscape, a pitiful spectacle of corruption and shallowness, and the truly American sensibility, developed and free, arising from the expression of American bards, "the poets, philosophs, literats here." His criticisms of the actual culture are harsh, his tone querulous and sarcastic. He derides America's unoriginal artists, and he bemoans the unformed tastes of the people. He excoriates the judicial system, the Congress, the churches, the attitudes and behavior of the entire nation: "I think there can never be again upon the festive earth more bad-disordered persons deliberately taking seats, as of late in These States, at the heads of the public tables — such corpses' eyes for judges — such a rascal and thief in the Presidency" (LG, p. 735).

Whitman had good reason to be distressed over the state of the nation in 1856. He was embittered by the passage of morally contemptible legislation that appeased the proslavery interests at the expense of free, white laborers and farmers, whose interests Whitman promoted as his own. The outworn Missouri Compromise, which had been adopted when Whitman was a baby, had not resolved basic constitutional and practical questions about the authority of Congress to limit or to extend slavery, and the entry of each new territory or state from Texas to California aggravated the conflict. Both Whigs and Democrats courted Southern votes in Congress, where the principles of democracy and political freedom were sacrificed in pragmatic efforts to avoid secession and civil war. New coalitions of powerful Democrats and Whigs adopted the Compromise of 1850, the Fugitive Slave Law of 1850, and the Kansas-Nebraska Act of 1854, each of which struck Whitman as a flagrant betrayal of the liberal idealism he had lately tried to preserve in the Democratic party. The disastrous effects of these desperate measures were immediately visible in the tragedy of "Bleeding Kansas," where proslavery and antislavery settlers made war on each other throughout 1855. Incensed over the failure of government, Whitman wanted to raise popular indignation against the political chicanery that was an outrage to American values. Adopting the role of the pamphleteer who rouses the nobler spirit of the nation — like his father's hero, Tom Paine, in an earlier crisis — Whitman wrote a tirade called "The Eighteenth Presidency" in which he urged young working men and women to usurp the power of political parties in the upcoming election.[4] The pamphlet was never printed, and Whitman's vehement call to action scarcely left his mouth. But a group of radical antislavery unionists had recently formed a third party along the lines Whitman was proposing, and in 1856 the new Republican party made a strong national showing. When four years later the party elected its candidate, Abraham Lincoln, to the presidency, Whitman's political view seemed to become national policy, and for a while he supported the Republican party.

His contentiousness in the preface and the pamphlet of 1856 also appears in the poem "Respondez!" in which Whitman ironically proposes reforms of a country sinking fast toward civil war. Originally titled "Poem of the Propositions of Nakedness," it is a bitter list of transpositions that reverse all the standards and values of meaningful life, which he alleges are constantly violated anyway in the behavior of a cruel, mindless, and corrupt society. Let us do away with the sham of our declared ideals and wisdom, he proposes, and then see the horrible truth of our present condition.

> Let us all, without missing one, be exposed in
>   public, naked, monthly, at the peril of
>   our lives! let our bodies be freely
>   handled and examined by whoever chooses!
>   (*LG*, p. 592)

If slaves can be exposed in public, then there is no standard that says other people should not be subjected to the same treatment. Through sixty similar verses, the poem suggests that the absurd propositions not only have the truth of ironic misstatement but also that they urge their mad, violent and catastrophic actions as an improvement over the nation's endless hypocrisies and self-delusions. The insistent parallelism of "Let..." at the beginning of each proposal implies a repudiation of responsibility to society, which is left to founder; and the sustained, archly moralistic ironies reveal a despairing anger that is inclined to destroy rather than amend the offensive civilization Whitman sees all around him. Perhaps more than anything else Whitman wrote about the spirit of his times, the poem reveals the qualities of willfulness and self-righteousness that prevailed in Whitman as well as in public policy throughout the North and South as they approached the ultimate solution to their differences. When he excluded the poem from the sixth edition of *Leaves of Grass* in 1881, Whitman removed an interesting social document that reflects the moral anguish of pre–Civil War America, but also implicates the poet in the nation's barbarism.

For the second edition of *Leaves* he also recast the 1855 preface into an uneven essay in verse about the definition of "These States." Originally titled "Poem of Many in One," it became "By Blue Ontario's Shore" after years of tinkering that never produced an entirely satisfactory poem, though he still considered it thematically important to his book. Many prose lines that rippled and shone in the original preface appear shrunk and denuded in the verses. The following lines, which are adapted from high points in the preface, lost their resonance and brilliance when transposed into poetry.

> These States are the amplest poem,
> Here is not merely a nation but a teeming Nation
>   of nations,
> Here the doings of men correspond with the
>   broadcast doings of the day and night,
> Here is what moves in magnificent masses careless
>   of particulars,
> Here are the roughs, beards, friendliness,
>   combativeness, the soul loves,
> Here the flowing trains, here the crowds,
>   equality, diversity, the soul loves.
>
>   (11. 60–65)

Though his polemical poetry is mostly sententious, the political problems of the nation so closely resembled emotional stresses in his family that current events beguiled Whitman into further projecting himself upon the entire social system. For this reason he is eloquent whenever he examines the undercurrents of his personal life through political events. In "By Blue Ontario's Shore," despite its overall flaccidity, Whitman recovers the vitality of poetic speech when he perceives that the main issue in a democracy is not a civic but an ontological problem. Democracy questions the existence of each individual, and it requires an answer from every citizen. As an unwitting illustration of the warnings of Carlyle, Tocqueville, and other contemporary commentators on democracy, Whitman while championing equality suffered from the absence of a structured social organization that defined limits among people. He embraced a mass democracy for its values of personal worth, but felt subverted by its effects of distance or obliterating closeness in his relations with the external world. As an exemplary American, he struggled to secure for himself the citizenship of individual being.

> I will not be outfaced by irrational things,
> I will penetrate what it is in them that is
>   sarcastic upon me,
> I will make cities and civilizations defer
>   to me,
> This is what I have learnt from America — it
>   is the amount, and it I teach again.
>   . . . . .
>
> I will confront these shows of the day and night,
> I will know if I am to be less than they,
> I will see if I am not as majestic as they,
> I will see if I am not as subtle and real as they,
> I will see if I am to be less generous than they,
> I will see if I have no meaning, while the
>   houses and ships have meaning,
> I will see if the fishes and birds are to be
>   enough for themselves, and I am not to
>   be enough for myself.
>
> I match my spirit against yours you orbs,
>   growths, mountains, brutes,
> Copious as you are I absorb you all in myself,
>   and become the master myself,
> America isolated yet embodying all, what is it
>   finally except myself?
> These States, what are they except myself?
>
> I know now why the earth is gross, tantalizing,
>   wicked, it is for my sake,
> I take you specially to be mine, you terrible,
>   rude forms.
>   (11. 293–296, 300–312)

This passage attempts a sublime moment in a leaking sieve of a poem. Each line asserts his determination to relate to a world that outfaces him with its vast disorder and inhuman complacencies, and the strong reiterations of his drive to be acknowledged as fit for life in the world echo with a wounded, plaintive quality. External things have already nearly done him out of his wits, out of his sense of personal orientation to reality. In this poem he does not mock the world of ordinary lives and troop away up the open road. Here *he* feels mocked by the separateness of a world that is supreme in its detachment, but cannot be rejected. He is sensitive to stances that are "sarcastic" or "subtle" or "irrational" in an exchange that has obliged him to "defer." The suggestion of chagrin or even humiliation gives this quandary a concrete pain. He is not less worthy or intelligent than the earth that unjustly diminishes him. But he is vulnerable to its harshness because he wants the earth to prove equal to *him* — though he does not admit this. He wants to discover in the world of external fragments the intricate mutuality of his subjective life: the continual responsiveness that should not be taken for weakness but strength. Involved in the world's great experiment in democracy, which allegedly promotes awareness of individuals, he must contend with alienation that causes heartache, futility and mental derangement. "I match my spirit against yours," he declares to obdurate nature; and he accepts earth's cruelty as a challenge to his further illumination, as if he was made to feel bad for his own good. Unfortunately, the complexity and force of this short passage are dissipated in the poem through interpolated and adapted lines that can scarcely hold their prose meanings.

In bearding the universe Whitman projects onto the world the contradictory attitudes that are identifiable in his poems as parental attitudes. The external world displays the impervious self-centeredness of his mother and the remote hostility of his father; yet at the same time the external world also embraces him with thrilling immediacy, like his mother, and it also prompts him to forge ahead in pursuit of receding goals, like his father urging on his sons in his failed ambitions. Impossible to fathom or to ignore, the external world shames him because he is responsive and vulnerable. His subjectivity is his tender spot, but he believes it can ultimately match the reality of objects. He confronts the universe with his demand for an acknowledgment of his equal power — but in most of the poems of 1856, the outer world remains rudely mute.

The major poem in which Whitman struggles to achieve his dignity in a world that pays no heed to him is "Crossing Brooklyn Ferry." It is also probably the most Emersonian of his poems, for in it he tries to poeticize a philosophical frame of mind. Originally titled "Sun-Down Poem," it is overtly about the crowds of people who hurry home at the end of the workday to their separate lives, withdrawing from him and from one another. He meditates on the clash between his intense separateness, which he finds an irrefutable fact of nature, and his need for acknowledgment as a living person. The poem is structured according to the contrast between his isolation and the human bond that has to be formed in the poem as well as in life. These different perceptions of life as either fundamentally fragmented or fundamentally cohesive fluctuate in the poem as Whitman ponders his connection to external things. He writes from two angles; the first is his strikingly vivid observation of external life in a style of realism that is unusual for him, and the other is his characteristic intuition that focuses more on personal insights than on logical abstractions. In the end, he rationalizes the opaque mindlessness of the world around him, because its ambiguous silences give him an important role as a poet, a translator of silent nature. His poetry dignifies the "old delicious burdens" that even the lesson of his "dear Master" could not persuade him to abandon. He reaches the limit of his willingness to follow Emerson's moral lead.

His isolation in the midst of life is conveyed by the realistic setting of the river between Brooklyn and Manhattan just before sunset. The ferryboat, which he often rides, is crowded at rush hour, but in the opening lines Whitman seems accustomed to finding himself alone with nature, no matter where he is. He begins with a direct address to the clouds above and the flood-tide below; he greets his inhuman familiars "face to face." But real faces show him his usual, self-conscious detachment from other people, who are "more curious to me" than they could suspect as he stands calmly meditating. He is not able to address himself as easily to them, innocently "face to face." The change from overt to covert salutation is the first questioning of his relationships in the poem.

> Flood-tide below me! I see you face to face!
> Clouds of the west — sun there half an hour
>   high — I see you also face to face.
>
> Crowds of men and women attired in the usual
>   costumes, how curious you are to me!
> On the ferry-boats the hundreds and hundreds
>   that cross, returning home, are more
>   curious to me than you suppose,
> And you that shall cross from shore to shore
>   years hence are more to me, and more in
>   my meditations, than you might suppose.
>   (11. 1-5)

The situation recalls Whitman's frequent melancholy over people "returning home." At the end of the day the "men and women attired in the usual costumes" give up their public roles as they hurry back to their private lives. Whitman again feels undermined by the receding of the observed world and the waning of any attention to him, which is a pattern of his experience. Already, the unregarding passengers are not conscious of him, despite his sustained thoughts of them. In line 4, their unawareness is passive and innocent: They do not "suppose" that he watches them. But in the intensification of the next line they seem to be minimizing his feelings in misconceiving his detachment: "you...are more to me...than you might suppose." In the repetition the other people gain a capacity for wrongful response. Their failure to recognize his presence is possibly a deliberate withdrawal based on their mistake about his attitude toward them. Even from this first glance, his human relations are a muddle.

The suggestion of apparent distance between people who may in fact be thinking intensely of each other leads Whitman to an obvious conclusion. The chaos of our understanding cannot comprehend the underlying cohesiveness of our existence. He contemplates the order of nature in which he finds "every one disintegrated yet part of the scheme." They all share the world of similar experience, however disjointed they appear; and he identifies with other observers of the river who for years ahead will take this journey every day and feel exactly as he does now. Relying on his exuberant heart to outleap time and place as well as the neglect of other people, he propels himself into the future with a change of verb tense in stanza 3.

> It avails not, time nor place — distance avails not,
> I am with you, you men and women of a generation, or
>   ever so many generations hence,
> Just as you feel when you look on the river and sky,
>   so I felt.
>
> (11. 20–22)

For seventy-two lines he imagines himself in the future, mixing his memories with the experience of people who may or may not know that he ever existed. Actually, this one-sided communion is exactly what he faces bleakly on board the ferry. But by adopting the perspective of memory he allows feelings from his past to define his connection with the present. As in his earliest memories in "There Was a Child Went Forth," the distance between him and what he loves becomes ever greater as the river grows dimmer in the twilight, buildings along the shore sink into shadow, and night covers the houses where people gather, leaving the streets deserted under the glare of foundry fires and his solitary gaze.

> I too many and many a time cross'd the river
>   of old,
> Watched the Twelfth-month sea-gulls, saw them
>   high in the air floating with motionless
>   wings, oscillating their bodies,

Saw how the glistening yellow lit up parts of
    their bodies and left the rest in strong
    shadow,
Saw the slow-wheeling circles and the gradual
    edging toward the south,
Saw the reflection of the summer sky in the
    water,
Had my eyes dazzled by the shimmering track of beams,
Look'd at the fine centrifugal spokes of light round
    the shape of my head in the sunlit water,
Look'd on the haze on the hills southward and
    south-westward,
Look'd on the vapor as it flew in fleeces tinged
    with violet,
Look'd toward the lower bay to notice the
    vessels arriving,
Saw their approach, saw aboard those that were
    near me,
Saw the white sails of schooners and sloops,
    saw the ships at anchor,
The sailors at work in the rigging or out astride
    the spars,
The round masts, the swinging motion of the
    hulls, the slender serpentine pennants,
The large and small steamers in motion, the
    pilots in their pilot-houses,
The white wake left by the passage, the quick
    tremulous whirl of the wheels,
The flags of all nations, the falling of them
    at sunset,
The scallop-edged waves in the twilight, the
    ladled cups, the frolicsome crests and
    glistening,
The stretch afar growing dimmer and dimmer, the
    gray walls of the granite storehouses
    by the docks,
On the river the shadowy group, the big steam-tug
    closely flank'd on each side by the
    barges, the hay-boat, the belated lighter,
On the neighboring shore the fires from the
    foundry chimneys burning high and
    glaringly into the night,
Casting their flicker of black contrasted with

wild red and yellow light over the tops
of houses, and down into the clefts of
streets.

(11. 27–48)

Whitman has brought the world emotionally close to him by turning
it into memory. But since he has found that neither time nor space creates
emotional distance, the question remains, as Whitman next asks, "What
is it then between us?" What separates us? He has dismissed all external
causes. Only a disorder in the heart could maintain this detachment
among individuals. The poem comes to a crucial focus on Whitman's
inference that only rancorous feelings, which he instantly claims are his
as much as anyone's, could cause isolation. "I am he who knew what
it was to be evil," he declares in a torrent of faults that he seems eager
to confess. No one, he assures his future travelers, could be more blame-
worthy than he had been in his time. The peculiar significance of his litany
of faults is that Whitman's tone remains unrepentant: His confession
expresses no contrition whatsoever. Instead, it is carried forward in high
spirits by his excitement over the prospect of instant reconciliation with
the world. The buoyancy of the passage expresses, not Whitman's shared
guilt, but his immense relief as he triumphs over the barriers in the heart
as easily as he triumphed over time and space. Belligerence and obtuse-
ness, he says, need not stand in the way of his ready sympathy.

> It is not upon you alone the dark patches fall,
> The dark threw its patches down upon me also,
> The best I had done seem'd to me blank and suspicious,
> My great thoughts as I supposed them, were they not
>   in reality meagre?
> Nor is it you alone who know what it is to be
>   evil,
> I am he who knew what it was to be evil,
> I too knitted the old knot of contrariety,
> Blabb'd, blush'd, resented, lied, stole, grudg'd,
> Had guile, anger, lust, hot wishes I dared not
>   speak,
> Was wayward, vain, greedy, shallow, sly, cowardly,
>   malignant,
> The wolf, the snake, the hog, not wanting in me,
> The cheating look, the frivolous word, the adulterous
>   wish, not wanting,
> Refusals, hates, postponements, meanness, laziness,
>   none of these wanting,

Was one with the rest, the days and haps of the
    rest,
Was call'd by my nighest name by clear loud
    voices of young men as they saw me approaching
    or passing,
Felt their arms on my neck as I stood, or the
    negligent leaning of their flesh against
    me as I sat,
Saw many I loved in the street or ferry-boat or
    public assembly, yet never told them a word,
Lived the same life with the rest, the same old
    laughing, gnawing, sleeping,
Play'd the part that still looks back on the
    actor or actress,
The same old role, the role that is what we make
    it, as great as we like,
Or as small as we like, or both great and small.

(ll. 65–85)

The resurgence of his sensual vigor in this passage leads him to pleasurable feelings and to anticipations of friendships and company; line 79 allows the first mention in the poem of anyone affectionately responding to him, and by the end of the passage he accepts the past with its falsity and hypocrisy. Elated to be warmly in touch, he reaches forward tenderly to the reader in one of those stunning passages of eerie intimacy.

Closer yet I approach you,
What thought you have of me now, I had as much of
    you—I laid in my stores in advance,
I consider'd long and seriously of you before you
    were born.

Who was to know what should come home to me?
Who knows but I am enjoying this?
Who knows, for all the distance, but I am as good
    as looking at you now, for all you cannot see me?

(ll. 86–91)

In the role of the disembodied spirit who dwells in poetry Whitman connects with people who are not actually there. His triumph in poetry perpetuates the solitude that he wants equally to escape and to preserve. But he feels vindicated because he chooses to become the unique, sensitive spokesman for a world that remains distant and unfathomable. In his elation he speaks with magisterial confidence as the interpreter of the world, changing to the imperative mood in the final thirty-two lines as if delivering a benediction upon all things that appear dead or heartless. Their disregard and remoteness have stimulated his imagination, he says, until he has intuited their orientation toward his soul. He says that the barriers of misunderstanding have fallen away from his heart: "We fathom you not — we love you," he announces to all external things.

> Appearances, now or henceforth, indicate what
> you are,
> You necessary film, continue to envelop the soul,
> About my body for me, and your body for you, be
> hung our divinest aromas,
> Thrive, cities—bring your freight, bring your
> shows, ample and sufficient rivers,
> Expand, being than which none else is perhaps
> more spiritual,
> Keep your places, objects than which none else
> is more lasting.
>
> You have waited, you always wait, you dumb,
> beautiful ministers,
> We receive you with free sense at last, and
> are insatiate henceforward,
> Not you any more shall be able to foil us, or
> withhold yourselves from us,
> We use you, and do not cast you aside—we plant
> you permanently within us,
> We fathom you not—we love you—there is perfection
> in you also,
> You furnish your parts toward eternity,
> Great or small, you furnish your parts toward
> the soul.
>
> (ll. 120–132)

The complacency of these lines is meretricious — one hears the stretching of truth in the gymnastic syntax of "being than which none else is perhaps more spiritual" — and Whitman's officious papal blessing misses the occasion in the poem to affirm his living worth and the value of personal relations. Instead of following Emerson's example of condemning all brutishness in society and nature, Whitman here puts a good face on the prospect of a world-without-change. He excuses and blesses the alienation he was made to feel, because he assumes that in order to remain a poet he must accept the emotional deprivation that spurred him to imaginative fulfillment. Despite his increasing desire for actual love, which his eroticized poetry continually heightened, he could not yet abandon the arrangement he worked out at the moment of his creative birth, when he seized upon imagination as compensation for relinquishing a very chancy world. Long after his childlike pact with the gods became redundant, Whitman held to his bargain. In sacramentalizing the status quo, this poem reinstates the forfeiture he complained about in "Song of the Broad-Axe": "Take the pay you approached for, / Take the white tears of my blood, if that is what you are after." Evidently, paying such tribute seemed necessary to forestall a greater penalty or calamity. Behind all his buoyant willingness to suffer repeated exposures in shame, behind his ingratiating readiness to march down endless roads alone, behind his winsome faithfulness to others who betray him, there was a deeper pain he would not face if he could avoid it. He chose for a while longer to elude the massive fear of annihilation that lay at the bottom of his heart. In the poems written for the second edition of *Leaves* he tried to accommodate the world's obduracy and its eternal demands. Certainly the burden of this responsibility to harmonize the universe was fundamentally "delicious" to him, but the deeper reinvestment of himself in the fortunes of a disturbed family and a warring nation could only further imperil the creativity that it fed.

5

The Frontiers of Sex, 1857–1858

WHITMAN INVESTED so much of himself in his poetry that he was destined to confront in his work the dilemma that had spurred his creativity in the first place. The crisis occurred in the years between the second and third editions of *Leaves of Grass* when for a time he felt dehumanized by writing poetry. From 1858 to mid-1859 while he edited the *Brooklyn Daily Times,* he apparently wrote no poetry. The dilemma that he believed he faced was that poetry falsified him and interfered with his direct pursuit of love; yet to give up writing poetry caused intolerable depression. He did not survive the crisis intactly; his creativity came to disaster over the problem of sex.

He approached his decisive ordeal with intuitive foreknowledge and his usual public announcements. Near the conclusion of his 1856 preface addressed to Emerson, Whitman declares that the most significant evil in the present deterioration of man and society is sexual denial and hypocrisy. In an age of zealous and loftily intellectual reform movements, he audaciously asserts that for the true reform of society and for the restoration of honest feelings in literature and painting, men and women should learn to give uncompromised expression to their natural sexuality. His voice conveys a religious and political fervor that most Americans would have considered misapplied, for he denounces the enervating and perverting effects of "infidelism about sex," and he argues that sex should be acknowledged as the wellspring of life, the foundation of "all that is worth being here for," especially in the new American world of freedom.

> To me, henceforth, that theory of any thing, no matter what, stagnates in its vitals, cowardly and rotten, while it cannot publicly accept, and publicly name, with specific words, the things on which all existence, all souls, all realization, all decency, all health, all that is worth being here for, all of woman and of man, all beauty, all purity, all sweetness, all

friendship, all strength, all life, all immortality depend. The courageous soul, for a year or two to come, may be proved by faith in sex, and by disdaining concessions.

(LG, pp. 737–738)

It is hard to imagine the effect of this manifesto upon the sensually reticent Emerson — of whom Henry James circumspectly once complained, "There were some chords in Emerson that did not vibrate at all." Whitman's stridency about sex may have precipitated Emerson's diplomatic silence about Whitman's second book even though the entire edition was dedicated to him; and an open disagreement between the two writers over Whitman's explicit sex themes a few years later, in 1860, marked their last meeting as kindred artists. Sojourning in Boston to oversee the printing of his third edition (1860) of Leaves of Grass, Whitman let Emerson look over the proof sheets. The two men walked on Boston Common while Emerson tried to dissuade Whitman from including the new "Children of Adam" poems about sexual love. They were too explicit and erotic, Emerson believed, to allow the rest of the book to receive a fair reception. Whitman listened and refused Emerson's advice without arguing. Thereafter, he discriminated sharply between Emerson's opinions, which he no longer held in awe, and the saintliness of the man he still revered; he also began to think of Emerson as nearly a generation older than he actually was. Whitman admired the reasonableness of Emerson's arguments on this occasion, but could easily resist them because the love poems were central to the aesthetic and moral integrity of the book. The third edition was expanded by 124 entirely new poems, and Whitman understood that Leaves of Grass was beginning to resemble in subject matter and internal order the full range of a man's life. He held to his purpose as a matter of social responsibility and public policy, for he viewed sexual fulfillment as the physical, natural foundation of democratic idealism.

Instead of a sexual mythology of compulsion, repression, and catastrophe, such as he recognized everywhere in the literature of the Old World, Whitman wanted to define an ideal of sex that reflected the personal freedoms of an expanding society in the natural abundance of the New World. He ascribed to sex a socially progressive, public utility that he often illustrated with topical imagery of westward expansion into the vast, undeveloped continent of natural resources waiting to be discovered and used. In his poetry he suggests that the communal enterprise of settling America will repay men and women with sensual rewards. The enormous energies and wild-hearted drives of the popular, puritanical, commercial spirit of his age meant almost nothing to him as indications of poverty or greed; he chose instead to define the goal of pioneering as gratification through physical health, sexual potency, and erotic pleasure. He implied that men and women working together to establish families, populate cities, and cultivate new lands enjoy an intimacy that surpasses traditional and polite expressions of love.

Of course, Whitman was writing idealistically about sex and about democracy at a time when slavery — with its sexual as well as political meanings — ruinously dominated American institutions and invaded private lives. Except for Whitman's works, American manners and literature during the mid-nineteenth century display an extreme denial of sexuality that surpasses any sexual repressiveness in mainstream European culture since the deterioration of medieval asceticism. Ascribing to standards of genteel purity and pragmatic efficiency, Americans looked away from the life of the body while the nation countenanced the grossest exploitation of millions of dehumanized slaves. The moral and emotional stress of this mass denial found expression in dreams of license beyond the boundaries of moral consequences, and the realm of traditional moral order appeared to end at the western frontier. In exploits of belligerence and possessiveness, any man could take masterful gratification from passive, bountiful, and unlimited lands beyond the edge of civilization. As long as slavery continued to defy the norms of sexual behavior and to upset the balance of monogamy (it was during this same period that the polygamous Mormons were massacred by other whites in slave-holding Missouri, their leaders lynched in free Illinois, and the entire population pushed further into the West), the course of territorial expansion was complicated by bloody rivalries between Northerners and Southerners who fought ostensibly over majority power in the Senate and killed each other over the unbroken prairies of Kansas. The country was imminently going to war over the status of blacks, whom most people in the North and South alike at that time did not much care for as people, whether enslaved or free. Against this social turbulence, all the more mystifying and catastrophic because its undercurrent of sexual meaning could not be identified, the myth of the West acquired its natively romantic features — as distinct from romantic ideas about the noble Indian and the harmony of the wilderness that Europeans earlier entertained. Americans developed the West's allure as an arena for strenuously combative exploits against man or nature in which every rival can win his separate glory. The symbol of the West resonated with sexual connotations of mastery over the ultimate slave, of lawlessness that was natural and condoned, and of envy that further inflamed fierce sectional jealousies. The West was the only lurid desire that nineteenth-century Americans admitted to having — and even that was disingenuously unsexed.

Whitman absorbed and reshaped the sexual meaning of his society's myth about the West. The glory that Whitman foresaw in the West was sensual domesticity. He tried to make the image of a robust, all-satisfying wife and mother preside over the strenuous work of pioneering and building that occupied Americans in his time. "Song of the Broad-Axe," the 1856 poem discussed in the preceding chapter, reveals his mixed feelings of admiration and antagonism toward such a woman as he extols her importance in the development of a cohesive, democratic society. He elevates her to divine equanimity above male restlessness and violence; she remains an aloof, single presence surrounded by troubled, potentially dangerous men. In another poem of the same year, "A Woman Waits for Me," Whitman deplores the decadence in woman's feminized role in society, and he welcomes women to more vigorous, companionable, and important activities. The woman who waits is really the woman who is awaited, not the woman who is at home; she is the expected glory of a new age. She waits in the potential of improved relationships between men and women who will enjoy health and equality by sharing the pleasure and responsibilities of sex.

> A woman waits for me, she contains all, nothing
>   is lacking,
> Yet all were lacking if sex were lacking, or if
>   the moisture of the right man were lacking.
>
> Sex contains all, bodies, souls,
> Meanings, proofs, purities, delicacies, results,
>   promulgations,
> Songs, commands, health, pride, the maternal mystery,
>   the seminal milk,
> All hopes, benefactions, bestowals, all the passions,
>   loves, beauties, delights of the earth,
> All the governments, judges, gods, follow'd persons
>   of the earth,
> These are contained in sex as parts of itself and
>   justifications of itself.
>
> Without shame the man I like knows and avows the
>   deliciousness of his sex,
> Without shame the woman I like knows and avows hers.
>
> Now I will dismiss myself from impassive women,
> I will go stay with her who waits for me, and
>   with those women that are warm-blooded and
>   sufficient for me,
> I see that they understand me and do not deny me,
> I see that they are worthy of me, I will be the
>   robust husband of those women.

They are not one jot less than I am,
They are tann'd in the face by shining suns and
blowing winds,
Their flesh has the old divine suppleness and
strength,
They know how to swim, row, ride, wrestle, shoot,
run, strike, retreat, advance, resist,
defend themselves,
They are ultimate in their own right—they are
calm, clear, well-possess'd of themselves.

(ll. 1-19)

The woman who is to be a good match for the representative American man will not be "impassive" with that treacherous superficial calm which is evident in "Song of the Broad-Axe" and which Whitman was at the moment specially distrusting in his mother. She will be wholly forthright and abundantly affectionate, and never will she withdraw from him, for he dismisses further contact with any woman who has wrung his heart with feelings of unworthiness to be her favorite. The new woman will be his complete companion. She promises to be all to him, for if "sex contains all" of the values of life, then "she contains all" of life's promise. She will be physically strong and athletic, and she will enjoy outdoor life the same as the man. While some of Whitman's lines in the poem are full of overweening boasting and male chauvinism — such as "It is I, you women, I make my way, / I am stern, acrid, large, undissuadable, but I love you" — his sexual preening indicates that he often feels powerless or competitive in relation to a feminine presence in his poetry. Often, indeed, he permits himself to become the woman because it seems to him that the balance may be against him as a man, since *she* "contains all." She already contains the future inside her, and she will bring forth "greater heroes and bards" that only he can germinate in her. Whitman presses himself into her, with an excused show of force that minimizes any sexual activity other than his own. Bracing himself for effectiveness, he dares not "withdraw" until he makes a "deposit" of riches long "accumulated." It is like breaking into a bank, not to steal but to return to the money. The treasure is the woman's fecundity, to which Whitman contributes his share. The fulfillment of their embrace is the germination and release of future generations. In the final nine lines of "A Woman Waits for Me" Whitman yearns for the responsive fertility of women who bring forth "loving crops" of boys and girls, whom he regards as "grafts" of himself. He loses all sense of the mutual relationship in sexual response as he describes draining rivers, grafting orchards, and planting crops to express his ultimate satisfaction in fathering America's future spirit.

Through you I drain the pent-up rivers of myself,
In you I wrap a thousand onward years,
On you I graft the grafts of the best-beloved
    of me and America,
The drops I distil upon you shall grow fierce
    and athletic girls, new artists, musicians,
    and singers,
The babes I beget upon you are to beget babes in
    their turn,
I shall demand perfect men and women out of my
    love-spendings,
I shall expect them to interpenetrate with others,
    as I and you interpenetrate now,
I shall count on the fruits of the gushing showers
    of them, as I count on the fruits of the
    gushing showers I give now,
I shall look for loving crops from the birth, life,
    death, immortality, I plant so lovingly now.

                        (11. 31–39)

The character of the woman in the poem changes from a robust, athletic, and equal companion to a passive and even unregarded vessel for impregnation. The diminishment in her stature, her depersonalization into a mere sexual utility, coincides with her increasing association with open lands and with man's mastery over natural fecundity. Whitman's reduction of woman to the status of a slave reflects the distortion that his society promoted for black and white, women and men.

Whitman's attitude changed dramatically as he drew closer to finding an authentic sensual life. The new love poems that he wrote for the 1860 edition of *Leaves* indicate a deepening sexual involvement with other people. Most strikingly, his solitary, autoerotic ecstasies over his own body and his advertisements of his sexual powers disappear entirely from his work after the poems of 1855 and 1856 such as "Song of Myself," "I Sing the Body Electric," "Spontaneous Me," and "A Woman Waits for Me." In at least one of the new poems written for the "Children of Adam" section, the sensual freedom that Whitman celebrates is expressed, not through mastery and dominance, but through recognition of his lover's feelings. "We Two, How Long We Were Fool'd" is his happiest and also his best poem about love for a woman. Much of its freshness comes from the stunning succession of wilderness metaphors that light upon the similarities of the lovers, their likeness not only to natural things but also to each other.

We two, how long we were fool'd,
Now transmuted, we swiftly escape as Nature
    escapes,
We are Nature, long have we been absent, but
    now we return,
We become plants, trunks, foliage, roots, bark,
We are bedded in the ground, we are rocks,
We are oaks, we grow in the openings side by side,
We browse, we are two among the wild herds spontaneous
    as any,
We are two fishes swimming in the sea together,
We are what locust blossoms are, we drop scent
    around lanes mornings and evenings,
We are also the coarse smut of beasts, vegetables,
    minerals,
We are two predatory hawks, we soar above and
    look down,
We are two resplendent suns, we it is who balance
    ourselves orbic and stellar, we are as
    two comets,
We prowl fang'd and four-footed in the woods, we
    spring on prey,
We are two clouds forenoons and afternoons driving
    overhead,
We are seas mingling, we are two of those cheerful
    waves rolling over each other and interwetting
    each other,
We are what the atmosphere is, transparent, receptive,
    pervious, impervious,
We are snow, rain, cold, darkness, we are each
    product and influence of the globe,
We have circled and circled till we have arrived
    home again, we two,
We have voided all but freedom and all but our
    own joy.

(LG, pp. 107–108)

By reiterating twenty-five times phrases like *we are this, we are that, we do such, we do so,* he affirms that both are responding the same way in their happiness. Whatever restraints and inhibitions they have had to escape, the equality of feelings between them is the revelation that delivers them from falsehood (''We two, how long we were fool'd'') to the recovery of their essential freedom and joy. In their passion, each returns to primal life. The predominate tone of the poem is tender and sensual, as in the delicate line: "We are what locust blossoms are, we drop scent around lanes mornings and evenings." This music returns in a variation seven lines later: "We are what the atmosphere is, transparent, receptive, pervious, impervious." There is nothing forced, threatening, or desperate even in the more vigorous assertions — "We prowl fang'd and four-footed in the woods, we spring on prey" — because the lovers in their delight are innocent toward each other. No other poem in "Children of Adam" expresses a similarly complete fulfillment.

Nearly everything else Whitman saw between men and women was shadowed with calamity despite his intention to celebrate the benefits of sex. In "From Pent-up Aching Rivers," for instance, he surveys an entire tributary system of eddying, converging rivers and tides of aching need and currents of sexual pleasure. As if dedicating a source of new power, he proclaims at the beginning of the poem that he is determined alone among men to make the maddening, fitful urges and the intense encounters of sex publicly acknowledged and illustrious. In a long series of prepositional phrases and participles that hold each line in suspense, Whitman ceremoniously approaches the headlong plunge of sex.

> From pent-up aching rivers,
> From that of myself without which I were nothing,
> From what I am determin'd to make illustrious,
>   even if I stand sole among men,
> From my own voice resonant, singing the phallus,
> Singing the song of procreation,
> Singing the need of superb children and therein
>   superb grown people,
> Singing the muscular urge and the blending,
> Singing the bedfellow's song, (O resistless
>   yearning!
> O for any and each the body correlative attracting!
> O for you whoever you are your correlative
>   body! O it, more than all else, you
>   delighting!)
> From the hungry gnaw that eats me night and day,
> From native moments, from bashful pains, singing
>   them,
> Seeking something yet unfound though I have
>   diligently sought it many a long year,
> Singing the true song of the soul fitful at
>   random,
> Renascent with grossest Nature or among animals,

Of that, of them and what goes with them my
    poems informing,
Of the smell of apples and lemons, of the pairing
    of birds,
Of the wet of woods, of the lapping of waves,
Of the mad pushes of waves upon the land, I
    them chanting,
The overture lightly sounding, the strain
    anticipating,
The welcome nearness, the sight of the perfect
    body,
The swimmer swimming naked in the bath, or
    motionless on his back lying and floating,
The female form approaching, I pensive, love-flesh
    tremulous aching,
The divine list for myself or you or for any
    one making,
The face, the limbs, the index from head to foot,
    and what it arouses,
The mystic deliria, the madness amorous, the
    utter abandonment,
(Hark close and still what I now whisper to you,
I love you, O you entirely possess me,
O that you and I escape from the rest and go
    utterly off, free and lawless,
Two hawks in the air, two fishes swimming in
    the sea not more lawless than we;)
The furious storm through me careering, I
    passionately trembling,
The oath of the inseparableness of two together,
    of the woman that loves me and whom I
    love more than my life, that oath
    swearing,
(O I willingly stake all for you,
O let me be lost if it must be so!
O you and I! what is it to us what the rest do
    or think?
What is all else to us! only that we enjoy each
    other and exhaust each other if it must
    be so;)

                            (11. 1–36)

This extended anticipation of a sexual embrace emphasizes the awesome power in the pent-up force of the river that is about to be unleashed. In yielding to this inner force, Whitman expresses misgivings over losing control of himself in the apparent recklessness of sex. His diction partly disavows his willingness, as the "deliria" and "madness" of desire impel him toward "abandonment." To engage in sex he must "escape," and to be satisfied he must become "lawless." While these nuances indicate the social attitudes that attribute license and depravity to all sexual pleasure, there is a deeper tone of personal anxiety as well. Actual sexual possession will deliver him to his nemesis, the fear of oblivion: "O let me be lost if it must be so!" he cries out in his ecstasy. The peak of erotic excitement includes the dread that he could be effaced by the passion that overwhelms him.

To limit the risk of destruction in the "furious storm" of emotion, in the final lines Whitman withdraws from intimate sexual contact in favor of his public role as the proselytizer of new sexual attitudes. Like the poet in "The Sleepers," he redirects his attention to daytime and public life while promising to return to the night in which his lover waits — just as his mother waited in his sleep until he assumed her identity in his dreams. Again as in the earlier poem, he takes care to see before he departs that he is expected back again: "(Yet a moment O tender waiter, and I return)." With this link to his lover confirmed and with his disengagement from her accomplished, he draws the long series of phrases into a grammatically complete statement.

> From the one so unwilling to have me leave, and
>   me just as unwilling to leave,
> (Yet a moment O tender waiter, and I return,)
> From the hour of shining stars and dropping dews,
> From the night a moment I emerging flitting out,
> Celebrate you act divine and you children prepared
>   for,
> And you stalwart loins.
>
> (11. 52–57)

For Whitman, sexual intercourse threatened the loss of the mindful self, the reduction of self-awareness that he feared as disintegration and personal oblivion. The loss of his knowing mind threatened a complete loss of being, an obliteration that might be symbolized by castration or engulfment. By contrast, masturbation or homosexuality did not rouse the specter of annihilation, because those sexual acts intensified his self-consciousness, especially with the power of fantasy. Actual sexual possession of a woman reduced him to unconscious life, which he only once celebrated in "We Two, How Long We Were Fool'd." Although he championed sexual love, he dreaded the overriding passion that would dislodge him from centering on his own sensations. He wanted to enter into absolute, sensual sympathy with others while maintaining his inviolable detachment from them. More than any other kind of experience, sexual love was likely to demonstrate the impossibility of achieving his cross purposes in life, except through poetry.

An identical cry of apprehensiveness occurs in the more private poem "One Hour to Madness and Joy," which is also full of prolonged, over-wrought anticipation of sex. Looking ahead to something like a stolen moment, Whitman imagines his complete gratification. He is impatient to be with his lover and to yield to their utmost passion, yet once again he distances actual intercourse through metaphors of the remote wilderness. He expects them to enjoy each other "in defiance of the world!" He is eager "to return to Paradise!" He is ready to depart for the outlands of experience, and seeks the unrestrained openness of the West within the pleasures of sex.

> O to speed where there is space enough and air
> enough at last!
> To be absolv'd from previous ties and conventions,
> I from mine and you from yours!
> To find a new unthought-of nonchalance with the
> best of Nature!
> To have the gag remov'd from one's mouth!
> To have the feeling to-day or any day I am
> sufficient as I am.
>
> O something unprov'd! something in a trance!
> To escape utterly from others' anchors and holds!
> To drive free! to love free! to dash reckless
> and dangerous!
> To court destruction with taunts, with invitations!
> To ascend, to leap to the heavens of the love
> indicated to me!
> To rise thither with my inebriate soul!
> To be lost if it must be so!
>
> (11. 11–22)

The last line here repeats his chronic worry over annihilation: "To be lost if it must be so!" Immediately, his jubilation turns into a narrowing and confining rapture that sounds consolatory over solitude and the loss of love, as if he has found himself not in paradise after all but in exile. His robust passion turns quaint and astringent, like Emily Dickinson's intoxication with self-denial. The poignancy of the final two lines lies in

Whitman's fore-knowing acceptance of so very little love as his meager portion of contraband joy on which he feeds himself and keeps alive.

> To feed the remainder of life with one hour of
>   fulness and freedom!
> With one brief hour of madness and joy.
>   (11. 23–24)

Whitman's anticipation of bleak fate hides in the disparity between the long, empty "remainder of life" and the single dole of concentrated pleasure that he counts on having. He seems ready enough to forfeit ongoing sexual love with a woman.

He titled this section of poems "Children of Adam" because though he believed that in the garden of the West the natural innocence of love could restore mankind to a new Eden, his idea of paradise was not passionate sexual union but perfect companionability, such as children and comrades might share. In the opening poem of this section Whitman's Adam is above all a resurrected child delighting in the recovered freshness of his senses, secure in Eve's company. The physical renewal and self-possession celebrated here occur only in suspended actions, producing a kind of hovering detachment that is supported by the web of present participles that forestall any definite contact.

> To the garden the world anew ascending,
> Potent mates, daughters, sons, preluding,
> The love, the life of their bodies, meaning
>   and being,
> Curious here behold my resurrection after slumber,
> The revolving cycles in their wide sweep having
>   brought me again,
> Amorous, mature, all beautiful to me, all wondrous,
> My limbs and the quivering fire that ever plays
>   through them, for reasons, most wondrous,
> Existing I peer and penetrate still,
> Content with the present, content with the past,
> By my side or back of me Eve following,
> Or in front, and I following her just the same.
>   (*LG*, p. 90)

For Whitman it was truly like the beginning of the world to welcome the sexual vitality of his body. But sexual intercourse with women threatened his precarious separateness.

For a year or more before writing the "Children of Adam" poems he had been writing lyrics of homosexual love, for in loving other men

Whitman temporarily found his goal of sensual sympathy and spiritual integrity. In loving other men Whitman could be wholly passionate, and he could endure even rejection by his lover or the pain of unreturned attentions, all without fearing that he would lose his own self or be destroyed by uncontrollable natural forces. Whitman experienced his emotions more freely and securely toward men than toward women. "Adhesiveness," as he called it, borrowing from phrenology the term for manly affection, seemed more authentically personal than ordinary sexual love. It gave him the pleasure of becoming like a generously caring mother toward specially beloved youths, who were like images and "grafts" of himself. It brought him romantic excitement without the undertones of emotional enslavement and domestic hypocrisy that he repudiated in conventional relationships. And best of all, it gave him affection that seemed, for the first time, entirely his own to keep for himself. All of Whitman's poems about homosexual love radiate with his momentous discovery of the wonder and beauty of intimate privacy.

In the "Calamus" section of *Leaves of Grass* Whitman begins with an emphatic change of scene as he ventures "away from the clank of the world" to roam "in paths untrodden," where he can contemplate feelings that are not acknowledged in public life. No longer blazing a trail for everyone, he turns away from exposure to common view. His turn toward seclusion in this section is symbolized in the first poem, "In Paths Untrodden," by the reference to calamus, a type of grass that does not grow everywhere alike but only by quiet ponds and marshes.

> In paths untrodden,
> In the growth by margins of pond-waters,
> Escaped from the life that exhibits itself,
> From all the standards hitherto publish'd, from
>   the pleasures, profits, conformities,
> Which too long I was offering to feed my soul,
> Clear to me now standards not yet publish'd,
>   clear to me that my soul,
> That the soul of the man I speak for rejoices
>   in comrades,
> Here by myself away from the clank of the world,
> Tallying and talk'd to here by tongues aromatic,
> No longer abash'd, (for in this secluded spot I
>   can respond as I would not dare elsewhere,)
> Strong upon me the life that does not exhibit
>   itself, yet contains all the rest,
> Resolv'd to sing no songs to-day but those of
>   manly attachment,
> Projecting them along that substantial life,
> Bequeathing hence types of athletic love,

Afternoon this delicious Ninth-month in my
    forty-first year,
I proceed for all who are or have been young
    men,
To tell the secret of my nights and days,
To celebrate the need of comrades.

                         (*LG*, pp. 112–113)

Since Whitman was capable of exhibiting himself in any sexual role, as his earlier poems fully illustrate, the setting of secrecy for singing his "manly attachment" and his "need for comrades" must be accepted as a deliberate, artful choice. In writing about homosexual love, whatever dangers of social opprobrium he faced, Whitman was primarily creative, not primarily reticent. In seeming to withdraw from open view, he is giving expression to something he positively wants for the fullness of love's satisfaction; he is not merely reflecting a social taboo. Though it is surely true that society's attitudes against homosexual feelings caused him confusion and pain, it is also evident that he usually faced social condemnation in any matter with stubborn resolution. And in one declamatory poem in the "Calamus" section, "For You O Democracy," he does attempt to celebrate "the manly love of comrades" for its contribution to the social cause of democratic idealism. As it happened, the eventual outcries against obscenity in Whitman's poems focused on the eroticism between men and women, never on the eroticism between men. As his adviser, Emerson had correctly assessed their era when he cautioned Whitman against the explicitness of the "Children of Adam" poems, rather than the subject matter of "Calamus." But Whitman chose to sound hushed and hidden in celebrating homosexuality because that particular style of expression indicated an avenue toward real fulfillment.

In "Calamus" he does not try to appear understood and accepted by the vast audience he usually addresses. In some of the poems he expects to be understood by only a special few, who will intuit meanings that will remain unclear to the general reader. His sympathy with men he loves is not just confidential, as in ordinary intimacy; it is designedly esoteric. And this stance allows him at times to exclude and reject the rest of the world — a stance that brings Whitman close to reversing his fundamental principles. In "Calamus" he resists identifying with the entire, democratic population he has hitherto felt obliged to absorb. He does not offer a universal gospel, as he did in "Song of Myself," for instance. Most people will now fail to understand him, he says in "Whoever You Are Holding Me Now in Hand." Nevertheless, he intends to escape from the clutches of the commonplace reader.

But these leaves conning you con at peril,
For these leaves and me you will not understand,
They will elude you at first and still more afterward,
    I will certainly elude you,
Even while you should think you had unquestionably
    caught me, behold!
Already you see I have escaped from you.

For it is not for what I have put into it that I
    have written this book,
Nor is it by reading it you will acquire it,
Nor do those know me best who admire me and vauntingly
    praise me,
Nor will the candidates for my love (unless at most
    a very few) prove victorious,
Nor will my poems do good only, they will do just
    as much evil, perhaps more,
For all is useless without that which you may guess
    at many times and not hit, that which I
    hinted at;
Therefore release me and depart on your way.

(11. 27–38)

He wants to be understood intuitively as a living person, and not as an abstract character created by words in his poems. His emphasis on the enigma of his personality is a familiar way of proclaiming his inexhaustible variety, like the many contradictory roles that he assumed in earlier poems; but here the dangers of being deadened or forced into a false self arise from the limitations of poetry itself. He sees himself possibly misunderstood by another's regard for him: An overly ready, superficial sympathy for his poems can distort him in the same way that conventions and hypocrisies distort life. Glib interpretations of his poems can yet take away the reality of his experience; and this kind of eroding, overpowering, half-invited intimacy became another kind of bondage to avoid. He portrays himself as a will-o'-the-wisp, escaping the poems that appear to contain him. The motif expressed by the words *elude, caught, escape*, and *release* voices his wish to break free from captivity. It repeats the personal myth of his enslavement and liberation that appears also in his longing for sensual freedom with a robust woman in the lawlessness of sex in the West. But in this instance he goes away and does not return in a better place or an elemental form: He does not wait in the grass under our boot-soles or walk in the garden after slumber. His final injunction to the reader suggests that fellowship with a select few is preferable to further poetic self-representation: "Therefore release me and depart on your way."

To win fame as a poet now seems repugnant to him. In "Recorders Ages Hence" Whitman's concern about public misapprehension is stated more sharply: Fame is not just inadequate, it is downright inaccurate. Fearing that his poetry might give a false idea of his true character, he instructs future historians to remember him as a lover of comrades.

> Recorders ages hence,
> Come, I will take you down underneath this impassive
>   exterior, I will tell you what to say of me,
> Publish my name and hang up my picture as that of
>   the tenderest lover,
> The friend the lover's portrait, of whom his friend
>   his lover was fondest,
> Who was not proud of his songs, but of the measureless
>   ocean of love within him, and freely
>   pour'd it forth,
> Who often walk'd lonesome walks thinking of his dear
>   friends, his lovers,
> Who pensive away from one he lov'd often lay sleepless
>   and dissatisfied at night,
> Who knew too well the sick, sick dread lest the one he
>   lov'd might secretly be indifferent to him,
> Whose happiest days were far away through fields,
>   in woods, on hills, he and another wandering
>   hand in hand, they twain apart from other men,
> Who oft as he saunter'd the streets curv'd with his
>   arm the shoulder of his friend, while the arm
>   of his friend rested upon him also.
>
> (*LG*, pp. 121–22)

In disdaining glory as a poet, Whitman objects to the abstraction of himself in poetry that reduces him to mere self-consciousness, that is, to a mere witness to experience. He wants people to recognize that he has the full range of feelings — affection, dread, longing, and happiness — that give him a personal life apart from the poems he writes. In wanting to be defined by his "measureless ocean of love," and not by his words alone, Whitman is repeating his chronic anxiety over his "affection that will not be gainsay'd." But here it is not unheeding parents who deny his heart; the danger now arises from the misrepresentation of himself through poetry, which presents a fixed, "impassive exterior" of his true self.

To preserve his inner self in a hidden flowering of privileged love,

Whitman had to maintain privacy from overpowering outsiders, and especially from a possessive woman. Consequently, in the "Calamus" poems Whitman treats homosexual love as a natural secret, a hidden dimension of life. It does not lead to immortality and to communion with a future world of readers. It does not lead him to propose social reforms, even though he surmises in "The Base of All Metaphysics" that the "dear love of man for his comrade" has practical benefits in the institutions of civilization. His love for comrades leads him away from his usual general experience, in which he shares the imagined consciousness of others, to consider the particularity of his own emotions. With a sense of security and privacy he views his experience as entirely individual, not commingled or representative or symbolic in any way, but merely similar to other people's private lives. He becomes what we call realistic.

His lyrics about secret love are more convincing and tender than his overweening pronouncements in "Children of Adam." They include many short poems that define a moment's sensation of desire, capture a nuance of pleasure, contemplate a stab of loneliness for an absent lover, or recognize a rush of delight at the mere sight or thought of his lover. He does not build up his emotions into events of national or metaphysical importance; in fact, he avoids running into abstractions. In reminding himself of his usual quandaries in the poem "Of the Terrible Doubt of Appearances," he dismisses the need for any confirmation or justification of reality except for the simple presence of his lover.

> When he whom I love travels with me or sits a
>   long while holding me by the hand,
> When the subtle air, the impalpable, the sense
>   that words and reason hold not, surround
>   us and pervade us,
> Then I am charged with untold and untellable
>   wisdom, I am silent, I require nothing
>   further,
> I cannot answer the question of appearances or
>   that of identity beyond the grave,
> But I walk or sit indifferent, I am satisfied,
> He ahold of my hand has completely satisfied
>   me.
>
> (11. 11–16)

The presence or absence of his real lover gives him a new focus on the external world. In "Calamus" he fixes his attention on objective things for considerably longer than a single line. He composes narratives of his experience, and he experiments with traditional literary forms. He imitates sonnets to express his love, beginning one poem with an echo of Shake-speare: "When I peruse the conquer'd fame of heroes." At an early stage in the composition of these poems, he toyed with arranging twelve of them into a cluster resembling an Elizabethan sonnet sequence. This group included "Hours Continuing Long," a lament over a lost love in which Whitman's grief is unconsoled. He does not attempt to deny the sheer misery he feels, or claim that it has meaning or use. Thus he can surren-der to the plain wretchedness: "Sullen and suffering hours! (I am ashamed — but it is useless — I am what I am)." Having love of his own, or losing love that was real to him, Whitman finds coherence in the objective world; and he seems indeed to settle into the world, accepting it as it is. He gives fuller, more analytical development to the single objects of his attention, as in "I Saw in Louisiana a Live-Oak Growing."

> I saw in Louisiana a live-oak growing,
> All alone stood it and the moss hung down from
>   the branches,
> Without any companion it grew there uttering
>   joyous leaves of dark green,
> And its look, rude, unbending, lusty, made me
>   think of myself,
> But I wondered how it could utter joyous leaves
>   standing alone there without its friend
>   near, for I knew I could not,
> And I broke off a twig with a certain number of
>   leaves upon it, and twined around it a
>   little moss,
> And brought it away, and I have placed it in
>   sight in my room,
> It is not needed to remind me as of my own dear
>   friends,
> (For I believe lately I think of little else
>   than of them,)
> Yet it remains to me a curious token, it makes
>   me think of manly love;
> For all that, and though the live-oak glistens
>   there in Louisiana solitary in a wide
>   flat space,
> Uttering joyous leaves all its life without a
>   friend a lover near,
> I know very well I could not.
>
> (*LG*, pp. 126–127)

The peculiar wonder of this poem is Whitman's soft-spoken, musing literalness as he fully develops the metaphor while disengaging himself from its power to define him. He talks his way out of his usual identification with everything, and stands clear of his usual projections and assumptions. The main thrust in the poem is his increasing awareness of his difference from the symbol that eloquently reflects his previous way of living. His encounter with the oak is placed in the past in faraway Louisiana, and the twig he has brought with him signifies how much his outlook has changed, or traveled, from what he once desired to what he now values. It is "a curious token" to him, like a relic of a former, outlived self. He disavows his initial identification with this symbol of his solitude, however sympathetically he still understands its meaning; and he turns toward lovers as more important to him than his art. By this gentle assertion of independence from the very element, poetry, that has defined him, Whitman steps closer to relinquishing his vocation for the sake of spontaneous loving. The life of actual love that he wistfully contemplated as an outgrowth of poetry in the conclusion of "Song of the Open Road" now seems a more reasonable goal. The "camerado" is no longer a remote, imaginary traveler, but rather someone he directly cherishes and cannot think of doing without, "a friend a lover near." The intimacy of poetry alone can no longer make him happy.

On the contrary, one of Whitman's best love lyrics implies that he is ready to turn to a life of loving without poetry. "When I Heard at the Close of the Day" reveals Whitman's dissatisfaction with his longstanding discipline of ambition and solitary creativity. His achievements, his acclaim, and his cronies no longer delight him, he says; he is happy only when he withdraws from it all to be with his lover at a rendezvous. But Whitman is not just on vacation: He dismisses the rewards of national fame and high accomplishments, and he emphasizes his perfect gratification in actual, private intimacy.

> When I heard at the close of the day how my name
>   had been receiv'd with plaudits in the
>   capitol, still it was not a happy night
>   for me that follow'd,
> Or else when I carous'd, or when my plans were
>   accomplish'd, still I was not happy,
> But the day when I rose at dawn from the bed of
>   perfect health, refresh'd, singing,
>   inhaling the ripe breath of autumn,
> When I saw the full moon in the west grow pale
>   and disappear in the morning light,

When I wander'd alone over the beach, and
    undressing bathed, laughing with the
    cool waters, and saw the sun rise,
And when I thought how my dear friend my lover
    was on his way coming, O then I was happy,
O then each breath tasted sweeter, and all
    that day pass'd well,
And the next came with equal joy, and with the
    next at evening came my friend,
And that night while all was still I heard the
    waters roll slowly continually up the
    shores,
I heard the hissing rustle of the liquid and
    sands as directed to me whispering to
    congratulate me,
For the one I love most lay sleeping by me
    under the same cover in the cool night,
In the stillness in the autumn moonbeams his
    face was inclined toward me,
And his arm lay lightly around my breast — and
    that night I was happy.

                   (*LG*, pp. 122–123)

The patient mood of assured love in this poem contrasts with the frenetic atmosphere in "One Hour to Madness and Joy." Furthermore, there are no overtones of apocalyptic passion or inequality or bereavement in the union, which seems to continue as a happy memory even in the final phrase, "that night I was happy." But in its own renegade or lawless way, the union is possibly subversive, aimed at undermining the values of society.[1] These lovers are not a pair of innocents in an idyllic garden from which they emerge to a world replenished by their love. They have no way to return their love to the world that, in "Children of Adam," expands to new boundaries in the West. Their only possible link to the world they have relinquished is Whitman's art, which is a *plan* that no longer commands his interest. The direct contrast made between "plaudits in the capitol" and the more meaningful "whispering" of the sea "to congratulate me" indicates that nature's way of recognition supersedes, at least in the poem, society's validation. Nature's style of cherishing, which is quiet and secret, supplants the noisy praise, which appears not only hollow but even antithetical to the kind of private experience he now desires.

In the "Calamus" poems Whitman is not merely insisting that he is "a simple separate person" who is also capable of defining himself as the representative of all mankind. He rejects that double role, and undertakes to extricate himself from America and from poetry. In a few poems of thrilled recalcitrance he abandons his career. He declares that he will no longer write poems, for he prefers to live in seclusion with his lover.

His most explicit rejection of a life dedicated to poetry appears in "I Thought That Knowledge Alone Would Suffice," which Whitman allowed to appear only once, in the first printing of the "Calamus" poems in the 1860 edition. He excluded the poem from later editions of *Leaves of Grass,* probably because it went too far in repudiating values he eventually resumed. The poem offers a complete justification for seeking happiness in love apart from the rest of mankind. His rejection of poetry sounds particularly convincing because Whitman presents the end of his poetic vocation as the final step in his moral development. He speaks as if the meaning of his past life as well as his present culminates in crossing this threshold to privacy and real love.

> Long I thought that knowledge alone would suffice
>   me—O if I could but obtain knowledge!
> Then my lands engrossed me—Lands of the prairies,
>   Ohio's land, the southern savannas,
>   engrossed me—For them I would live—I
>   would be their orator;
> Then I met the examples of old and new heroes—
>   I heard of warriors, sailors, and all
>   dauntless persons—And it seemed to me
>   that I too had it in me to be as dauntless
>   as any—and would be so;
> And then, to enclose all, it came to me to strike
>   up the songs of the New World—And then
>   I believed my life must be spent in
>   singing;
> But now take notice, land of the prairies, land
>   of the south savannas, Ohio's land,
> Take notice, you Kanuck woods—and you Lake Huron—
>   and all that with you roll toward Niagara—
>   and you Niagara also,
> And you, Californian mountains—That you each
>   and all find somebody else to be your
>   singer of songs,
> For I can be your singer of songs no longer—
>   One who loves me is jealous of me, and
>   withdraws me from all but love,

With the rest I dispense—I sever from what I
    thought would suffice me, for it does
    not—it is now empty and tasteless to me,
I heed knowledge, and the grandeur of The States,
    and the example of heroes, no more,
I am indifferent to my own songs—I will go with
    him I love,
It is to be enough for us that we are together—
    We never separate again.

                    (LG, pp. 595–596)

It is like a letter of resignation from a dutiful employee who thought there would never be anything better in life than the job he now happily rejects. In deciding to go away with his lover, Whitman spends most of the poem trying to explain that his decision has to do with the emptiness of the great ambitions he earlier entertained. The story emphasizes a series of goals that promised to be all-sufficing, but the narrative indicates their insufficiency as one unfulfilling aspiration just rolls into another: "Long... Then...Then...And then...And then...." His pursuits were naively passionate and dedicated; even the youthful desire for knowledge is recalled as an exclamatory longing to achieve complete fulfillment in this noble purpose. His intention to follow a public career is recalled also as a readiness for absolute dedication to selfless values. Heroes inspired him to take on their attributes; and, having attempted many roads, he fused together all his previous ideals and ambitions by becoming the nation's poet: "And then I believed my life must be spent in singing." The rapid summary of his life emphasizes that he has paid his dues to society by a succession of responsible roles. He has given full service, and is now morally free to cast off all claims except the claim of love. In developing this rationalization, he is writing off his debt to others. But he is also claiming superiority over those symbolic lands from which he did not receive as much as he gave. Their debt to him was never paid. There are signs of anger and reproach in the lines that beard America; he refuses any longer to be taken for granted, to be assumed by others, to be not noticed:

    But now take notice...
    Take notice, you...and you...and all that
        with you...and you...also,
    And you...That you each and all find somebody
        else to be your singer of songs,
    For I can be your singer of songs no longer...
    ... — it is now empty and tasteless to me.

The vehemence of his direct address conveys considerable acrimony toward the symbolic lands, suggesting that he feels overburdened and misused by unappreciative people. The repetition of the phrase "your singer of songs" slightly mocks the counterfeit dignity it conveys, and the irony implies Whitman's chagrin that he was kept subordinated and that the poet's role itself is undervalued. Now he can reject his taskmasters, The States, to go with someone who will repay him properly with reciprocated love and inseparable union. He does not need to work for paltry or withheld compensation any longer.

But even this rejection of his vocation ends by weaving together two conflicting goals that show he will not stray far. While he carefully explains that he is free of his duty to art and society, he reveals that he probably cannot turn away from the imaginary parents who hold him in thrall to poetry. Even as he decides to give up his "empty and tasteless" labors as a poet, he reveals an undercurrent of reproach against those who begrudged him love in return for the love he offered them. Both his uneasy love and his unvented anger prevent him from accepting this injustice — and this in turn will prevent him from abandoning poetry. He will continue to seek to redress the imbalance, to obtain what is owed him, to coerce love from the selfish, to claim equality with the overpowering master, to pursue fulfillment through imaginary instead of actual relationships. He may also have discovered simpler, more rational grounds for failing to act on his decision to give up poetry for a lover who was jealous of his divided attention; but if he thought at any time that such a trade would be a bad bargain, he did not write poems about his preference for art over love. After the romantic escapade of "Calamus," he wrote poems that express with increasing remorse his loneliness and grief in this life.

The idea of himself as a single Dionysian "kosmos" no longer suited him, and he thought he had extricated himself from the charm of those mossy branches in "I Saw in Louisiana a Live-Oak Growing." In taking the next logical step in his self-definition Whitman believed that he was completing *Leaves of Grass*, and consequently that he was dying away from the personality expressed in the book. He was leaving himself solid and intact in those poems, and if he wrote other poems, they would not similarly center on inward explorations of Personality. He would find other themes, perhaps in natural science and current history, he surmised. Convinced he was rounding off what he had set out to accomplish, he wrote a happy farewell address to the future. "So Long!" sparkles with giddy wit as he displays his talent in a final entertainment — "To conclude, I announce what comes after me" — and, like Prospero, he summons his magic in order to abjure it.

It appears to me I am dying.

Hasten throat and sound your last,

Salute me—salute the days once more. Peal the
old cry once more.

(11. 33–35)

He kept this poem as the concluding piece in the 1860 edition and in all later editions of *Leaves of Grass* (and continued it garrulously in two appendixes). It is made to be a memento, dated like a photograph taken years ago. It celebrates an earlier myth of himself that he recalls as a picture of his prime. Once again, flamboyantly and for the last time, Whitman engages his readers in the communion of his consciousness offered for us to share. It was truly the last celebration of his protean self.

What is there more, that I lag and pause and
crouch extended with unshut mouth?
Is there a single final farewell?

My songs cease, I abandon them,
From behind the screen where I hid I advance
personally solely to you.

Camerado, this is no book,
Who touches this touches a man,
(Is it night? are we here together alone?)
It is I you hold and who holds you,
I spring from the pages into your arms—decease
calls me forth.

O how your fingers drowse me,
Your breath falls around me like dew, your pulse
lulls the tympans of my ears,
I feel immerged from head to foot,
Delicious, enough.

Enough O deed impromptu and secret,
Enough O gliding present—enough O summ'd-up past.

Dear friend whoever you are take this kiss,
I give it especially to you, do not forget me,
I feel like one who has done work for the day
to retire awhile,
I receive now again of my many translations,
from my avataras ascending, while others
doubtless await me,
An unknown sphere more real than I dream'd,
more direct, darts awakening rays about
me, *So long!*

Remember my words, I may again return,
I love you, I depart from materials,
I am as one disembodied, triumphant, dead.

(11. 49–71)

This ingenious, hearty farewell shows Whitman's pleasure over the anticipated change in his life. The poem is full of extravagant happiness over concluding his poetic role with such grandeur, affection, and freedom. But the elation is only temporary: Despite his intention to quit writing poems about his solitary self, Whitman could not let the subject rest. The deepest source of his creativity was not his desire for happiness and fulfillment; more fundamentally, he wrote to maintain his individual being, and poetry expressed the depth of his struggle just to exist. Love for either sex could not entirely free him from his quarrel with his parents because his challenge to them was also his defense against oblivion.

His new poems of sexual love for men waited to appear in a third edition of *Leaves of Grass*, for which Whitman could not find a publisher. After he completed them by early 1858, Whitman wrote no poetry for perhaps as long as a year and a half. Busily employed as the editor of the *Brooklyn Daily Times* in the late 1850s, he easily produced editorials and other daily journalism, but he suffered a kind of writer's block in his creative life. His notebooks show that he stoked the old pipe dream of making a living from his poetry by becoming a wandering minstrel and orator-teacher. Actually, he spent much of his time adrift in bohemian conviviality with the literary and theatrical crowd that met nightly at Pfaff's saloon. He liked being the champion thoroughbred in that stable, though his role was mainly to observe the cleverness of others and to receive their admiration. His eccentric appearance made him look like the embodiment of *Leaves of Grass*, but inwardly he was not sure of his next step. He wavered between his spiritual definition as a poet and his sensual independence from poetry. Perhaps, for the sake of a kind of happiness he never attained, Whitman might have given up writing poetry in the late 1850s to live thereafter on Long Island in anonymity with a lover. Obviously, he could not; but the "Calamus" poems indicate that writing poems had become repetitive and repugnant to him. Creativity threatened him with emotional falsification and it reimposed repeated heroic struggles for integrity, all of which lay behind him and awaited him on the page as well. His art had come to reproduce an old trap for Whitman, who by sharing his existence so fully with others, and having his existence so invaded by the "understanding" of others, found once again that he retained nothing real about his separate self. He thought he had to choose between writing poetry and living life.

6

Cradle and Coffin, 1859

WHITMAN'S INSPIRED compromise was to construct a new identity. In a brief surge of creativity in mid-1859, he wrote two great poems in which he held onto his vocation by changing his conception of himself.

The identity he had ambitiously and joyously constructed in the poems of his first two editions had impelled him toward an autonomous life: first, within the subjective, symbolic world of his imagination, and then in the actual world through sexual fulfillment. The idea of himself as a god capable of recovering, renewing, and sharing all imaginable experiences was the myth through which he accepted his paradoxes and identified with the diversity of the nation. But the myth pushed him farther than he could freely go. He relinquished the idea of himself as an ecstatic poet who had miraculously emerged from the loving fusion of contrary parts of himself as he lay on the grass one summer morning. He rewrote his life story with an entirely new focus on his childhood, and the identity that emerges is quite literally not his old self anymore. In returning closer to childhood, he gave up much of his fight against sadness and dependence, which he had resisted by striving for autonomy through his poetry.

In rethinking himself, he wrote the only two poems that directly and explicitly portray his conflicts with his parents as the main issues in his creative life. Though he dealt implicitly with these relationships in nearly all of his major poems, in the two great "Sea-Drift" poems he examines at length his childhood responses to his mother and father. Considered together, "As I Ebb'd with the Ocean of Life" and "Out of the Cradle Endlessly Rocking" indicate Whitman's self-analytical response to his crisis of identity. In both poems he confronts an obsessive early memory of abasement and neglect, in order to answer his present self-questioning, and to choose, as he felt forced to do, between degrading submission and utter oblivion.

Both poems center on the ocean and the shore, which had loomed in his imagination since his young daydreams on the Long Island beaches. The seashore became part of his night dreams as well, and it remained throughout his life the single most haunting image in Whitman's memory, for the suggestiveness of the place never diminished for him. As an old man reminiscing in *Specimen Days* he was still curious about its ambiguity and persistence.

> Even as a boy, I had the fancy, the wish, to write a piece, perhaps a poem, about the sea-shore—that suggesting, dividing line, contact, junction, the solid marrying the liquid— that curious, lurking something, (as doubtless every objective form finally becomes to the subjective spirit,) which means far more than its mere first sight, grand as that is—blending the real and ideal, and each made portion of the other. Hours, days, in my Long Island youth and early manhood, I haunted the shores of Rockaway or Coney Island, or away east to the Hamptons or Montauk. Once, at the latter place, (by the old lighthouse, nothing but sea-tossings in sight in every direction as far as the eye could reach,) I remember well, I felt that I must one day write a book expressing this liquid, mystic theme. . . .
>
> There is a dream, a picture, that for years at intervals, (sometimes quite long ones, but surely again, in time,) has come noiselessly up before me, and I really believe, fiction as it is, has enter'd largely into my practical life—certainly into my writings, and shaped and color'd them. It is nothing more or less than a stretch of interminable white-brown sand, hard and smooth and broad, with the ocean perpetually, grandly, rolling in upon it, with slow-measured sweep, with rustle and hiss and foam, and many a thump as of low bass drums. This scene, this picture, I say, has risen before me at times for years. Sometimes I wake at night and can hear and see it plainly.[1]

His recollection in old age includes innumerable but possibly misleading suggestions of a primal scene of sexual intercourse that a child, waking at night, might misinterpret as distress or even interrupt with mortifying consequences. Whatever his memory contained, its internal effects were examined in the "Sea-Drift" poems. Both poems treat the seashore as the domain of parents who are in great distress that affects their child with anguish and grief he can hope to master only through poetry. In "As I Ebb'd with the Ocean of Life," he attributes to his parents, to his "mother" and "father," who personify the ocean and land, the turbulence of the setting and its harshness toward him. Here the seashore evokes a moment of bitter chagrin for a boy old enough to feel that embarrassment and injustice are catastrophes.

Whitman deals openly with his loss of faith in himself as a poet. He cannot write poems now, and even his earlier work appears shallow and false to him. Demoralized and ironic, he walks along the seashore in a self-conscious effort to recover poetic inspiration, but he criticizes even this effort as mere egotism: "Held by this electric self out of the pride of which I utter poems," he says disparagingly. He is despondent over his dry spell and hopeless about even wanting to write. The ocean (in earlier, happier poems it was called "my lover the sea") appears old and cross, its raspy voice grating on his spirit, and the debris drifting everywhere signifies the wreckage of all lives. The ocean is filled with the evidence of universal disintegration and death that it deposits on the shore. "The fierce old mother endlessly cries for her castaways," he observes, and the ambiguity of that metaphor leaves room for the dark thought that the castaways are not simply lost from her but also discarded by her. Her moaning, whether in grief or anger, resounds in "hoarse and sibilant" accusations — the adjectives convey the accusatorial whisper that he too is but mournfully worthless debris.

The ocean that is filled with the voices of the dead makes him mindful of his death to come, and he is plunged into despair over the futility of his artistic intentions and his accomplished work. In the most bitter, self-chastising lines in all of Whitman's poetry, his language resonates with a humiliating repudiation, suggesting not only the punishing conscience of a middle-aged poet but also the mortification of a youngster who had "dared" — the verb is used twice — to defy his parents, who retaliate with scorn and belittling.

> O baffled, balk'd, bent to the very earth,
> Oppress'd with myself that I have dared to open
>   my mouth,
> Aware now that amid all that blab whose echoes recoil
>   upon me I have not once had the least idea who
>   or what I am,
> But that before all my arrogant poems the real Me
>   stands yet untouch'd, untold, altogether
>   unreach'd,
> Withdrawn far, mocking me with mock-congratulatory
>   signs and bows,
> With peals of distant ironical laughter at every
>   word I have written,
> Pointing in silence to these songs, and then to the
>   sand beneath.

I perceive I have not really understood any thing,
   not a single object, and that no man ever can,
Nature here in sight of the sea taking advantage of
   me to dart upon me and sting me,
Because I have dared to open my mouth to sing at all.
                      (11. 25–34)

The pain that sears him comes from mockery — "mocking me with mock-congratulatory signs and bows"; and from ridicule — "all that blab"; and blame — "my arrogant poems" (in the first version his poems were "insolent"); and disdain — "peals of distant ironical laughter." He feels exposed in front of others and wrung with embarrassment: "here in sight of the sea taking advantage of me to dart upon me and sting me." His merciless "real Me" makes a trite gesture in the reminder that his poems are writ on sand, and this single clichéd expression is a clue to one source of his emotions. This is a revision of a line in which he felt his cruelly vindictive "Me" "Striking me with insults till I fall helpless upon the sand" (*Variorum*, II, p. 320). Throughout the passage Whitman evokes the sharp wound of a child's sensibility, and he reacts with futile efforts to appease his attacker. Unlike other exposures to shame in earlier poems, this confrontation does not lead to a deliciously erotic exhibition of his nakedness, nor does it prompt any show of independent bravado or inspire him to create alternative means of gratification to console himself. In this poem he suffers without turning his pain into a triumph of the spirit, and he dwells mostly on the wretched hopelessness of his attempts to regain love from his parents.

Stanzas 3 and 4 describe in almost literal terms a conflict that appears scarcely altered from an actual, nearly violent family argument. Whitman beseeches his parental land and ocean to put an end to this atmosphere of reproachfulness that he does not really understand. But his earnest demands for a comforting embrace frighten them into even greater coldness and misunderstanding. Whitman throws himself upon the shore and clings to his "father" for a kiss and an answer that will acknowledge him and restore him; but his imploring is received more like an assault, for his father remains aloof, while his worried, angry mother, who has not sided with the boy, moans and blames him for behaving so badly. They think he attacks them, he thinks they condemn him. It is the wretchedness of childhood.

3

You oceans both, I close with you,
We murmur alike reproachfully rolling sands and
   drift, knowing not why,

These little shreds indeed standing for you and
    me and all.

You friable shore with trails of debris,
You fish-shaped island, I take what is underfoot,
What is yours is mine my father.

I too Paumanok,
I too have bubbled up, floated the measureless
    float, and been wash'd on your shores,
I too am but a trail of drift and debris,
I too leave little wrecks upon you, you fish-shaped
    island.

I throw myself upon your breast my father,
I cling to you so that you cannot unloose me,
I hold you so firm till you answer me something.

Kiss me my father,
Touch me with your lips as I touch those I love,
Breathe to me while I hold you close the secret of
    the murmuring I envy.

4

Ebb, ocean of life, (the flow will return,)
Cease not your moaning you fierce old mother,
Endlessly cry for your castaways, but fear not,
    deny not me,
Rustle not up so hoarse and angry against my feet
    as I touch you or gather from you.

I mean tenderly by you and all.

(11. 35–55)

The land and sea remain unforthcoming despite Whitman's protestations
of love. He tries to be conciliatory by accepting their terms for him — "I
close with you" (as in a business deal, a term his parents would com-
monly use). He submits to the meagerness of their bounty of shreds and
debris, claiming for himself only the diminished life available underfoot
and equally his father's lot. He will concede every personal goal except
that of being recognized and accepted by them. His demand increases
until it clamors like a threat: "I throw myself upon your breast my father,
/ I cling to you so that you cannot unloose me, / I hold you so firm till
you answer me something." But his insistence is met with only silence
and fear. To pursue his desire is to risk losing contact with them
altogether: "Deny not me," he implores his angry and frightened mother,

who has apparently already moved to cast him away. He soothes and coaxes her in her dark mood to accept his sympathy and good intentions, for he means to serve both parents "tenderly," not violently as they evidently supposed.

The passage expresses Whitman's heartsick disappointment over his father, whose blessing never materializes despite his son's beseeching. Instead, the poem confirms a frightening and implacable resistance in the inscrutable old man. Invoking him no more, Whitman turns away from his father, whose limitations have been searingly exposed. In devaluing his father's image he rejects as well the radical idealism that Whitman wanted his father to symbolize. He turns away bitterly, from the ideal as well as from the man. It is no longer love but scorn that guides the resolution of the poem.

The ocean that withdrew from him remains the only promise of love and faith, and Whitman humbles himself before his mother as he prepares to wait, half expecting a return to his old self. He gathers together bits of wreckage to display to the reader, for whose sake he has continued to slave away at poetry, he says. His continuing depression is evident in the emotional discord of the conclusion. Antagonism that can no longer be diluted with hope and directed safely against his father now turns bitter and is randomly misdirected — just as his father's umbrage against fate probably had been. He stuns the reader with lurid images of his decomposing corpse. He speaks angrily to the reader, whom he addresses with taunting subservience as a remote "phantom," and calls out churlishly to future readers as if they were insensitive Brobdingnagians, "You up there walking or sitting, / Whoever you are, we too lie in drifts at your feet." His habitual stoicism has become disingenuous; he gibes at the reader, and his self-pity falls on yet another deaf ear.

> I gather for myself and for this phantom looking
>   down where we lead, and following me and
>   mine.
>
> Me and mine, loose windrows, little corpses,
> Froth, snowy white, and bubbles,
> (See, from my dead lips the ooze exuding at last,
> See the prismatic colors glistening and rolling,)
> Tufts of straw, sands, fragments,
> Buoy'd hither from many moods, one contradicting
>   another,
> From the storm, the long calm, the darkness, the
>   swell,
> Musing, pondering, a breath, a briny tear, a dab
>   of liquid or soil,

Up just as much out of fathomless workings fermented
    and thrown,
A limp blossom or two, torn, just as much over waves
    floating, drifted at random,
Just as much for us that sobbing dirge of Nature,
Just as much whence we come that blare of the
    cloud-trumpets,
We, capricious, brought hither we know not whence,
    spread out before you,
You up there walking or sitting,
Whoever you are, we too lie in drifts at your feet.
                           (11. 56–71)

    The attitudes of his parents have combined to undermine his creativity. The mocking tones and betrayal of the shore and sea remain with him in the end to blight the poem with a ragged conclusion. He cannot justify his parents, but neither can he renounce them — not even after he has exposed and verbalized their cruelty. But he does shift his allegiance to a more exclusive sympathy with his mother. All his Oedipal striving for equality with his father felt pointless: not purposeless, just futile. Denied comradeship and confirmation from his father, Whitman had no recourse except to align himself in partial defeat but secure intimacy with the feminine side of his nature. In devaluing his father's idealized image, he let go of the obligation to choose between poetry and autonomy in experience. He regressed to identify more closely with his mother, on a pre-Oedipal level of attachment. In his creative life he reorganized his ideal self to reflect his thwarted goal and fundamental grief. In life and in his later poems Whitman clings to the voice of the maternal sea, which oppresses but also comforts him. In the two "Sea-Drift" poems, the ocean of life does not rush back with lilting, buoyant affection; when it returns it brings intimacy but also gloom. And nothing else in nature — not his usual "objects" or "electric" bodies, not his beloved comrades or his impulsive masculine soul — ever rushes forward to revive his elation over existence. Even the heart-stopping thrills of his fleeting glances into his past are supplanted by deliberate and somber retrospection.

    In the second "Sea-Drift" poem Whitman completes his deeper identification with his mother. In "Out of the Cradle Endlessly Rocking" he reinterprets his spiritual origin and poetic destiny by yielding to feelings of emptiness and loss, from which, as he now says, his entire creative activity arises. As a direct antithesis to "Song of Myself" (and to the other poems that further develop the identity he constructs there), "Out of the Cradle Endlessly Rocking" dedicates a new self. This account of his life was as important to him as the earlier life story it revokes, because writing

it was a ceremony of emotional compromises and self-revision that probably saved him from withdrawing completely from the larger world. He
bestows great dignity upon the form of the poem itself, which is unusual
for Whitman, who alleged that poems fell from him like seeds in nature.
Now he needs to sacramentalize art; and for that purpose this poem is
an operatic production. "Out of the Cradle Endlessly Rocking" crystallizes the definitive tragedy of his experience, and he dramatizes this
through operatic characters who alternate with arias and recitative passages. The long overture, initially entitled the "Pre-Verse," reflects the
themes of "As I Ebb'd with the Ocean of Life," for Whitman again in tears
throws himself upon the sand and again confronts the waves. But this
time he does not suffer the childhood despair that led him to feel defeated
in his adult, creative life. The overture suggests that Whitman is returning
to his childhood to interpret the pain that arises from the past. His
"reminiscence" introduces a child whose imagination is awakened by
his privileged insight to the grief in everyone's life.

> Out of the cradle endlessly rocking,
> Out of the mocking-bird's throat, the musical
>   shuttle,
> Out of the Ninth-month midnight,
> Over the sterile sands and the fields beyond,
>   where the child leaving his bed wander'd
>   alone, bareheaded, barefoot,
> Down from the shower'd halo,
> Up from the mystic play of shadows twining and
>   twisting as if they were alive,
> Out from the patches of briers and blackberries,
> From the memories of the bird that chanted to me,
> From your memories sad brother, from the fitful risings
>   and fallings I heard,
> From under that yellow half-moon late-risen and
>   swollen as if with tears,
> From those beginning notes of yearning and love
>   there in the mist,
> From the thousand responses of my heart never to
>   cease,
> From the myriad thence-arous'd words,
> From the word stronger and more delicious than any,
> From such as now they start the scene revisiting,
> As a flock, twittering, rising, or overhead passing,
> Borne hither, ere all eludes me, hurriedly,
> A man, yet by these tears a little boy again,

Throwing myself on the sand, confronting the waves,
I, chanter of pains and joys, uniter of here and
    hereafter,
Taking all hints to use them, but swiftly leaping
    beyond them,
A reminiscence sing.

                                            (11. 1–22)

The overture comes to an end when it scrupulously differentiates the
adult poet from the boy he remembers having been. The carefully delin-
eated, realistic distinction between the child and the man is the key element in the emotional and rhetorical structures of the poem, for the climax
is an intimate reconnection between the poet and the boy. Whitman
separates them in the overture so that he can meaningfully fuse them
in the resolution, which he does by submitting to the outlook of childhood. In this poem the vivid past does not rush forward to the adult,
passive Whitman, bringing him the comforting intimacy of the
remembered world. Rather, Whitman actively reaches back to comfort
the boy he was; with maternal, self-sacrificing solicitude for a stricken
child, he pledges to give up the themes and goals of his earlier poetry
in order to express the pain and jubilation of the child's tender heart.
He stays *with the boy* to write about the grief he felt as a solitary child;
and his reunion with the boy includes a surrender to the limitations and
worldview of childhood. He does not feel thwarted in his aims as a man
and poet; instead, he accepts the inhibited aims of childhood as his
fundamental lot. The potential victory of a diminished self over a larger
self always threatened to upset Whitman's psychological balance and his
poetic identity. It is not a new pitfall in his life or in his poetry; it does
not signify specific guilt for his recent homosexuality or his self-assertive-
ness or any other particular behavior of the moment. Rather, this surge
of guilt has always been countered by efforts to oppose his doom — until
this poem. Here he regresses to a compromised life in which his childhood sensibility wrests fuller control over his imagination and his poems.

The operatic action opens on a scene of secure domesticity and fragrant
springtime as Whitman recalls a succession of mild days when as a child
he watched two mockingbirds nesting. He sees himself as a carefully
respectful, curious, deferential but intent boy whose attention is engrossed
by secretly viewing the birds' home life, which is ordinarily hidden.

And every day the he-bird to and fro near at hand,
And every day the she-bird crouch'd on her nest,
    silent, with bright eyes,

And every day I, a curious boy, never too close,
    never disturbing them,
Cautiously peering, absorbing, translating.

(11. 28–31)

In this opening recitative passage the boy's demeanor is noticeably subdued — like that of a withdrawn youth. His perspective creates the child's inner vista of secret, suppressed response that distances the boy from the experience he absorbs. His summer-long fascination with the bird remains emotionally flat until he finally admits that the male bird's songs define his own true feelings. In contrast to the boy's initial detachment from his feelings, the male bird sings the aria passages with rhapsodic daring that displays the range of his swiftly changing moods and the intensity of his passions. The bird sings with the brashness of a young lover who expects his happiness to defy all misfortune, expressing the usual romantic self-confidence that to any sober listener conveys the usual portents of disappointment. The bird's foolish but charming over-estimation of the power of his feelings reflects Whitman's ironic view of the egotism of his earlier poetry. Now disenchanted with his work, he allows the naive arrogance of the bird to represent his own former bravado.

> *Shine! shine! shine!*
> *Pour down your warmth, great sun!*
> *While we bask, we two together.*
>
> *Two together!*
> *Winds blow south, or winds blow north,*
> *Day come white, or night come black,*
> *Home, or rivers and mountains from home,*
> *Singing all time, minding no time,*
> *While we two keep together.*

(11. 32–40)

When misfortune immediately follows in the lines after the bird's arch, first song, the calamity is compressed into a brusque report that the female bird suddenly disappeared and never appeared again. Whitman devotes the largest part of the poem to songs of woe from the summer-long ordeal in which the bird's romantic defiance of fate changes into torments of worry over the mate that fails to return, and then into acceptance of grief itself as the underlying fate that strips away all arrogant delusions. He focuses on the bird's throes of invented hope, mistaken explanations, false sightings of her, fears of being forgotten — pathetic efforts to deny the calamity and then to stave off his wild grief. Like the bel canto singers he adored, Whitman adopts a virtuoso, artful style to indicate unguarded expressiveness: He imitates a mockingbird's song, which passes rapidly from twittering, to trilling, to full-throated warbling.

> O night! do I not see my love fluttering out among
>   the breakers?
> What is that little black thing I see there in the
>   white?
>
> Loud! loud! loud!
> Loud I call to you, my love!
>
> High and clear I shoot my voice over the waves,
> Surely you must know who is here, is here,
> You must know who I am, my love.
>
> (11. 79–85)

The bird's anguish is presented with the restrained pity of dramatic irony, since we have already been informed that the mate is forever lost. This extended ironic perspective is unusual for Whitman, who almost never tells a story in his poetry; when he does elsewhere occasionally speak as a narrator, he fully identifies with his characters and mingles his knowledge with theirs. Here too the story he tells is clearly his own early experience of loss and confusion; the bird is, as he says, his "brother." But here Whitman observes the drama as a narrator with full knowledge of the outcome. His own recitative passages maintain his sympathetic but detached omniscience: "He call'd on his mate, / He pour'd forth the meanings which I of all men know" (ll. 59–60). Like the boy, the narrator holds back his immediate, direct response.

Whitman ultimately allows the bird's chaotic search to subside into permanent mourning.

> O past! O happy life! O songs of joy!
> In the air, in the woods, over fields,
> Loved! loved! loved! loved! loved!
> But my mate no more, no more with me!
> We two together no more!
>
> (11. 125–129)

As the bird songs cease the perspective of dramatic irony melts away, for Whitman does not view the child's sudden distress with similar, knowing restraint. There is a rush of emotion that is marked by a shift of verb-tense into present-participial phrasing for fourteen lines when the child can no longer suppress his feelings and he plunges into tears: "The love in the heart long pent, now loose, now at last tumultuously bursting "(1. 137). Casting aside any differentiation of viewpoints, Whitman allows the boy to identify with the bird's grief while Whitman adopts the perspective of the child and allows the boy to speak for him as an adult poet. When the boy recognizes at last that he has been hearing his own sadness in the cries of the bird, the boy instantly understands the meaning of his fascination with the bird's tragedy and accepts his destiny to become the poet of "the cries of unsatisfied love," even responding in a bardic stance of apostrophe to the bird that has touched his very soul.

> Demon or bird! (said the boy's soul,)
> Is it indeed toward your mate you sing? or is it
>   really to me?
> For I, that was a child, my tongue's use sleeping,
>   now I have heard you,
> Now in a moment I know what I am for, I awake,
> And already a thousand singers, a thousand songs,
>   clearer, louder and more sorrowful than
>   yours,
> A thousand warbling echoes have started to life
>   within me, never to die.
>
> O you singer solitary, singing by yourself, projecting
>   me,
> O solitary me listening, never more shall I cease
>   perpetuating you,
> Never more shall I escape, never more the reverberations,
> Never more the cries of unsatisfied love be absent
>   from me,
> Never again leave me to be the peaceful child I was
>   before what there in the night,
> By the sea under the yellow and sagging moon,
> The messenger there arous'd, the fire, the sweet
>   hell within,
> The unknown want, the destiny of me.
>
>   (11. 144–157)

Whitman promises to correct his mistaken, naive attitudes. He pledges fidelity to the fundamental griefs that he will "never more" — that is, never any longer — fail to commemorate. The refrain of "never more" and "never again" revokes his earlier arrogant predilection to celebrate his happiness and to assume the fulfillment of love. The reiterated "never more'' does not express the sudden ambitiousness of a young child but rather, more fittingly, the resolve of an adult poet who has lived long enough to attempt ''escape'' from his woes and finds that he can't. He will ''never more'' be so foolish as to imagine that ''the cries of unsatisfied love'' could possibly ''be absent from me.'' He will not abandon his art, for there is no fulfillment outside poetry itself. By accepting the male bird's sad experience as his own he also accepts the bird's solitude: the stern fact is repeated in ''O you singer solitary, singing by yourself, projecting me, / O solitary me listening.'' The destiny of solitude and poetry (which he thought he rejected in the ''Calamus'' poems) settles upon him as a restored continuity with his past. His own childhood contains the imperative that renews his poetic vocation. Whitman's implicit rationalization is that his true identity antedates the birth of the ''kosmos,'' the erotic liberator in stanza 5 of ''Song of Myself.'' What he now feels as the lack of sensual satisfaction, the sexual ''fire, the sweet hell within,'' was part of the deprivation that defined his identity in childhood. With this revised conception of his central self, he will find fulfillment in songs that show the painful truth of his father's life: There is no achieving one's desires anywhere in nature. That distant masculine Muse, newly understood in the sad mockingbird, proclaims the fate of all ardent but naive expectations to realize one's ideals in the actual world.

For this tragic vision the boy-poet seeks the new theme, or ''the clew,'' that will give coherence to his flood of feelings in this fresh illumination. Like the man-poet born in ''Song of Myself,'' the boy-poet needs to learn how to express the insight that redefines his entire being. The word, or idea, comes to him from ''the fierce old mother incessantly moaning.'' Her ''angry moans'' and other troubled sounds have always suggested this possible motif, whose full meaning he now grasps as a sign of a special tenderness between them. When the heaving and swelling ocean gives him the key, it supersedes the other shibboleths of *Leaves of Grass*; it is not Love or Sex or Nature or Freedom or America or the vastness of Personality itself.

> A word then, (for I will conquer it,)
> The word final, superior to all,
> Subtle, sent up—what is it?—I listen;
> Are you whispering it, and have been all the time,
>   you sea-waves?
> Is that it from your liquid rims and wet sands?
>
> Whereto answering, the sea,
> Delaying not, hurrying not,
> Whisper'd me through the night, and very plainly
>   before daybreak,

Lisp'd to me the low and delicious word death,
And again death, death, death, death,
Hissing melodious, neither like the bird nor
    like my arous'd child's heart,
But edging near as privately for me rustling at
    my feet,
Creeping thence steadily up to my ears and laving
    me softly all over,
Death, death, death, death, death.

Which I do not forget,
But fuse the song of my dusky demon and brother,
That he sang to me in the moonlight on Paumanok's
    gray beach,
With the thousand responsive songs at random,
My own songs awaked from that hour,
And with them the key, the word up from the waves,
The word of the sweetest song and all songs,
That strong and delicious word which, creeping to
    my feet,
(Or like some old crone rocking the cradle, swathed
    in sweet garments, bending aside,)
The sea whisper'd me.

(ll. 160–183)

In these lines we are moved, not by a lamentation over death, but by his awe and gratefulness for the restored security with a mothering ocean. The sea-washes at his feet may have earlier sounded fierce and angry, but now the tide of her fleeting tenderness returns with melodious hissing. Since he has repudiated his rebellious effort to escape from her — vainly desiring the more manly company of a lover, a comrade, or an ideal father — he feels forgiven and privileged to be accepted again by her majestically unstoppable, enveloping flood of intimacy. Beyond all quarrels or ebbing moods between them, the ocean remains there to caress him and to receive him. His mother's love flows back in "The sea whisper'd me," a line that perfectly concretizes her exquisite mixture of ardor and narcissistic identification with him. Assured that there is nothing else in the fallen world except the lasting reality of "unsatisfied love," the poet resumes the "delicious" melancholy of his childhood as he returns to lonely sympathy with the possessive crone in his art.

    The reconceptualization of himself in "Out of the Cradle Endlessly Rocking" commits Whitman to a consistently elegiac mode of expression in the best of his subsequent works. He will remain the poet of death in the years through the Civil War and into his old age. The protean self that energized his life and art coalesces into "a great tender mother-man," which is how John Burroughs, who met Whitman a few years later in Washington, remembered him as having always been.[2] He wasn't always so. Nor was it inevitable that his earlier goals of sensual autonomy in life and explorative freedom in poetry had to be foregone. The great sea change in his sensibility grew out of a conflict of allegiances that his art had intensified and that he was inclined to resolve with art alone. Whitman rescued his poet's vocation only by holding true to the burden in his mother's voice.

7

Perishing Unions, 1860–1892

THE COMPOSITION of his two great seashore poems in 1859 did not immediately bring Whitman back to work vigorously writing new poetry. In the short run those journeys to the bottom of his soul appear to have been exhausting and perhaps dispiriting. He had, after all, lost part of himself in the redefinition of his poetic identity, and he did not yet clearly know what he would become. At the same time in 1859, he had also lost, or given up, his job as editor of the *Brooklyn Daily Times*. He may have quarreled with the owner over an editorial titled "Beecherolatry," which attacked the vanity and hypocrisy of the popular and glamorous New York minister Henry Ward Beecher.[1] Such a target surely suited Whitman's mood after his deflation of his father. But perhaps he was not fired; he may have simply quit, for he was clearly losing interest in all current events. He felt in general that his life had become unreal, and he lacked any sense of direction or strong purpose. According to his notebooks, he repeatedly tried to rouse himself from a "Slough" of fecklessness, but to no avail.[2] After leaving the *Daily Times* he found no steady employment. Perfunctorily, he wrote his most vapid, superficial journalism as piecework while current national events resonated with the louder and louder significance of John Brown's raid in October 1859; his execution in December, which inflamed even Emerson into fury; and the presidential campaign in 1860, leading to the election of Lincoln. But even these momentous events could not rouse him from "my New York stagnation," as he called it later.[3] He felt dissociated from nearly everything he had claimed to embody. When the new firm of Thayer and Eldridge offered to become his publishers, Whitman went off to Boston to spend the entire spring of 1860 overseeing the publication of the third edition of *Leaves of Grass*. For the frontispiece he chose a portrait by one of his bohemian friends from Pfaff's saloon that shows him with curly hair and beard, wearing a soft round collar and a big bow tied in his dark silk scarf.

It is an outlandishly literary, or painterly, costume, presenting Whitman as he never was — yet it shows him certainly out of touch with his book and his era.

In the following April when war broke out between the states, Whitman resolved to stir himself to inspiration by purifying his body: "I have this day, this hour, resolved to inaugurate for myself a pure, perfect, sweet, clean-blooded robust body, by ignoring all drinks but water and pure milk, and all fat meats, late suppers — a great body, a purged, cleansed, spiritualized, invigorated body."[4] But the regimen, if he practiced it, was not much use. Six weeks later he noted his forty-second birthday with general dissatisfaction over his achievements. He wanted most of all to resume his writing, and he projected another book of poems that would differ from the *Leaves*. He encouraged himself by writing an introduction in advance: "I write this introduction on my birthday after having looked over what has been accomplished. So far, so well, but the most and the best of the Poem I perceive remains unwritten, and is the work of my life yet to be done. The paths to the house are made — but where is the house itself?"[5] His disaffection from current political issues left him without a link to the public world. "Quicksand Years," written in 1861 or 1862, expresses his alienation from his times, as well as his anxious resolve not to lose his strong sense of self.

> Quicksand years that whirl me I know not whither,
> Your schemes, politics, fail, lines give way, substances
>   mock and elude me,
> Only the theme I sing, the great and strong-possess'd
>   soul, eludes not,
> One's-self must never give way—that is the final
>   substance—that out of all is sure,
> Out of politics, triumphs, battles, life, what at
>   last finally remains?
> When shows break up what but One's-Self is sure?
>   (*LG*, p. 448)

In a period of severe disenchantment inwardly, and nothing but the maddest chaos in the world around him, he feared he might personally disintegrate. He had reclaimed his vocation in the poems of 1859, but he was still not writing extensively or well. In his poems of the early 1860s he is blatantly conventional, and often he imitates other poets, as if seeking inspiration from the popular appeal of their verse. "Pioneers! O Pioneers!" celebrates the march of westward expansion as if civil war were not a serious threat (he eventually removed the poem from *Drum-Taps*, his book of Civil War poems, where it was wholly inappropriate). The poem's diction, sentiment, and meter echo Longfellow, and Whitman obviously wrote it to the over-loud accompaniment of "Hiawatha" dinning in his head:

> Raise the mighty mother mistress,
> Waving high the delicate mistress, over all the
>   starry mistress, (bend your heads all,)
> Raise the fang'd and warlike mistress, stern, impassive,
>   weapon'd mistress,
> Pioneers! O pioneers!

(11. 41–44)

On occasion in the 1860s, he imitated his earlier work, like "Out of the Cradle Endlessly Rocking," by creating dramatic characters in his poetry, but generally this poetry is sententious and trite. Among these attempts to produce a colloquy of voices, his most interesting experiment is an imitation of Browning in a dramatic monologue. "The Centenarian's Story" reveals a fruitful new direction for Whitman's free verse, for it includes lines that minimize his usual repetitiveness and omit the cumulative phrasing that suspends each line separately. These superb lines introduce a new rhythm:

> It sickens me yet, that slaughter!
> I saw the moisture gather in drops on the face
>   of the General.
> I saw how he wrung his hands in anguish.
>
> Meanwhile the British manoeuvr'd to draw us out
>   for a pitch'd battle,
> But we dared not trust the chances of a pitch'd
>   battle.
>
> We fought the fight in detachments,
> Sallying forth we fought at several points, but
>   in each the luck was against us,
> Our foe advancing, steadily getting the best of it,
>   push'd us back to the works on this hill,
> Till we turn'd menacing here, and then he left us.
>
> That was the going out of the brigade of the youngest
>   men, two thousand strong,
> Few return'd, nearly all remain in Brooklyn.
>
> That and here my General's first battle,
> No women looking on nor sunshine to bask in, it

did not conclude with applause,
Nobody clapp'd hands here then.

But in darkness in mist on the ground under a chill
    rain,
Wearied that night we lay foil'd and sullen,
While scornfully laugh'd many an arrogant lord off
    against us encamp'd,
Quite within hearing, feasting, clinking wineglasses
    together over their victory.

So dull and damp and another day,
But the night of that, mist lifting, rain ceasing,
Silent as a ghost while they thought they were
    sure of him, my General retreated.

I saw him at the river-side,
Down by the ferry lit by torches, hastening the
    embarcation.

                                          (11. 64–86)

Even though he sensitively heard Browning's prosody and could reproduce it in his own idiom, Whitman did not go on to perfect the fluidity
of colloquial speech that later poets, like Ezra Pound, developed from
his and Browning's examples. Whitman passed by this threshold to renewed innovative creativity even though he had the words in his mouth;
literary history records no clearer, sadder instance of a poet turning his
back on his genius to hang onto something buried in his old work.

   Apparently willing in the early 1860s to follow any crowd — other poets,
the gang at Pfaff's, or the military hysteria — Whitman wrote a number
of patriotic "reveille" poems to praise the vigor and purposefulness of
war. He became apologetic about them in later years, not only because
they are mediocre but mainly because their sentiments embarrassed him.
He wrote a retraction in 1871:

        Aroused and angry,
        I thought to beat the alarum, and urge relentless
            war;
        But soon my fingers fail'd me, my face droop'd,
            and I resign'd myself,
        To sit by the wounded and soothe them, or silently
            watch the dead.

                                          (*LG*, p. 309)

These lines indicate the direction Whitman followed to recover himself during the war years. He began to find the true voice of his later poetry when he started frequenting a Manhattan hospital in 1860 or 1861 to comfort sick and injured workmen. He was led to this not only by friendship for his usual crowd of stage drivers and carters; he was also fascinated by the hospital procedures and the operations, which he was permitted to watch. This more or less routine association with death soon came to objectify and confirm the poetic role he had redesigned for himself in "Out of the Cradle Endlessly Rocking." Among the wounds, the amputations, the fevers, the sobs, and the repeated deaths, Whitman steadied himself to look at the unbearable. It is this attitude of supreme fortitude in witnessing death that he adopts for the remainder of the war (and beyond it, in the better poems of his later years). It is also the way he spent the rest of the war years as a hospital nurse visiting soldiers in Washington, for Whitman suddenly cast off his "New York stagnation" in December 1862, and never again took up permanent residence in the city. He initially went to the battlefield to look for his brother George, who had been wounded; when he found him alive and well, Whitman nevertheless remained in Washington. He had at last left home for good, at the age of forty-three, though he made frequent visits and once came back to treat an illness for seven months. In Washington he took up an arduous routine as a volunteer hospital aide, comforting young soldiers in their pain, loneliness, and, often, their final agony; and in his poetry he traced the implications of "the low and delicious word death" that had awaited his full attention for the past three years. In responding to the Civil War, he extended the murmuring embrace of the sea-crone and the pathos of the wounded boy.

Most of the poems Whitman wrote during the war years were published first in 1865 as a separate volume entitled *Drum-Taps* and later incorporated into his fourth edition of *Leaves of Grass*, in 1867. His voice is sorrowful and compassionate as he grieves over losses that are tragic revelations, not just misfortunes. Suffering crystallizes reality, stripping away the delusions of victory, or defeat, of individuality in life or the fantasy of union with nature in death. He is kind toward all who suffer in the war, with the privileged intimacy that only calamities make possible. He is never provoked to moral judgment of North or South; he maintains strict neutrality over the inflammatory issues that drove the whole nation to civil war, tacitly dismissing them as trivial concerns. The definitive poems in *Drum-Taps* do not imply that liberal political principles are necessary expressions of human decency — even worth dying for — which is an extraordinary omission of a viewpoint Whitman vigorously upheld in earlier works. He appears indifferent to any particular social values. Or, to see it from what was possibly his perspective, he could no longer accept the brutalities of his nation as reflections of his inner life except as occasions to mourn. History had become a family disgrace.

In "The Wound-Dresser" he expressly draws the reader away from the chronicles of war and heroism — "I dwell not on soldiers' perils or soldiers' joys" — to enter a reverie that goes beyond reported, national experience. Like an old man remembering the terrible past, Whitman recounts without flinching his exposure to hospital gore. He forces himself to open door after door of forgotten things, as if steadying his memory to focus on the wounds. Conjuring up the past — that is, adopting the perspective of a "reminiscence" — has become his most effective tool for developing pity for his subject, partly because a reminiscence always looks at oneself. He watches himself maintain composure while his soul burns.

> On, on I go, (open doors of time! open hospital
>   doors!)
> The crush'd head I dress, (poor crazed hand tear
>   not the bandage away,)
> The neck of the cavalry-man with the bullet
>   through and through I examine,
> Hard the breathing rattles, quite glazed already
>   the eye, yet life struggles hard,
> (Come sweet death! be persuaded O beautiful
>   death!
> In mercy come quickly.)
>
> From the stump of the arm, the amputated hand,
> I undo the clotted lint, remove the slough,
>   wash off the matter and blood,
> Back on his pillow the soldier bends with curv'd
>   neck and sidefalling head,
> His eyes are closed, his face is pale, he dares
>   not look on the bloody stump,
> And has not yet look'd on it.
>
> I dress a wound in the side, deep, deep,
> But a day or two more, for see the frame all
>   wasted and sinking,
> And the yellow-blue countenance see.
>
> I dress the perforated shoulder, the foot with
>   the bullet-wound,
> Cleanse the one with a gnawing and putrid gangrene,
>   so sickening, so offensive,

While the attendant stands behind aside me holding
    the tray and pail.

I am faithful, I do not give out,
The fractur'd thigh, the knee, the wound in the
    abdomen,
These and more I dress with impassive hand, (yet
    deep in my breast a fire, a burning flame.)

                              (11. 39–58)

The shock-effect of so much misery around him narrows his vision onto
each small effort to endure pain. Even when Whitman assumes the
soldier's identity in many of the war poems in *Drum-Taps*, he expresses
no vindications of his cause, no bitterness about war's delusions, and
no hysteria over the violence — which is unusual for battlefield responses
to war, even in poetry. He concentrates on the pathos of death. The best
war poem in *Drum-Taps* concerns Whitman's vigil beside the body of his
fallen comrade. "Vigil Strange I Kept on the Field One Night" opens at
the moment his comrade falls wounded; the two men look at each other
with shocked eyes, and their helpless love passes through their fleeting
touch. The wound that is mortal for one man is immortal for the other.

Vigil strange I kept on the field one night;
When you my son and my comrade dropt at my side
    that day,
One look I but gave which your dear eyes return'd
    with a look I shall never forget,
One touch of your hand to mine O boy, reach'd up
    as you lay on the ground,
Then onward I sped in the battle, the even-contested
    battle,
Till late in the night reliev'd to the place at
    last again I made my way.

                              (11. 1–6)

Finding the body, Whitman begins his vigil without tears or words of
misery. Remorseful for having sped onward in his duty while leaving
the younger comrade to die alone, Whitman finds that the vigil is not
full of anguish but is "strange," "curious," "wondrous," "mystic," and
"sweet" — almost entirely enigmatic and revelatory. His mourning gives
him full title to father and mother and lover of the fallen boy, qualifying
him to take part in sacred acts of devotion.

Found you in death so cold dear comrade, found
    your body son of responding kisses, (never
    again on earth responding,)
Bared your face to the starlight, curious the
    scene, cool blew the moderate night-wind,
Long there and then in vigil I stood, dimly around
    me the battlefield spreading,
Vigil wondrous and vigil sweet there in the fragrant
    silent night,
But not a tear fell, not even a long-drawn sigh,
    long, long I gazed,
Then on the earth partially reclining sat by your
    side leaning my chin in my hands,
Passing sweet hours, immortal and mystic hours with
    you dearest comrade—not a tear, not a word,
Vigil of silence, love and death, vigil for you my
    son and my soldier,
As onward silently stars aloft, eastward new ones
    upward stole,
Vigil final for you brave boy, (I could not save
    you, swift was your death,
I faithfully loved you and cared for you living,
    I think we shall surely meet again,)
Till at latest lingering of the night, indeed just
    as the dawn appear'd,
My comrade I wrapt in his blanket, envelop'd well
    his form,
Folded the blanket well, tucking it carefully over
    head and carefully under feet,
And there and then and bathed by the rising sun,
    my son in his grave, in his rude-dug grave
    I deposited,
Ending my vigil strange with that, vigil of night
    and battle-field dim,
Vigil for boy of responding kisses, (never again on earth responding,)
Vigil for comrade swiftly slain, vigil I never forget,
    how as day brighten'd,
I rose from the chill ground and folded my soldier
    well in his blanket,
And buried him where he fell.

                                   (11. 7–26)

    The stark literalness of the concluding line puts an end to the suggestive atmosphere of luminous, animate night that expresses Whitman's inner spaciousness in the center of the poem. His sweet communion in the starlight occurs between traumatic events at the beginning and end: the abruptly dealt wound, the death look, and the brutally plain burial. These details occur as shocks, defining the limits of time and reality around the boundless sympathy (in the center of the poem) that reaches across death and upward to the stars. The return to the harsh fact of death underscores Whitman's new attitude that love never reaches its objects; it swells in the solitary heart, creating a cavern of voiceless grief and tenderness.

This poignant poem resembles Whitman's elegy on the death of Lincoln, "When Lilacs Last in the Dooryard Bloom'd," in which Whitman struggles to accept death with unsentimental fortitude. In the poem he vacillates between sore-hearted grieving over Lincoln (and all the dead) and writing a memorial poem, between absolute grief as a sensual experience and the poetic expression of grief that has been transformed into a special sensibility for living. The poem reactivates Whitman's old conflict over his truth or falsehood as a person who is defined by the imaginative sympathy that his poetry required. This issue was revived by his response to the traumatic experience of hearing about Lincoln's death and then disciplining himself to write about it. He was visiting at home in Brooklyn when General Lee surrendered and the end of the war was assured in early April 1865. On the morning of Easter Saturday, April 15, he read in the newspaper that the president had been assassinated the night before. His behavior over the next few days suggests a slow release of his immeasurable grief. At home he and his mother could say nothing to each other all day Saturday. Stunned and horrified, they read all the editions of the papers, which came out as frequently in those days as the hourly news, "and pass'd them silently to each other," he recalled.[6] He mingled a good deal with the silent New York crowds; and then, apparently on Sunday night, he returned to Washington. He did not go to see Lincoln's body lying in state in the White House or later in the Capitol. Flaring up again in his solitary grieving, his old conflict over his emotional authenticity reappears in Whitman's greatest Civil War poem as an obsession with guilt and self-justification.

Like the earlier poem about the fallen soldier, Whitman's personal vigil over the dead Lincoln is similarly framed by shocks of death that the mourner learns to accept as the ultimate reality. In the opening lines Whitman looks back to Lincoln's death and then in the same sentence jumps forward to the moment of writing to express his ongoing mourning. The poem maintains the present tense until its emotional climax, when Whitman suddenly resumes the past-tense narrative, in stanza 14. At that point, as he returns to the event, he has gained enough strength to face his complex response to Lincoln's death.

> When lilacs last in the dooryard bloom'd,
> And the great star early droop'd in the western
>   sky in the night,

I mourn'd, and yet shall mourn with ever-returning
    spring.

Ever-returning spring, trinity sure to me you bring,
Lilac blooming perennial and drooping star in the
    west,
And thought of him I love.

(11. 1–6)

In stanzas 2 and 3 the irony of death paralyzes him. He is locked in grief by the "harsh surrounding cloud that will not free my soul." Distraught that he is "helpless," he sees in the lovely vitality of April's lilacs the innocent beauty that must be made to express his pain. He breaks a sprig of lilac with its heart-shaped leaves, strong perfume, and delicate blossom to signify his stricken world. Intruding upon this mood as if from a distance, the song of a thrush is overheard in stanza 4. It does not call to Whitman; rather, it seems to pass along the edge of his attention. The thrush dwelling in seclusion and constantly warbling rekindles Whitman's purpose, but he remains transfixed by the spectacle of death spreading over the land. Lincoln's funeral train journeys through fields and orchards whose beauty cannot conceal the graves in all the earth. It passes through cities that are plunged into rites of mourning, where thousands of voices rise in "dirges pour'd around the coffin." Swept along with the public show of love for Lincoln, Whitman steps forward to place his sprig of lilac on the coffin.

In a parenthetical aside — a device that often indicates his most breathless, anxious utterance — he touches the coffin and immediately experiences a slight rush of recognition. He extends his love to all the dead, and he brings roses and lilies and more lilacs to cover the coffins. This outpouring of his abundance of devotion is more intense and more private than the thousands of "mournful voices of the dirges pour'd around the coffin." His gesture seems more personal and more delicate than theirs — the grief of crowds looks messy. As Whitman transforms Lincoln's death into a personal loss, his devotion echoes with the voice of the child in "As I Ebb'd with the Ocean of Life," who knew that his father would never embrace him. Like that child, Whitman tries to explain that his assertive action is a tender, not hostile, gesture toward *you and all*.

(Nor for you, for one alone,
Blossoms and branches green to coffins all I bring,
For fresh as the morning, thus would I chant a song
    for you O sane and sacred death.

All over bouquets of roses,
O death, I cover you over with roses and early
    lilies,
But mostly and now the lilac that blooms the first,
Copious I break, I break the sprigs from the bushes,
With loaded arms I come, pouring for you,
For you and the coffins all of you O death.)
(ll. 46–54)

He wants to see death as a comforter, not a destroyer of men; and this effort helps him to accept Lincoln's terrible remoteness in death. He gains sympathy for the heavy-heartedness that burdened Lincoln while he lived and now suggests a tragic inevitability about his death. In stanza 8 Whitman addresses the western star, acknowledging what it had long been trying to tell him about the woe that finally struck down Lincoln. Whitman in fact believed that the deepest element in Lincoln's character, as he explained later, "was sadness bordering on melancholy, touched by a philosophy, and that philosophy touched again by a humor, which saved him from the logical wreck of his powers.[7] This extraordinary empathy with Lincoln's melancholy leads to a reconciliation between the remote star and the forlorn mourner. Whitman speaks to the star like the shade of a troubled father, whose sorrow he now perceives, but whom he failed to understand.

O western orb sailing the heaven,
Now I know what you must have meant as a month
    since I walk'd,
As I walk'd in silence the transparent shadowy night,
As I saw you had something to tell as you bent to
    me night after night,
As you droop'd from the sky low down as if to my
    side, (while the other stars all look'd on,)
As we wander'd together the solemn night, (for
    something I know not what kept me from sleep,)
As the night advanced, and I saw on the rim of the
    west how full you were of woe,
As I stood on the rising ground in the breeze in
    the cool transparent night,
As I watch'd where you pass'd and was lost in the
    netherward black of night,

As my soul in its trouble dissatisfied sank, as
    where you sad orb,
Concluded, dropt in the night, and was gone.
                            (11. 55–65)

This expression of pained forgiveness suggests the willing but helpless
love of a child for a father whose sullenness holds unexplained meaning.
But the star left Whitman still dissatisfied, and his bruised resentment
of his father's abruptness endures in tones of hurt in the brusque phrasing
of the end line.

As my soul in its trouble dissatisfied sank, as
    where you sad orb,
Concluded, dropt in the night, and was gone.

There is a deeper grief he has yet to uncover — and he senses it. Steadily
the sound of the thrush arises again to urge him to conquer his uncontrollable distress, his failure to accept the naturalness and sweetness of
death; but he cannot give up his attachment to the dead man. He is
"detain'd" by the "lustrous star"; he does not know yet how to satisfy
his grief. In the following three stanzas he decks himself in perfumes and
decorates the grave with sentimental images of a serene nation. Then he
again hears the dolorous birdcall floating to him from a dim swamp; and
Whitman promises to relinquish the savoring of wounds that still detain
him, and to join in the "liquid and free and tender" song of the thrush.
An element of suspense gathers around Whitman's long-delayed
departure for the dusky swamp; his apparent reluctance to end this suffering suggests the avoidance of a sharper pain.

The climax occurs in stanza 14, when the poem suddenly shifts to the
past tense as Whitman recalls the shock of learning about Lincoln's death.
At the beginning of stanza 14 he is complacent in the midst of natural
beauty — "the large unconscious scenery of my land" — until he is struck
along with the entire land by the descending cloud of death.

— lo, then and there,
Falling upon them all and among them all, enveloping
    me with the rest,
Appear'd the cloud, appear'd the long black trail,
And I knew death, its thought, and the sacred knowledge
    of death.

Then with the knowledge of death as walking one
    side of me,
And the thought of death close-walking the other
    side of me,
And I in the middle as with companions, and as holding
    the hands of companions,
I fled forth to the hiding receiving night that
    talks not,
Down to the shores of the water, the path by the
    swamp in the dimness,
To the solemn shadowy cedars and ghostly pines so
    still.

(11. 116–125)

In these ambiguous lines the stricken poet is guided by his understanding of death as a part of experience ("the knowledge of death") as well as something to write about ("the thought of death"). He is led forward and also away by his companions, who hold his hands while he flees from the world to where no voice intrudes on him. In his bitterest line he describes his panic over being exposed both to crudely overweening sympathy and to blame: "I fled forth to the hiding receiving night that talks not." Whitman's remorse was tied to his belief that anyone he loved must leave him. And when tragedy came, his fear was again confirmed: He *knew* it all along, and that painful prescience indicates his sense of guilt. But in the further link between Lincoln's melancholy and his own father's remoteness, Whitman had to reexperience what he feared and hated in both men, who commanded love but never responded. Lincoln's sensibility made him the special target of Whitman's ambivalent hope that his father would embrace him or die.

Wretched enough to want to die himself in the swamp, Whitman at last translates the thrush's song of praise for death, turning to his "dark mother" for comfort and expecting death to soothe him with maternal tenderness. Again caroling like a bird, he hopes to be "gratefully nestling" close to his mother; he is ready to be gathered into "the sureenwinding arms of cool-enfolding death." Oddly, the long carol is flat and static; and no matter how attentively one reads it, its effect is much like a passage one skips over. The death carol so blandly takes easy comfort in the thought of death that there seems to be no need for relief from living. The lapse of feeling in the carol tends to confirm the view that Whitman's underlying goal in the poem was to set the record straight, to make sense out of his complicated reaction to Lincoln's death, and to gain the peace not of forgetfulness but of exoneration. For this purpose, it is not Mother Death — who loves him with blame in her heart — but the nation of mourners who must proclaim his innocence.

After the song of the thrush, Whitman has a vision that helps him understand the horror on the battlefield: "My sight that was bound in my eyes unclosed, / As to long panoramas of visions." In stanza 15 he sees all of the other deaths in the war. The war has transformed the nation because the vast grief of it has awakened every heart. America is not to be henceforth represented by charming pictures of life-as-usual, which he earlier sought, in stanza 11, to put in Lincoln's tomb. (That coldly unheeding memorial better reflects the family's constrained response to his father's death, when household life went on as usual and Whitman rejoiced over the first publication of his poems.) Now every household grieves, and the great upheaval of national suffering defines as well as unites the mourners. The surviving Americans — "the wife and the child and the musing comrade" — reveal their spiritual depth and sweetness of soul as they forever suffer.

> While my sight that was bound in my eyes unclosed,
> As to long panoramas of visions.
> And I saw askant the armies,
> I saw as in noiseless dreams hundreds of battle-flags,
> Borne through the smoke of the battles and pierc'd
>   with missiles I saw them,
> And carried hither and yon through the smoke, and
>   torn and bloody,
> And at last but a few shreds left on the staffs,
>   (and all in silence,)
> And the staffs all splinter'd and broken.
>
> I saw battle-corpses, myriads of them,
> And the white skeletons of young men, I saw them,
> I saw the debris and debris of all the slain soldiers
>   of the war,
> But I saw they were not as was thought,
> They themselves were fully at rest, they suffer'd not,
> The living remained and suffer'd, the mother suffer'd,
> And the wife and the child and the musing comrade
>   suffer'd,
> And the armies that remained suffer'd.
>
> (11. 169–184)

The expansion of his grief into the dimensions of history removes the politics and ideology from the Civil War. No principle was redeemed, no cause upheld, no side victorious or defeated. It was a family tragedy, and the pity of it drowns all other issues. Everyone mourns; no one is blamed. In this enlightened perspective, cleansed of petty judgments, there is no longer any reason for Whitman to die in a swamp. In stanza 16 he emerges to speak again of Lincoln, and he concludes the poem by turning away from the lilacs, the star, and the bird, which were his "retrievements out of the night" — his recollections of the trauma he experienced. Now he accepts Lincoln's death as the epitome of the whole war, and like other casualties there was nothing willed or intended about it. It was inevitable, considering the circumstances. And that particular, unstated point of murder is what he finally succeeds in denying. He never acknowledges the assassination. He writes the entire poem as if Lincoln died naturally, worn out by the war, even suggesting that Lincoln knew he was declining because of an inner sorrow or illness. All the cruelty and terror surrounding the assassination are excluded, because the grandeur he felt in his guilt kept him from externalizing the crime. He is relieved and uplifted by mourning, for in a hopelessly torn world sorrow is the only avenue to closeness.

> Passing, I leave thee lilac with heart-shaped
>   leaves,
> I leave thee there in the door-yard, blooming,
>   returning with spring.
>
> I cease from my song for thee,
> From my gaze on thee in the west, fronting the
>   west, communing with thee,
> O comrade lustrous with silver face in the night.
>
> Yet each to keep and all, retrievements out of
>   the night,
> The song, the wondrous chant of the gray-brown bird,
> And the tallying chant, the echo arous'd in my soul,
> With the lustrous and drooping star with the countenance
>   full of woe,
> With the holders holding my hand nearing the call
>   of the bird,
> Comrades mine and I in the midst, and their memory
>   ever to keep, for the dead I loved so well,
> For the sweetest, wisest soul of all my days and
>   lands—and this for his dear sake,
> Lilac and star and bird twined with the chant of
>   my soul,
> There in the fragrant pines and the cedars dusk
>   and dim.

(11. 193–206)

Treating Lincoln's assassination as a death in the family, he reduced the entire Civil War to a domestic scale — and that, in fact, is how he chose to see current history. He is compassionate toward all who suffer, and is never provoked to moral judgment of one side or the other. His only verse expressing indignation over the outrage of Lincoln's assassination is a trivial, four-line epitaph, "This Dust Was Once a Man," in which he denounces "the foulest crime in history known in any land or age" (*LG*, p. 339). No other line in *Leaves of Grass* suggests that Lincoln's death resulted from malice in individuals or society at that time. In a minor prose piece written many years later and delivered several times as a lecture to augment his income, Whitman treats the death of Lincoln as a murder, and even adds the impression that he personally witnessed the shooting at Ford's Theater.[8] But in the poems about the Civil War, even though the subject is national experience, he does not weigh the values of democracy and equality that so concerned him ten years earlier. Whitman perceived the Civil War as a family conflict that reaffirmed and intensified family unity, but did not introduce new political conditions or alter the social composition of the nation. The issues and consequences of the war were less visible to him than the reflection it gave of a single consciousness of national identity — that is, of *nationality*. "I have myself, in my thought, deliberately come to unite the whole conflict, both sides, the South and North, really into One," he wrote, "and to view it as a struggle going on within One Identity.... What is any Nation, after all— and what is a human being—but a struggle between conflicting, paradoxical, opposing elements—and they themselves and their most violent contest, important parts of that One Identity, and of its development?"[9] From an empyrean perspective this may seem true enough, but there are more humane ways to view the war that would admit reasons for averting, beginning, or ending it at any point in the struggle. He was all for ending it early because he was repelled by the casualties of the war, but he never felt that the war represented anything important except the convulsions of union. This narrowing of vision weakened his poetry; it also made him insensitive in his advancing age to the moral commitments of other people who more clearly differentiated between public wrongs and their private griefs.

Because of his indifference to the issues, he appeared conservative to his generally radical friends in Washington, particularly in the matters of Abolition and Reconstruction. Though he opposed slavery, he was in no hurry to scrap the practice where it could be safely and usefully contained; and he had no impatient indignation for the sake of blacks. He held to his opinions through endless arguments during his ten years in Washington, and these opinions played a part in the collapse of the best friendships he ever enjoyed.

In Washington Whitman was the center of a small circle of literary friends who shared the intense camaraderie that he had always wanted. In the household of William and Ellen (Nelly) O'Connor he found the daily company of strong-willed, intelligent, sophisticated, educated people who valued his work, upheld its ideals, and adored him personally. The O'Connors were "my understanders, my lovers...my family," he told Traubel passionately when he compared the O'Connors to his own family that had failed to appreciate him. But the murky conflation of *lovers* and *family* brought out complications of his submerged past that finally burst beyond language. The story of his friendship with the O'Connors repeats the story in his poems as the material disintegrated back into the disorder of actual events. The intensity of the love that flowed in both directions, between Whitman and the O'Connors, stirred the three of them to a conflict of overwrought longings and inhibitions that precipitated the angry dissolution of the O'Connors' marriage, directly followed by Whitman's stroke and a severe depression. The argument that divided the three of them was ostensibly over slavery, but this concealed a deeper struggle about sex and family roles. Their ambiguous triangle dramatizes the sense of family life that possessed Whitman's imagination from the earliest development of his creativity. When his involvement with the O'Connors threatened not merely to fulfill forbidden dreams but even to invade his poetic realm and deprive him of his singular inwardness, he again chose to save his inner self.

Whitman had first met O'Connor briefly in Boston in 1860 when Whitman answered Charles Eldridge's offer to publish a third edition of *Leaves of Grass*. Whitman was instantly struck by O'Connor's vitality and magnetism; looking back on their first meeting, he recalled his flush of excitement over O'Connor, who "was personally and intellectually the most attractive man I had ever met." In the same memoir, which was written to preface a volume of O'Connor's posthumously published tales and essays, Whitman reconstructs his early attraction and the early signs of trouble, though he does not mention his later rift with O'Connor.

> As I saw and knew him then, in his 29th year...he was a gallant, handsome, gay-hearted, fine-voiced, glowing-eyed man; lithe-moving on his feet, of healthy and magnetic atmosphere and presence, and the most welcome company in the world. He was a thorough-going anti-slavery believer, speaker and writer, (doctrinaire,) and though I took a fancy to him from the first, I remember I fear'd his ardent abolitionism — was afraid it would probably keep us apart. (I was a decided and out-spoken anti-slavery believer myself, then and always; but shy'd from the extremists, the red-hot fellows of those times.)[10]

Whitman met both Eldridge and O'Connor again in Washington in December 1862, when he needed assistance in locating his wounded brother George. Eldridge's publishing firm had gone bankrupt, and the war had drawn both men separately to Washington, where as government clerks they continued their friendship. When Whitman decided to stay in Washington, it was partly in response to this opportunity for new friendship. He moved into the same rooming house with the O'Connors and took his meals in their apartment. It was from this center of home-life that Whitman with unflagging energy carried out his grueling work in the hospitals. When the tenants of the rooming house were required to move, Whitman took a one-room hovel and adopted a style of shocking penury — copying his mother, who was then living in the basement of her own house and eating stewed tomatoes while she wrote to Walt to complain about the rest of the family. Whitman centered his life around the O'Connor household; as Eldridge recalled, "We met at O'Connor's house every night for months at a time with hardly a break, and we talked of everything that the human mind could conceive."[11] The O'Connors had parties on holidays, and Eldridge and Whitman also shared Sunday dinner with them. During their endless talks O'Connor defended Edgar Allan Poe's writings, the significance of Victor Hugo, Bacon's authorship of "Shakespeare's" plays, and the natural equality of blacks. The group toyed with founding a new periodical to be called The Pathfinder, alluding to James Fenimore Cooper's tale of adventure and allegiance between a young frontiersman and his Indian companion.

Whitman was enthralled and overwhelmed by O'Connor's forcefulness. The man's fiery, voluble, and generous temperament roused Walt's admiration, which could still be heard in his idealizing descriptions of O'Connor in his talks with Traubel.[12] William was like "a torrent," "an avalanche," more vast than "twenty thousand Niagaras"; he was "a constant marvel...like the sun every morning, like the stars every night." The expression of his opinions, aversions, and sympathies "resembles a natural law: he is beyond appeal: he delivers himself without apologies: he kills and saves, mercilessly, gently." His literary knowledge and brilliance were "infinitely comprehensive"; in short, "William could not do even the comparatively innocent things without the air, the authority, of a sovereign will." He was also turbulent, moody, "hypochondriacal." He often plunged into weeks of silence: "Depression! that is O'Connor!" O'Connor's combination of commanding vitality and withdrawn vulnerability made him doubly attractive to Whitman.

In his eyes, O'Connor was also exquisitely refined and beautiful. In matters of taste, William "was gifted beyond us all: was sensitive in the last degree to beauty." The man's air of loveliness attracted Whitman to the very movements of O'Connor's body: "He was one of the most graceful of men: agile, easy: yet also virile, vigorous, enough. William came along the street this way...I can liken it to nothing but the movements of a beautiful deer — a fawn: his body swung along with such strength, his step was so light, his bearing was so superbly free and defiant." Whitman was dazzled by O'Connor the way most men are dazzled by a woman.

O'Connor was wonderful also because he had an exceptionally keen literary sensibility, which he used to help Whitman perfect his poems. He cared about the finest points of Whitman's poetic style, and he made Whitman pay attention to polishing details that would increase the precision and subtlety of his lines. O'Connor "would fly into a fury over my literary sins — would give me hell about some comma I did use or some comma I didn't use."[13] Under O'Connor's watchful eye Whitman completed the first systematic, comprehensive revisions of his poetry. The results of these efforts appear in the so-called Workshop Edition, the fourth edition of *Leaves of Grass*, published in 1867, which shows Whitman's effort on nearly every page to improve his phrasing and to give greater coherence to the book as a record of a whole life. Some of the revisions are masterful, as, for instance, the improved first stanza of "Starting from Paumanok," a poem Whitman had haplessly struggled with for many years. Other changes included the deletion of those poems that announced he would abandon poetry to go away with a lover. Finding at last a comrade in creativity, Whitman removed those earlier expressions of rebellion against the isolating and undermining effects of writing poems.

While under O'Connor's literary guidance Whitman got into trouble with censorious authorities, and O'Connor loyally and instantly came to his aid. Whitman was marking his revisions into an earlier edition of *Leaves*, and this "Blue Book" of planned changes was discovered in his desk at his bureaucratic job in the Department of Interior (an aptly named place that O'Connor found for Whitman to hold a sinecure). Shocked by the explicit sexuality of such poems, Secretary Harlan dismissed Whitman in June 1865. O'Connor stood ready to spend his energies and his meager fortune to defend Whitman's work. O'Connor immediately helped him obtain another government post, and then undertook to denounce the cabinet secretary who had found *Leaves of Grass* obscene and had cashiered the author. O'Connor's pamphlet, *The Good Gray Poet*, which he published at his own expense the following January, fanned a public controversy over artistic freedom, the merit of *Leaves of Grass*, and the integrity of Whitman's character; O'Connor's spirited defense surrounded the poet in clouds of obfuscating notoriety and idolization for decades. O'Connor then sought out opportunities to review the new *Leaves*, and he worked steadily to make the poems prevail in the spiritual experience of mankind. In 1869 he again publicly championed Whitman, now called by some The Bad Gray Poet. He was also active at that time in promoting Whitman's reception among the Rossetti circle in England.

His constant enthusiasm and brilliant daring on Whitman's behalf made O'Connor a dream come true — just as Emerson had once seemed to be, but better. O'Connor was Whitman's masculine ideal, the very Soul of his poet, his muse, his loyal comrade, his intelligent and fiery defender, and from the first stages of their long friendship, he was also his tender and beautiful lover. The love between the two men was charged with sexual feelings that made their communications electric with suggestiveness. Their erotic response to each other was further heightened and complicated by Nelly's equally strong erotic involvement with Whitman, toward whom she was enticingly, soothingly maternal, suggesting a sexually roused counterpart to his mother. The most intricate and most consequential romantic involvement in Whitman's adult life needs yet to be fully recognized in this welter of sensitive love and displaced passions among three emotionally deprived idealists who came together in the upheaval of war. Against Washington's brutal chaos, they fashioned an imaginative world of tenderness for one another, and then they suffered for their temerity.

At one point in 1864, when Whitman was forced by illness and exhaustion from his hospital work to return to Brooklyn to recuperate, the O'Connors were desolated by his absence. They had lost an infant son shortly before they met Whitman, who noted in his memoir that their sense of parental loss was raw: "O'C. was yet feeling serious about it." Apparently it remained memorable to Whitman too, who would have heard in that death an echo of his own family's history. Both William and Nelly wrote self-revealing, affectionate letters to Whitman during his seven-month absence. In William's first letter he writes, "Many thoughts of you have come to me since you went away, and sometimes it has been lonely and a little like death. Particularly at evening when you used to come in." He speculates enticingly over the life they will lead when they are reunited.

> I wonder what the future for us is to be. Shall we triumph over obscurities and obstacles and emerge to start the Path-finder, or whatever the name of it is to be? I wonder if it is so written on the iron leaf. Shall you live to publish many great poems amidst recognition and tumults of applause? Shall I live to write my Shakespeare book and a score of gorgeous romances? Or shall we never meet, never work together, never start any Pathfinder, never do anything but fade out into death, frustrated, lost in oblivion?[14]

By spinning out the uncertain alternatives of glory or oblivion, O'Connor certainly knew how to mesmerize Whitman. O'Connor elaborated his loneliness into a friendship of apocalyptic dimensions, and his fanciful musings over the future invite a pledge of steadfastness from Whitman, who recognized the invitation but responded with reserve: "as to the future & as to our meeting again, I have no doubt we shall meet again & have good times."[15]

Three days after William wrote, Nelly described her loneliness even more strongly.

> It will be two weeks to-morrow since you left us, and I have missed you terribly every minute of the time. I think I never in my life felt so wholly blue and unhappy about any one's going away as I did, and have since, about your going. I began to be really superstitious I felt so badly. I did not think that you were going to die, but I could not possibly overcome the feeling that our dear and pleasant circle was broken, and it seemed to me that we four should not be together any more as we have been.... Ah! Walt, I don't believe other people need you as much as we do. I am *sure* they don't need you as much as *I* do.[16]

Both letters toll with forebodings that were sure to make Whitman feel anxious over possibly not seeing the O'Connors again, and the expressions of insecurity in love and home life would draw him further into their family. Nelly's sweetly drawn distinction indicates that she and William appealed to Whitman's love according to their separate needs. Perhaps they were jealously competitive. Nelly could be more overtly dependent, but William could be entertaining through colorful descriptions of friends and incidents in Washington, which give amusing proof of his constant thoughts of Walt.[17] When Whitman was ready to return to Washington, William wrote that he was busying himself to find a government post for him, and that the family had missed him all through the recent holidays of Thanksgiving and Christmas (1864).[18]

O'Connor dwells on the insufficiency of his many expressions of love and esteem for Whitman, apologizing that he can never say enough or say exactly the right things. After his praise in *The Good Gray Poet*, which even Whitman's detractors called a polemical literary monograph unparalleled in America, O'Connor told Whitman that he meant more in his heart than he had said. Even this ardent support fell short of his true feelings for Whitman as a poet, O'Connor pointed out in a letter about the progress of his defense: "But oh, Walt, the literary shortcomings of it oppress me. It is not the thing that should be said of your book — not the thing that it is in even me to say — as I feel. However."[19] It is implied that Whitman will know, and that anyway those feelings need to be left unsaid.

The protestations from both O'Connors grew more fervid and provocative during the late 1860s when William visited Whitman in Brooklyn and met Walt's mother. Whitman later wrote to tell him what a warm impression he had made. O'Connor's reply includes some coyly flirtatious posturing: "Your letter was very sweet. I think a young girl finding herself beloved or admired by some one unsuspected before, must feel as I did when I read how the household thought of me. But I didn't lay myself out at all, as you say, and, moreover, the evening I was there I had a shocking headache."[20] This girlishness, even to the point of feigning the vapors, suggests that Whitman was not merely projecting his unconscious wishes when he discerned "a fawn" in O'Connor's beautiful body. When Whitman again visited his mother the next year, the O'Connor household awaited his return with alluring expressions of longing. This time Nelly writes like a betrothed girl: "Dear Walt, we long for you, William sighs for you, and I feel as if a large part of myself were out of the city. I shall give you a good big kiss when you come, so depend upon it. My love to your good noble mother, whom I shall some day know. Kiss her for me—and tell her that I love her boy Walt."[21] The phrase "so depend upon it" means: you mustn't not let me.

While Nelly seems determined to win Walt's love for herself, William with flirtatious whimsy excludes Nelly from his comradeship with Walt. Perhaps they were vying to overreach each other in demonstrations of affection for their friend, or perhaps there was now a more serious rivalry over Whitman's love. The O'Connors' marriage was already severely strained by their disagreement over William's restless ambition to write and Nelly's insistence that he remain in government service. According to her niece, Nelly's stubborn will destroyed O'Connor's genius and their marriage.[22] Nelly turned to Whitman with a seductiveness that was less humorous, more plaintive, and more explicit than William's. Her love became insistent and sexual when she wrote to Whitman from her sister's house in Providence, Rhode Island, where she was staying for a time, possibly in a temporary estrangement from her husband. Her letter of November 20, 1870, invites Walt to declare the love that she knows he feels for her — her conviction that she knows his true feelings is evident in her insistence — and she urges him to take advantage of this special opportunity for them to be together.

> Dear Walt,
>   My very dear friend — it is good to feel so assured of one's love as not to need to express it, & it is very good to know that one's love is never doubted or questioned, & for these

reasons it is I am sure that we do not write to each other. I always know that you know that I love you all the time, even though we should never meet again, my feeling could never change, and I am *sure* that you know it as well as I do. I do flatter myself too, that *you* care for *me*, — not as I love you, because you are great and strong, and more sufficient unto yourself than any woman can be, — besides you have the great outflow of your pen which saves you from the need of personal love as one feels it who has no such resource. You could not afford to love other than as the Gods love; that is to love *every body*, but no one enough to be made unhappy, or to lose your balance. You know that Hector Tyndale was always preaching that to us, to be like the Gods. But however it is with you, it is very good sometimes for me to try to tell those that are very dear to me how I like them. And ever since I left home I have had it in my heart to write you, — but it has been postponed, waiting for the more fitting time. It is only when I am away from you that I am conscious of how deeply you have influenced my life, my thoughts, my feelings, my views — *my self* in fact, in every way, you seem to have permeated my whole being. And knowing you as intimately as I do I find myself constantly wondering and thinking how such or such a thing seems to you, what your ideas are in relation to this or that.

I find too that the estimate in which persons hold you is a sort of test of them to me all the time. . . .More than all your poems, more than all you ever can write, *you* are to me; yet they were very much to me before I knew you. It is good to have my love for them sounded by knowing you, and finding my feeling and thought about you justified. I have sometimes suffered very deeply, but I feel that I have been dealt very kindly by, and had more than fullest compensation in the great privilege of knowing you, and being permitted to be with you as I have. I hope that the good angels who take care of us will for long, long yet spare us to each other. And you must be very good and come often to see us, you must not neglect the golden opportunity of letting me love you and see you all that is possible. I think that I must have been very good at some time to have deserved such a blessing.

Very soon I hope to see you now, very soon.[23]

After describing her feelings for Whitman, Nelly adds an odd postscript that again, indirectly, invites Whitman's confession of love. She includes a newspaper clipping of the final diary entry of a man who froze to death in a mountain pass, and she pointedly relates his loneliness to Whitman's solitude.

It is such a scene, he alone in that mountain pass with no hope
of escape and the snow falling in fearful quantities. It is one
of the *loneliest* pictures that I ever conceived. As I read it I
thought of you.

Good by again.

With love Nelly

Whitman's emotional temperature at this moment was nowhere near
freezing; it was raised very high, as Nelly evidently intuited, though she
mistook the meaning of his excitement. Nelly's letter implies that
Whitman has been silent because he has restrained his love for her, and
on this assumption she coaxes him to come forward at last as her lover.
The "golden opportunity" that she says is now at hand never led to an
affair, as far as anyone knows, but her invitation to engage in a romance
with his best friend's wife indicates that for a long time before this letter
Whitman and the O'Connors had been living in a hothouse atmosphere
of compromising attentions among the three of them. Whitman may have
been drawn into an exclusive sympathy with the charming and jealous
Nelly, but he was more ardently attracted to William, who trained all his
powerful glamour on Whitman's vulnerable heart. In the half-suppressed
erotic confusion of their friendship, Whitman's sexual desires suddenly
soared into misdirected release, which ironically was safer in that dangerous situation. In the months preceding Nelly's letter Whitman found
himself fighting down unwelcome homosexual desires for Peter Doyle,
a lonely young companion who for four years had been like a son to
Whitman. In the summer of 1870, Whitman had to make vehement
resolutions to maintain his sexual rectitude. His notebook shows him con-
quering an upsurge of "adhesiveness" toward Doyle, whose initials he
encodes as 16(P) 4(D). Along with underlinings and printer's marks that
he added for emphasis, Whitman changed the pronouns from masculine
to feminine.[24]

> REMEMBER WHERE I AM MOST WEAK, & most lacking. Yet
> always preserve a kind spirit & demeanor to 16. But PURSUE
> HER NO MORE.
> . . .
> It is IMPERATIVE, that I obviate & remove myself (& my orbit) at
> all hazards from this incessant enormous & PERTURBATION
> . . .
> TO GIVE UP ABSOLUTELY & for good, from this present
> hour, this FEVERISH, FLUCTUATING, useless undignified pur-
> suit of 164—too long, (much too long) persevered in,—so humili-
> ating—It must come at last & had better come now now—(It can-
> not possibly be a success)

LET THERE FROM THIS HOUR BE NO FALTERING, NO
GETTING [word erased] at all henceforth, (NOT ONCE, under
any circumstances)—avoid seeing her, or meeting her, or any talk
or explanations—or ANY MEETING WHATEVER, FROM THIS
HOUR FORTH, FOR LIFE.

After these confessions, Whitman added general admonishments, possibly later in the summer.

> Depress the adhesive nature
>
> _____
>
> It is in excess—making life a torment
>
> _____
>
> All this diseased, feverish disproportionate
> adhesiveness

   Although it is never safe to explain or to discount anyone's sexual be-
devilment, Whitman's desperate self-reviling sounds off-key. He had
spent the hospital years indulging in similar sentimental attachments to
young soldiers, and mooning over them in affectionate letters after they
left Washington. The boys were his pets, darlings, lovers, and dear sons.
He was hurt and demoralized by any sign of coldness, like that he received
from one Tom Sawyer. These erotically heightened friendships may have
been substitutes for an active sexual life or perhaps they show his fanciful
overvaluing of superficial affairs. Whitman exaggerated their romantic
complexity in his constant worrying about the return of his affections.
But his homosexual excitement never wrung him with fear and loathing
over his "perturbation." His troubled feelings over Doyle lasted for only
a few months in the middle of a relationship that was generally placid
for years before and after his turmoil. It seems clear that the crisis arose
in response to the strain in the O'Connor household. By midsummer of
1870 he found himself once more in the role of a guilt-ridden son enjoying
an unwarranted preeminence in the home of parents who were virtually
estranged from each other, and who were (this time) *both* overtly
showering him with their possessive love.
   One response to the situation was to get away frequently, just as he
resolved in the notebook to do. He had reasonable excuses for going away,
since he was no longer the robust and indefatigable man who had spent
the war years nursing the wounded; he was now bothered by chronic
dizziness and a general loss of stamina. Over the next two years he took
several leaves of absence from his clerkship for no overtly compelling
reasons, sometimes hiring a substitute for his duties in the attorney
general's office while he stayed for weeks at a time in Brooklyn. This way

of dealing with the crisis seems to have reduced immediately his distress over Peter Doyle, but Whitman nevertheless continued to flee and return to both his families.

He completed "Passage to India" in midsummer of 1870 when his perturbation over Doyle was at its peak, and the poem, like the notebook, indicates that he badly wanted to get away from the disturbance within him, the strong sexual compulsion that he repudiated. In the poem Whitman longs to escape to a mythical innocence of mind in which the joys of companionship will be safely beyond reproach. His homosexual desires are generalized into the yearnings for affection that have motivated all people throughout history, and the poem is essentially a prayer for deliverance from the painful restlessness of human strivings. He expects that the future will reproduce the primal paradise from which mankind wanders lost and confused, drawn magnetically forward through bewilderment and despair by the lure of recoverable innocent affection. In the opening lines he proclaims that he was always inclined toward the past, which is now speeding forward, ready to be recovered.

> Singing my days,
> Singing the great achievements of the present,
> Singing the strong light works of engineers,
> Our modern wonders, (the antique ponderous Seven
>   outvied,)
> In the Old World the east the Suez canal,
> The New by its mighty railroad spann'd,
> The seas inlaid with eloquent gentle wires;
> Yet first to sound, and ever sound, the cry
>   with thee O soul,
> The Past! the Past! the Past!
>
> The Past—the dark unfathom'd retrospect!
> The teeming gulf—the sleepers and the shadows!
> The past—the infinite greatness of the past!
> For what is the present after all but a growth
>   out of the past?
> (As a projectile form'd, impell'd, passing a
>   certain line, still keeps on,
> So the present, utterly form'd, impell'd by
>   the past.)
>
>   (ll. 1–15)

In the argument of the poem Whitman foresees that a great poet will someday complete the work of all the voyagers toward India, the origin and the goal of every human endeavor, for the poet with his revelations of the heart will encircle the globe with sympathy. Whitman implicitly looks back over his own early poetic journeys in which he championed the "Affection that will not be gainsay'd"; his restless quest will ultimately be vindicated.

> All affection shall be fully responded to, the
>   secret shall be told,
> All these separations and gaps shall be taken up
>   and hook'd and link'd together,
> The whole earth, this cold, impassive, voiceless
>   earth, shall be completely justified.
>   (11. 108–110)

But Whitman takes early leave from the march of mankind; he cannot wait until the millennium to see his purpose fulfilled. He eagerly begins his own passage to safe haven by launching out with his soul in a spirit of innocent jubilation. The lover who embraced him in his youthful, solitary ecstasies returns as his chosen final companion. Nearly drunk with happiness over the recovery of companionship, Whitman gives himself to an epic adventure of soul mates voyaging toward apocalyptic destinies.

> O Soul, repressless, I with thee and thou with me,
> Thy circumnavigation of the world begin,
> Of man, the voyage of his mind's return,
> To reason's early paradise,
> Back, back to wisdom's birth, to innocent intuitions,
> Again with fair creation.
>
> O we can wait no longer,
> We too take ship O soul,
> Joyous we too launch out on trackless seas,
> Fearless for unknown shores on waves of ecstasy
>   to sail,
> Amid the wafting winds, (thou pressing me to thee,
>   I thee to me, O soul,)
> Caroling free, singing our song of God,
> Chanting our chant of pleasant exploration.
>
> With laugh and many a kiss,
> (Let others deprecate, let others weep for sin,
>   remorse, humiliation,)
> O soul thou pleasest me, I thee.
>   (11. 169–184)

This rapturous description of journeying to a symbolic India renowned in history and literature was not inspired by sickly Doyle's small promise of ecstasy. This glamour was always O'Connor's. The love between these two men who each commanded vast imaginative powers to comprehend the whole earth reawakened Whitman's dream of perfect soul-sharing. Lying beyond India, heaven itself still promises to reward desire.

> As fill'd with friendship, love complete, the
> Elder Brother found,
> The Younger melts in fondness in his arms.
> (11. 222–223)

The romance of Cooper's Pathfinder and his natural companion lies in the background of "Passage to India," just as it appeared in Whitman's plans to edit a new periodical with O'Connor. But Whitman's dream of perfect sharing was shattered by a violent quarrel that evoked his profoundest dread of domestic rivalry. In August 1872 Whitman and O'Connor quarreled over the constitutional amendment to ensure voting rights for blacks in the upcoming presidential election. Offended by Whitman's stubborn conservatism, O'Connor denounced him. Whitman later complained to Traubel that on the antislavery question O'Connor "would go for — go for me in the fiercest way — denounce me — appear to regard me as being negligent, as shirking a duty."[25] O'Connor's language could have been mild, but no other charge, however phrased, would have seemed more unfair to the devotedly dutiful Whitman. It was the kind of complaint about "shirking a duty" that his father had often held against him, and so there was a deep bruise in Whitman on this score. Further, it recalled arguments with his father on the subject of slavery, but now Whitman was unfairly cast in his father's illiberal role. Whitman erupted with indignation. They both said brutal things to each other, for Whitman's temper was as abusive and volcanic as O'Connor's. Nelly jumped in to take Whitman's side, and this egregious disloyalty goaded both men to wound each other. Whitman may have remarked on O'Connor's own negligence and "shirking" of Nelly, or in some other way may have asserted a superior sexual role. It appears that O'Connor felt that he had suddenly lost his wife and his best friend; and leaving them to face each other he stormed out of their lives. He did not return to Nelly for sixteen years, until he fell mortally ill in 1888. For ten years he also shunned Whitman, who was horrified and ready to make up the next day. They finally resumed an amiable literary correspondence in 1882, but they never discussed their estrangement and they never saw each other again.

This violent and unresolved quarrel left Whitman to face his worst feelings about himself, for here was the uncontrollable passion and devastation he had always feared. The failure of this over-charged friendship unleashed the flood of Whitman's guilt, and for a while he went down in it. Overcome with remorse and still outraged at O'Connor's reaction, Whitman sank into a depression and contemplated his own death. He made a will in October 1872, and sent it to his brother George, perhaps as a sign of his despair. His emotional state contributed to his collapse in January 1873, when he suffered a paralytic stroke. He had been plagued with headaches during much of his time in Washington, and the strain of the past few months brought on a massive attack. A sympathetic physician who attended him concluded at the time that his emotional state precipitated the stroke, as Whitman later recalled to Traubel: "Without having any particular theory to account for the breaking-up [the stroke], I can, I think see pretty clearly what brought it about: my good Doctor— Doctor Drinkard—(oh! he was very good—I think the best Doctor that ever was!)—Doctor Drinkard seemed to understand me well: he charged it to the emotional disturbances to which I was subjected at that time: I do not know that he exactly formulated it that way—laid it down as indisputable—but he looked on that as the one sufficient explaining cause."[26] Evidently, Whitman was inclined to accept this explanation without dispute.

When troubles come, they...for Whitman also, they came like the furies, for he was beset by other shocks in 1873. In February his beloved sister-in-law, Mattie, died in St. Louis, where she and Jeff had moved after living with Mrs. Whitman in Brooklyn for nine years. In May the ultimate blow fell: His mother died in Camden, New Jersey, soon after she arrived to live in George's household. In Whitman's depressed state, he could not possibly have differentiated these disasters that fell in rapid succession, swiftly eroding his home life. In Whitman's mind, they must have seemed connected and overlapping, consequences of his turbulent deeds. Still lame after his stroke and bereft of the four people dearest to him, Whitman sat by his mother's body, rocking in grief and crashing his heavy cane again and again on the floor through the night. He was entering the bitterest period of his life — and O'Connor angrily withheld his help and sympathy.

Before he eventually recovered his emotional and physical strength, Whitman spent years in "unspeakable" anguish; he survived another stroke in 1875, but did not begin to regain his strength and morale until early May 1876, when he went off for a prolonged stay in the country at the Stafford farm and enjoyed his happiest summer in many years. The turning point coincides exactly with a gesture of esteem from O'Connor. Though they were still estranged, O'Connor wrote a letter to the *New York Tribune,* printed on April 22, 1876, in which he again defended Whitman from calumny in the American press. O'Connor's article "Walt Whitman. Is He Persecuted?" joined in the outcries coming from England in March that the United States stupidly neglected its greatest poet. The New York literary press thought otherwise, and said so in shallow rationalizations of its prejudice. When Burroughs and O'Connor separately wrote long letters to argue the merit of his works and character, Whitman heard the tonic praise that could restore his spirit. The controversy also led to a financial windfall, for his English admirers collected a testimonial for him. The entire episode renewed him morally, and he remained forever grateful for "the blessed gale from the British Isles." O'Connor championed *Leaves of Grass* again in 1882, when a new issue was banned in Boston, and this time O'Connor warmly resumed their friendship through correspondence.

In the long months when both old men were usually bedridden and ill, the thirty-year-old Horace Traubel began his daily visits to Whitman, during which he recorded nearly every word of their conversations and entered Whitman's life with the complete sympathy of boyish adoration. Traubel was Whitman's factotum, his official chronicler, one of his literary executors, his visible immortality among the young, and his last son and darling, whom he loved to kiss and embrace. Hardly a day went by when Whitman did not mention something about O'Connor or talk about him lovingly. When he had spells of mental confusion, he rambled about William, and sometimes about Nelly. Once he imagined that William had come to see him and was being detained downstairs.[27] In the last days of O'Connor's life, Traubel became their emissary. The most moving and yet most turbulent entry in the six volumes of Traubel's daily record is March 2, 1889, when he traveled for the first time to Washington to meet O'Connor before he died. Traubel's account of his arrival in the city and journey across town reveals his excitement at experiencing the locations of Whitman's earlier life that are hallowed for him by long devotion to the man and his poems.

> Of course everything made me think of W. The buildings every-
> where. The Capitol. The Treasury. Here O'C. worked, and W.,
> and Burroughs. It was all W.'s stamping ground. It has been
> the environment of his daily life. Was in his books. In his
> memories as he talked to me from day to day. I felt all sorts
> of things as I went and looked about. Just as we had been
> saying: "This is America!" I found myself saying: "This is
> Walt: Walt is this!"[28]

The reverential tone mixes with suspenseful agitation in quick, subdued sentences as Traubel then enters O'Connor's house and is led by Nelly up to William's room, where William exclaims over Traubel as the wonder child of the entire Whitman fellowship (which includes Nelly). As soon as they are left alone, O'Connor passionately kisses him and calls him the child of his brotherhood with Walt (which excludes Nelly). Traubel is unnerved by the fervid embrace but he recognizes that he is there in place of Walt and that he must carry O'Connor's soul and the imprint of his body back to Whitman. O'Connor and Traubel are moved to tears over this symbolic reconciliation.

It was apparently satisfying to Whitman too, as Traubel reports. Soon after O'Connor's death, Whitman wrote the preface to the volume of O'Connor's stories published posthumously. Free of any grudge, the preface is a tribute to his friend and ends: "Thrice blessed be his memory!" In all of his recollections of O'Connor, Whitman bore no rancor after he emerged from the dark period of the 1870s — what bitterness he may have felt at that time he probably could not truthfully recall. His friendship, like his poetry, clearly came from fidelity to underlying, earlier experience, and he preserved his attachments. He loved O'Connor with creative inspiration.

Though the sexual passions of their triangle were never far from Whitman's dreams and mind-wanderings, he wanted to remember the O'Connors as his true family, as the ones who recognized and made a home for his real self, the person who is expressed in *Leaves of Grass*. In comparison with the O'Connors, the Whitman family scarcely knew him, he told Traubel when he gave one of Nelly's letters into Traubel's keeping. The recollection of Washington days made him weep as he spoke.

> The O'Connor home was my home; They were beyond all others — William, Nelly — my understanders, my lovers: they more than any others. I was nearer to them than to any others — oh! much nearer. A man's family is the people who love him — the people who comprehend him. You know how for the most part. I have always been isolated from my people — in certain senses I have been a stranger in their midst. . . . Who of my family has gone along with me? Who? Do you know? Not one of them. They are beautiful, fine: they don't need to be apologized for: but they have not known me: they have always missed my intentions. . . . Blood tells sometimes against a man as well as for a man: they say that blood is thicker than water: but what does blood mean in a case like this? . . . When I think of what my own folks by blood didn't do for me. . . I don't make much of the family diamonds or the inherited crown.[29]

He is still astonished that the family he grew up in did not become the lovers of his adult spirit. He speaks like the wounded adolescent he had been, not ready to take his life elsewhere, but resentful that his parents did not satisfy him. With good reason, he lived defensively on guard among them like a Jew in Russia, yet he wanted them to come closer than anyone could. One sympathizes also with his parents. Beset by failure, they refused to listen to the turmoil he attended to in his heart. Wanting to achieve an American dream of success, they had the greatest poet in America growing in their child, and they missed the significance of their lives together. They always missed his intentions, as he says. They have not known me, he says. His complaints show how long the quarrel continued. But only the poems survive.

At the end of his life Whitman never failed to believe in the great significance of his spirit expressed in *Leaves of Grass*, and he never deteriorated into indifference over the details of his work. In 1891 he prepared an "authorized edition," in which he enjoined future editors to preserve his text exactly as he left it. Committed to the integrity of his book, Whitman did not want his arrangement of poems disregarded or any selection of his poems to supersede the entirety of *Leaves of Grass*. He protected to the last the poetic identity that alone defined his true, inner nature. His formal existence in the book was more authentic to him than any other, chronological, experience of life. When he died in March 1892, he had thirty-two years earlier in "So Long!" uttered his final words:

> I love you, I depart from materials,
> I am as one disembodied, triumphant, dead.

Notes

Chapter 1.

1. "Notes from Conversations with George W. Whitman, 1893: Mostly in His Own Words," *In Re Walt Whitman*, edited by Horace Traubel, Maurice Bucke, and Thomas Harned (Philadelphia, 1893), pp. 35–36.

2. Horace Traubel, *With Walt Whitman in Camden* (hereafter cited as WWC), 6 vols. (1906–1982), I, p. 227.

3. Ibid., III, pp. 525–526.

4. Ibid., IV, pp. 473–474.

5. "Conversations with George W. Whitman," p. 34.

6. After a visit to the Whitman household on November 9, 1856, Bronson Alcott recorded this comment by Louisa Whitman: "Walt...had no business but going out and coming in to eat, drink, write, and sleep." *The Journals of Bronson Alcott*, selected and edited by Odell Shepard (Boston, 1938), p. 289.

7. Grace Gilchrist, "Chats with Walt Whitman," *Temple Bar Magazine*, 113 (February 1898): 208.

8. Ibid., p. 210.

9. *WWC*, II, pp. 113–114.

10. The turmoil surrounding Andrew's death is carefully discussed by Randall Waldron in *Mattie: The Letters of Martha Mitchell Whitman* (New York University Press, 1977), pp. 31–32.

11. Whitman commented on the effect of reading romances in a newspaper article in the *Brooklyn Eagle*, October 11, 1847, which is quoted in Joseph Jay Rubin, *The Historic Whitman* (Pennsylvania State University Press, 1973), pp. 22–23. Whitman's recollections of his reading in the law offices of the Clarke brothers are in *Specimen Days*, collected in *Prose Works 1892*, edited by Floyd Stovall (New York University Press, 1963), I, p. 13.

12. An American Primer, edited by Horace Traubel (Boston: Small, Maynard & Co., 1904), p. 16.

13. *WWC*, III, p. 109.

14. "Our Future Lot" is the earliest known published poetry by Whitman. *The Early Poems and the Fiction*, edited by Thomas Brasher (New York University Press, 1963), p. 28.

15. Quoted in Gay Wilson Allen, *The Solitary Singer: A Critical Biography of Walt Whitman* (New York University Press, 1967), p. 32.

16. Ibid., pp. 54–55.

17. Ibid., p. 37.

18. "Ourselves and the *Eagle*," *The Uncollected Poetry and Prose of Walt Whitman* (hereafter cited as *UPP*), edited by Emory Holloway, 2 vols., (New York, 1932), I, pp. 114–117.

19. *The Correspondence*, edited by Edwin Haviland Miller, 5 vols., (New York University Press, 1961), I, p. 33.

20. Ibid.

21. Whitman's stories are discussed in Stephen Black, *Whitman's Journeys into Chaos* (Princeton, 1975), pp. 16–31.

22. For a perceptive discussion of Whitman's correspondence with John Addington Symonds, to whom Whitman told this lie, see Black, *Whitman's Journeys*, pp. 175–182.

23. *UPP*, II, p. 66.

24. Whitman's views about "heart-music" are summarized in Rubin, *The Historic Whitman*, pp. 278–280; and in Justin Kaplan, *Walt Whitman: A Life* (New York, 1980), pp. 175–176.

25. Allen, *Solitary Singer*, p. 114.

26. *WWC*, II, pp. 173–174.

27. Rubin, *The Historic Whitman*, p. 282.

28. Ibid., p. 283.

29. Whitman's cranial survey is included in John Davies, *Phrenology: Fad and Science* (Yale University Press, 1955), pp. 123–124. Whitman's response to phrenological ideas is discussed in Harold Aspiz, *Walt Whitman and the Body Beautiful* (University of Illinois Press, 1981), pp. 109–133.

30. Whitman's consoling pronouncements here and in the following paragraphs are quoted from *UPP*, II, pp. 63–68.

31. Richard M. Bucke, *Cosmic Consciousness* (New York, 1901), p. 227.

32. *UPP*, II, p. 69.

Chapter 2.

1. Allen, *Solitary Singer*, p. 131.

2. For a detailed publishing history of *Leaves of Grass*, see Gay Wilson Allen, *The New Walt Whitman Handbook* (New York University Press, 1975).

Chapter 3.

1. Neruda's talk at a P.E.N. dinner in New York City is printed in *Walt Whitman: The Measure of His Song,* edited by Jim Perlman, Ed Folsom, and Dan Campion (Minneapolis, 1981), pp. 139–141.

2. *WWC,* II, pp. 113–114.

Chapter 4.

1. Richard Maurice Bucke, *Walt Whitman* (Philadelphia, 1883), p. 26. O. L. Triggs follows Bucke's report in his assertion that "this period was the happiest of his life." *Complete Writings* (1902), VII, p. 105.

2. Allen, *Solitary Singer,* p. 151.

3. John Burroughs, *Notes on Walt Whitman as Poet and Person* (New York, 1867).

4. *Walt Whitman's Workshop,* edited by Clifton Furness (New York, 1964), pp. 87–113.

Chapter 5.

1. This point is made in the excellent discussion of Whitman's homosexuality by Joseph Cady, "Not Happy in the Capitol: Homosexuality and the *Calamus* Poems," *American Studies,* 19 (Fall 1978): 5–22.

Chapter 6.

1. *Prose Works 1892,* I, pp. 138–139.

2. In his journal for January 28, 1903, Burroughs responded indignantly to Colonel Thomas Wentworth Higginson's attacks on Whitman for failing to serve in the army during the Civil War. "Think of belittling him because he did not enlist as a soldier and carry a musket in the ranks! Could there be anything more shocking and incongruous than Whitman killing people?. . .He was not an athlete, or a rough, but a great tender mother-man, to whom the martial spirit was utterly foreign." The entire passage is quoted in Clara Barrus, *Whitman and Burroughs, Comrades* (Boston, 1931), p. 339.

Chapter 7.

1. Allen, *Solitary Singer,* pp. 214–215.

2. *UPP,* II, p. 91, n. 1.

3. In a letter to Emerson, dated December 29, 1862, Whitman stated that his recent removal to Washington, D.C., ended "and for good, my New York stagnation." *Correspondence,* I, p. 61.

4. Allen, *Solitary Singer,* p. 272.

5. *Workshop*, p. 135.

6. *Prose Works 1892*, I, p. 31.

7. *WWC*, I, p. 4.

8. *Prose Works 1892*, II, pp. 497–509.

9. Ibid., I, pp. 325–326.

10. Ibid., II, p. 690.

11. Allen, *Solitary Singer*, p. 370.

12. This sampling of Whitman's remarks about O'Connor is taken from various conversations with Traubel in *WWC*; see I, pp. 33, 51, 162, 179, 362, 465; II, p. 12; III, pp. 76, 127, 263, 428.

13. *WWC*, II, p. 15.

14. Letter of July 2, 1864; *WWC*, IV, p. 366.

15. *Correspondence*, I, p. 236.

16. Ibid., I, p. 234, n. 99.

17. A letter of August 13, 1864, gives an entertaining description of life in Washington; *WWC*, III, pp. 337–340.

18. Letter of December 30, 1864; *WWC*, II, pp. 400–403.

19. Letter of October 19, 1865; *WWC*, I, pp. 83–85.

20. Letter of May 9, 1867; *WWC*, III, p. 522.

21. Letter of November 21, 1868; *WWC*, III, pp. 524–525.

22. A memoir by Grace Ellery Channing, quoted in Florence Freedman, "New Light on an Old Quarrel: Walt Whitman and William Douglas O'Connor, 1872," *Walt Whitman Review*, 11 (June 1965): 27–52.

23. Unpublished letter in the Library of Congress; portions quoted by Freedman and Kaplan (see chapter 1, note 24).

24. *UPP*, II, pp. 95–96.

25. *WWC*, III, pp. 77–78.

26. Ibid., IV, p. 472.

27. Ibid., I, pp. 295–297.

28. Ibid., IV, p. 253.

29. Ibid., III, pp. 525–526.

Index

David Cavitch is professor of English and
former chairman of the English department
at Tufts University. He is author of *D. H.
Lawrence and the New World,* a member of
the executive board of the D. H. Lawrence
Society, and has held a Senior Fellowship
from the National Endowment for the
Humanities.